Daseinsanalysis

ALICE HOLZHEY-KUNZ

Translated by Sophie Leighton

FAB

FREE ASSOCIATION BOOKS

First published in 2014 by
Free Publishing Limited

English language Copyright © 2014 Sophie Leighton

A CIP Catalogue of this book is available from
the British Library

ISBN: 978-1-8534322-5-5

Typeset in Bembo 11pt by
www.chandlerbookdesign.co.uk

Printed and bound by CPI Group (UK) Ltd, Croydon, CR0 4YY

CONTENTS

II Philosophico-psychological aspects

III Mental suffering

IV Therapeutic conclusions

Preface to the English edition

The English-speaking reader may wonder why this book is appearing under the foreign-sounding title 'Daseinsanalysis' instead of 'Existential analysis', the familiar term that is used in the Anglophone world. There are two critical reasons for this: first, Rollo May introduced the term 'existential analysis' into American psychiatry and psychotherapy in 1958 because he (mistakenly) believed this was an appropriate translation of the specialist term 'Daseinsanalyse'. 'Daseinsanalyse' was already at that time a highly regarded movement in psychiatry in continental Europe, which was principally associated with the name Ludwig Binswanger. Binswanger himself borrowed the name 'Daseinsanalyse' from Martin Heidegger's philosophical work *Being and Time*. It is a historical irony that Heidegger's book was not yet available in English in 1958 and it was therefore possible to make the error of translating Heidegger's concepts of 'Dasein' and 'daseinsanalytic' as 'existence' and 'existential'. Thanks to Rollo May, the English-speaking world therefore became familiar with the writings of the founder of daseinsanalysis at an early stage, only unfortunately under the misleading title 'existential analysis'. The book itself, containing Binswanger's writings, bore the title 'Existence'. This book had a huge impact in the English-speaking world since it led to the emergence of the psychotherapeutic movement that has been called 'existential analysis or 'existential therapy' to this day.

This brings us to the first reason for publishing this book under the title *Daseinsanalysis* in the English translation as well: what is said in Part II about basic themes of human existing and in Part III about basic forms of mental suffering is philosophically largely based on Heidegger's ontological reflections on human 'dasein'. Therefore this book remains in the daseinsanalytic tradition, even though it has moved a long way away from the intellectual approaches of its two founding fathers, Ludwig Binswanger and Medard Boss. However, looking at the 'existential analysis' movement in the Anglophone world there are certainly many references to existential philosophical ideas, although these are rarely consistent and do not generally serve a theoretical analysis of phenomena but the quest for a practical therapeutic orientation.

The second reason is that daseinsanalysis has regarded itself in therapeutic terms since its beginnings as a 'psychoanalysis from daseinsanalytic perspectives' (Binswanger). The present book works out in detail in Part IV why the therapeutic procedure of daseinsanalysis should adhere to Freud's technical fundamental rules and therefore to 'analysis' in the Freudian sense. This constitutes a further important difference from what is understood therapeutically in English-speaking regions as 'existential analysis'. For here the reference to existential philosophy led away from Freud's psychoanalysis to a form of counselling that is guided by ideas from existential philosophy.

Alice Holzhey-Kunz

Daseinsanalysis
Daseinsanalysis
Daseinsanalysis
Daseinsanalysis
Daseinsanalysis
Daseinsanalysis

Historical Part

Daseinsanalysis
Daseinsanalysis
Daseinsanalysis
Daseinsanalysis
Daseinsanalysis
Daseinsanalysis

Introduction

t is highly debatable whether Ludwig Binswanger alone should be called the founding father of daseinsanalysis or whether this title should be shared with Medard Boss. From a purely chronological perspective, the facts of the matter are certainly ambiguous. From 1943, Binswanger termed his theory, which he first began to develop in 1930, *Daseinsanalyse*—daseinsanalysis—or the daseinsanalytic school of thought in psychiatry. It was not until after 1950 that Boss, a former student of Binswanger put forward his own new version of 'daseinsanalysis'. This, however, comprised not only a wholesale rejection of Binswanger but also the demand that Binswanger should abandon the label 'daseinsanalytic' for his theory on the basis that he had misunderstood and therefore misused this term drawn from Martin Heidegger's philosophy.

The history of daseinsanalysis therefore cannot be traced back to one single origin, although the two trends arose in succession. In fact, they share two identifiable reference-points: both make a positive connection with Martin Heidegger's philosophy and diverge critically from Sigmund Freud's psychoanalysis; and both claim to use the phenomenological method dating back to Edmund Husserl, which sets out to observe 'the things themselves' instead of subordinating them to theoretical constructs. These common reference-points certainly give rise to a similar terminology but not to any agreement in terms of content. Binswanger has a different understanding from

Boss of Heidegger's philosophy, and has another perspective on Freud and a different conception of phenomenology. Furthermore, Binswanger's daseinsanalysis focuses mainly on psychiatric research, while Boss places the main emphasis on psychotherapeutic practice.

1

Ludwig Binswanger: daseinsanalysis as an exact examination of world-projects

I n 1910, Ludwig Binswanger (1881–1966) took over as medical director of the Bellevue Sanatorium in Kreuzlingen at Lake Constance, founded by his grandfather in 1857, which had already gained an international reputation as a private psychiatric clinic. Previously Binswanger had trained in psychiatry under Eugen Bleuler at the Burghölzli psychiatric clinic in Zurich, where he also became acquainted through C. G. Jung with Sigmund Freud's psychoanalysis, to which he initially adhered. Various journeys to Freud in Vienna and a return visit from Freud to Kreuzlingen in 1912 formed the basis of a lifelong friendship, as the correspondence published in 1992 demonstrates (Fichtner, 2003).

However, Binswanger's theoretical interests soon developed beyond his initial attachment to psychoanalysis.[1] His first book, *Eine Einführung in die Probleme der allgemeinen Psychologie* [introduction to the problems of general psychology], published in 1922, 2010), is philosophically grounded primarily in Paul Natorp's Neo-Kantianism and Edmund Husserl's phenomenology.

Binswanger's prime concern from the outset was to establish psychiatry as a science and to overcome its bleak condition as a mere conglomeration of disconnected sub-disciplines. He considered that this task could be accomplished only if psychiatry was orientated

---

[1] For an overview of the three stages of Binswanger's thought, see Holzhey-Kunz, 2006.

towards the 'whole human being' rather than the brain or the mind, and in doing so took as a basis a philosophically determined concept of human being. As Binswanger conceived it, the daseinsanalysis he developed achieves precisely this: it contains the philosophical anthropology that can lay the foundations for a scientific psychiatry and it has at its disposal a method for obtaining scientifically exact knowledge concerning mental illnesses. This also already anticipates something that Binswanger's daseinsanalysis neither achieves nor sets out to achieve: it claims neither to provide a philosophical justification for Freud's psychoanalysis nor to be a movement in psychotherapy.

Binswanger's work would be inconceivable without the preceding philosophical achievements of both *Edmund Husserl* and *Martin Heidegger*. In Husserl, Binswanger finds the investigative method that can yield 'scientifically exact' knowledge and therefore constitutes a valuable alternative—*phenomenology* (Binswanger, 1922)—to the prevailing natural scientific method in psychiatry. And in Heidegger's 1927 work *Being and Time* (Heidegger, 1966), Binswanger finds a philosophical definition of the human being as '*Dasein*', which enables the psychiatrist to consider the mentally ill person not only as the bearer of symptoms, but as an entire *human being*.[2]

1.1 Scientifically exact investigation of world-projects

The originality of Binswanger's achievement consists in his introduction into psychiatry of the concept of the *world-project*, drawn from Heidegger's lecture 'The essence of reasons'.[3] The concept of the 'world' used in it refers not to the universe of things or the so-called external world but to the broad *horizon* within which a human being operates, thinks and acts. This concept of the world is familiar from everyday language, since in history we refer to the mediaeval world in contrast to the modern world, in sociology to the peasant-agrarian world in contrast to the bourgeois-urban world, in developmental

---

[2] Binswanger even makes the provocative statement that psychiatry can only become an 'autonomous science' if it is based on the ground 'of the human being' (1956, p. 57).

[3] For the first time in his 1947 essay, 'Über die daseinsanalytische Forschungsrichtung in der Psychiatrie' (1992-1994, Vol. 3, p. 235f, published in English as 'The existential analysis school of thought' in May et al., 1994, pp. 191–213.

psychology to the young child's world and so on. This always refers
to the horizon of meaning into which an era, a social stratum or the
human being at a particular developmental phase is integrated—
the horizon that both makes possible and restricts *the way in which*
something becomes accessible to experience.

In this sense, for Binswanger every individual human being also
inhabits a special 'world' or rather a special individual 'world-project'
in which various social and cultural worlds clash and overlap. If,
however, the diversity of individuals consists in their various world-
projects, then the same applies to the different nature of mentally ill
people: it is 'the world-designs as such [that] distinguish the mentally
ill from the healthy (*ibid.*, p. 213)'. This enables us to give a clear
definition of daseinsanalytic investigation: it means 'to examine and
describe how the various forms of the mentally ill, and each one for
himself, design world' (*ibid*, p. 198, fn.19).

This methodological procedure has two notable characteristics:

1. Instead of being guided in the usual psychiatric way
    by the dominant medical categories of healthy and
    ill and assessing what the mentally ill person lacks in
    comparison to the healthy person, the focus here is on
    what is positively present: on the different world-project.

2. This method requires no empathy with the experience
    of another human being because the world-project to
    be explored, as will be explained in more detail, lies at
    the basis of all experience. Binswanger can therefore
    claim that the description of world-projects proceeds
    in a rigorously 'methodological' way and thus conveys
    scientifically exact and verifiable knowledge.

1.2 The example of the 'heel-phobia'

Binswanger's methodological procedure can be illustrated by a case
example that he had already published in 1911, as Freud's most recent
pupil at that time, and cites again in 1945 to present an overview of
the daseinsanalytic school of thought that he had by then developed.

'I shall report the case of a young girl who at the age of five experienced a puzzling attack of anxiety and fainting when her heel got stuck in her skate and separated from her shoe. Ever since, the girl—now twenty-one years of age—suffered spells of irresistible anxiety whenever a heel of one of her shoes appeared to loosen or when someone touched the heel or only spoke of heels. (Her own had to be nailed to her soles). On such occasions, if she could not get away in time, she would faint' (May et al., 1994, pp. 202–3).

The starting-point is clear. The girl is reacting to an intrinsically harmless incident as if it were an extreme threat—and is therefore reacting 'pathologically'. The anxiety attack, the subsequent fainting and the ensuing phobia are all completely inappropriate reactions and therefore cannot be understood from the actual context. For Binswanger the daseinsanalytic task therefore consists in discovering the world-project to which this girl's apparently absurd reactions belong and within which they have a comprehensible meaning despite all appearances to the contrary. The daseinsanalytic question is therefore: within which world-project does something as harmless as the separation of a heel from a shoe represent a life-threatening danger, to which anxiety, fainting and phobia would constitute *appropriate* reactions? Binswanger reaches the conclusion that this is a world-project that is one-sidedly governed by the *category of continuity*, so that discontinuous phenomena have no place in it. Someone who lives in such a world has absolutely no means of understanding separations that inevitably occur and processing them appropriately. This results in every separation, however innocuous, having the potential to become a traumatic experience because anxiety always arises when someone's world is threatened with destruction. The girl's phobic reactions and compulsive rituals are therefore appropriate defence mechanisms with which she is seeking to protect herself from any further experiences of discontinuity and their traumatic impact.[4]

---

[4] I shall return to the heel phobia example in Part III, Chapter 2 to test out an alternative daseinsanalytic interpretation.

1.3 The relationships between daseinsanalysis, psychoanalysis and psychiatry

The heel phobia example shows how far Binswanger has moved away from psychoanalysis. Certainly there remains one important common point: like Freud, Binswanger seeks to discover and interpret the hidden meaning of presenting symptoms instead of merely describing them as phenomena indicating a deficiency. The difference consists in the fact that Freud relates the manifestly meaningless symptoms to the (repressed) childhood history and thus discovers their 'historical' meaning, whereas Binswanger makes recourse to the world-project, which in his view not only lies at the basis of the unconscious discovered by Freud but represents a 'transcendental *a priori*' in the Kantian sense. If, however, the world-project has an *a priori* nature, then it also cannot originate from childhood but must instead characterise it from the outset because it prescribes the child's developmental possibilities (May et al., 1994, p. 247). Nevertheless, the daseinsanalytic investigation of the world-project does not seek to replace the psychoanalytic exploration of childhood development but only to deepen it (and thus relativise it). For Binswanger psychoanalysis remains indispensable because it alone can explain (1) why it is specifically the incident on the ice that instigates the neurotic development and (2) what separation the girl most fears at the time of the incident, namely parting from her mother (*ibid.*, p. 245).

Traditional psychiatric investigation is also validated (to some extent) according to Binswanger. Daseinsanalysis wants merely to adduce this, which means that the psychiatrist should begin by conducting a daseinsanalytic examination of the patient's world-project. This is because it is only in this way that the ill person can be perceived as a complete individual, which conventional psychiatric psychopathology has never managed to achieve, instead reducing the patient from the very outset to a 'case of x' concerning which a 'biological value judgement' is pronounced by means of diagnosis. Once the daseinsanalytic examination of the individual world-project has occurred, this should be followed by a 'psychopathological-clinical analysis' from a daseinsanalytic perspective. Binswanger adhered to this view even in his studies of schizophrenia, while to every daseinsanalytic investigation he appended an analysis that accorded with the prevailing psychiatric criteria of the time.[5]

1.4 Binswanger's conception of the human being

The conception of the human being developed by Binswanger diverges both from Freud and from Heidegger.

Drive or mind?

Binswanger criticises Freud's conception of the human being as naturalistic.[6] By this he means that Freud accords a false absolute status to the drives, overstating their importance along with that of biological facts for mental life in general and, furthermore, subordinates all mental processes to natural scientific thinking.[7] This is why psychoanalysis leaves no room either for spirituality and religiosity as autonomous phenomena that do not originate from the needs of the drives or for human 'being-a-self', which can be understood only in quantitative rather than qualitative terms. Freud responds to these objections with a resolute and humorous attitude in a personal letter to Binswanger: 'I have never ventured beyond the ground floor and basement of the building.—You maintain that if one changes one's point of view one can also see a higher floor, in which there live such distinguished guests as religion, art, etc. ... If I still had a lifetime of work ahead of me, I should dare to assign a home in my lowly little house to those highborn personages' (Fichtner, 2003, p. 212, letter of 8.X.36).

---

[5] Binswanger's studies of schizophrenia were published in a collected volume (1957), for which he provided a detailed introduction.

[6] Cf. Binswanger's commemorative lecture on Freud's 80th birthday in Vienna: 'Freuds Auffassung des Menschen im Lichte der Anthropologie' (Freud's conception of the human being in the light of anthropology) (1955 [1947], Vol. 1, pp. 159–189).

[7] Both Boss and Binswanger see Freud far too much as a natural scientist, so that their criticism relates much less to psychoanalysis itself than to its 'self-misunderstanding' (Habermas) as a natural science.

Care or love?

Highly as Binswanger praises the methodological approach of
Heidegger's work *Being and Time* for its structural analysis of human
dasein, he is equally harsh in criticising its conception of the human
being. In his view, Heidegger completely misjudges the nature
of the human being, because he characterises it only as 'care' and
thus neglects to consider the highest possibility that constitutes
the only way in which the human being can truly become human,
namely love. Binswanger therefore sees it as his task to rectify this
fundamental defect in Heidegger's anthropological approach. His
600-page major work *Grundformen und Erkenntnis menschlichen Daseins*
(Basic forms and knowledge of human dasein) was published in
1942 (Binswanger 1992–1994, Vol. 2). It represents a counter-model
to *Being and Time* in its understanding of the human being in terms
of 'loving being-together' rather than 'care'. This implies the thesis
that the 'anxiety', 'guilt', 'singularity' and 'finitude' that in Heidegger
are part of the human being's intrinsic nature can be overcome in
love. For Binswanger, the theoretical possibility of love proves that
the human being—albeit seldom *de facto*—is thus nevertheless *by his
nature* healthy and whole: not an isolated 'I' but a loving 'we' and in
love no longer abandoned but domiciled, no longer finite but infinite,
no longer temporally bound but eternal. It follows from this that
anxiety, guilt, solitude and abandonment emerge when the conduct
of a particular human life falls short of the possibility of this loving
being-together. Binswanger certainly knows how rare true love is,
but he insists that rather than inferring the nature of human being
from material circumstances, instead we must understand from his
nature the possibility of falling short of this in actual life. In fact, this
criticism from Binswanger received a response, although Heidegger
did not formulate it directly to him but presented it in the 'Zollikon
seminars', held jointly with his opponent Medard Boss (Heidegger,
2001a, pp. 115–116).

Now despite all the differences, Heidegger's and Freud's
conceptions of the human being converge in regarding him as a
radically finite being that is trapped in irresoluble contradictions
and intrinsically disposed to flee the truth about himself in illusions.

So Binswanger is only being consistent when he ultimately criticises both authors on the same basis, namely for elevating a deficient, pathological form of existence into the nature of the human being. Against both Heidegger and Freud, Binswanger champions a perfection of the human being in accordance with his nature. For him, the human being is 'flawless' by nature, which is why any gap or discontinuity already indicates an adversely modified world-project.

Binswanger's investigation of pathological world-projects is therefore based strictly speaking not on Heidegger's philosophical definition of dasein as 'being-in-the-world' but on his own counter-model of 'being-in-the-world-beyond-the world'. He formulates programmatically that 'knowledge of dasein' is 'intrinsically rooted in the loving being-together of I and you' (1992–1994,Vol. 2, p. 13). The postulate of love has a methodological meaning here, however, and in no way contradicts the requirement for moderation and scientific rigour (Vol. 2, p. 452f.). Binswanger does not claim that the doctor should love the patient but only that the presenting symptomatology should be explored from the standpoint of love, in order to ascertain in structural terms the extent of the 'modification' and thus also the existing shortfall of actual human being. He applies this method paradigmatically above all in the schizophrenia studies published between 1944 and 1952, most clearly in the Ellen West case study.[*] There he traces step by step the increasing contraction process that reduces the 'world' inhabited by Ellen West to the 'hole-world of mere desires' in which love only continues to feature as an extreme form of decay.

1.5 Daseinsanalysis as research and as psychotherapy

Binswanger emphasises that unlike psychoanalysis daseinsanalysis emerged from a purely scientific investigative interest rather than a therapeutic impetus. Thus he draws a clear distinction between things that for Freud were indissolubly connected—namely 'research' and 'healing'. Daseinsanalytic investigation can certainly be placed retrospectively in the service of psychotherapy, but it nevertheless is

---

[*] Republished in 1992–1994,Vol. 4, p. 73–209; also in May *et al.*, 1994, pp. 237–364.

and remains pure investigation. This again testifies to the ideal of 'exact' science. Insights gained in the context of an analytic-therapeutic setting under the conditions of transference and countertransference cannot satisfy scientific criteria. Daseinsanalytic investigation is therefore fundamentally based on 'credible autobiographical and biographical documents and testimonies', originating both from the patient's direct factual investigation and from reports made by his close family or friends and doctors or other caregivers.⁹ It is therefore no surprise that Binswanger makes only a few references to the relationship between daseinsanalysis and psychotherapy.¹⁰ He never fails to emphasise on these occasions that the daseinsanalyst conducting psychotherapy cannot dispense with psychoanalysis. Nevertheless, 'psychoanalysis conducted from a daseinsanalytic perspective' has a different focus for him because, instead of seeking to reconstruct the patient's childhood history, it aims to convey to him 'the experience of insight into his own daseins-structure'. It is therefore not the retrieval of repressed material but the experience of having 'fallen short of the structure of dasein' that becomes the driving force of the therapy. Accordingly, the therapeutic goal consists in 'enabling the patient to find his way back from his neurotically or psychotically eccentric, obsessive, hole-filled or cranky and so on mode of dasein and world into the freedom of having his own existential possibilities at his disposal' (1992–1994, Vol. 3, p. 262f.).

---

⁹ Binswanger wrote his schizophrenia studies on the basis of case histories from the 'Bellevue' that extended back over the previous twenty years.

¹⁰ Cf. 'Daseinsanalytik und Psychiatrie' (Daseinsanalysis and psychiatry), 1955, Vol. 2, p. 293f., 'Daseinsanalyse und Psychotherapie' (Daseinsanalysis and psychotherapy) (1992–1994 [1954]), Vol. 3, p. 259–263 and 'Existential analysis and psychotherapy', in Fromm-Reichmann and J. L. Moreno (eds.), 1956, Vol. 1. pp. 144–148. His highly regarded 1935 lecture on psychotherapy (1992–1994, Vol. 3, p. 205–230) shows the influence of Heideggerian thinking, but does not deploy the daseinsanalytic concept of the world-project that was only developed later.

2

Medard Boss: daseinsanalysis as the endeavour to overcome possessive subjectivism

2.1 Friendship and collaboration with Heidegger

After his training in psychiatry and psychoanalysis, Medard Boss (1903–1990) worked for a short period as the medical director of a private psychiatric clinic before establishing his own psychoanalytic practice first in Zurich and then nearby in Zollikon. At first, he was a convinced supporter of Freud and he also remained a member of the Swiss Psychoanalytical Society throughout his life. In the early 1940s, he turned to Ludwig Binswanger's theories; in 1947, he qualified as a lecturer at the medical faculty of Zurich University with a thesis on the meaning and content of the sexual perversions. Although the first edition of this book was still entirely indebted to Binswanger's ideas, the second edition four years later was based on a completely new daseinsanalytic theory (Boss, 1951). This reorientation resulted from Boss's encounter in the meantime with Martin Heidegger, which led to a lifelong friendship and collaboration. In the following years, Boss constructed his new starting-point for thought and developed a daseinsanalytic method of dream interpretation (1957, 1977), as well as a daseinsanalytic psychosomatics (1954).

Boss understood daseinsanalysis from the outset as a psychoanalytic practice, albeit one purged of Freud's theoretical errors. It was therefore only logical that in 1970 he created a training centre in Zurich for 'daseinsanalytic psychotherapy and psychosomatics'. His claim, however, went far beyond this, as is already clear from the title of his major work, *Grundriss der Medizin und Psychologie*.[11] With daseinsanalysis, a new more 'human-appropriate' foundation was to be laid for the whole of medicine and psychology; the specifically daseinsanalytic psychotherapy formed a field of application for the new theory.

The Zollikon seminars

Heidegger's participation in the development of daseinsanalysis was not restricted to philosophical guidance. In conjunction with Boss, he conducted the Zollikon seminars between 1959 and 1969 in a loose sequence. These were attended mainly by psychiatrists in training.[12] The explanations he gave there were recorded in shorthand by Boss and to a large extent incorporated directly into the emerging text of the *Existential Foundations of Medicine and Psychology*. If we also consider that Heidegger corrected all the philosophical passages of this book in minute detail and wrote parts of them himself, it becomes clear that the *Foundations* was a joint work by the psychiatrist and the philosopher.

What was Heidegger's motivation for this involvement? It seems likely that he saw the collaboration with Boss as an opportunity to give his inherently somewhat inaccessible thought a 'practical' application. In the Zollikon seminar of 8 July 1965, he declared that there was 'the highest need for doctors who *think* and who do not wish to leave the field entirely to scientific technicians' (2001a, *loc. cit.*, p. 103). Heidegger is careful to address the participants consistently as 'doctors', regardless of whether they are treating patients somatically or psychically. His interest lies not specifically in psychiatry and psychotherapy but in medicine in general and indeed in its modern form as an applied natural science. He believes that he can exert an influence as a philosopher by informing scientifically orientated

---

[11] Published in English as *Existential Foundations of Medicine and Psychology* (Boss, 1994).

[12] The seminars were given this name because most of them took place in Boss's house in Zollikon. They were published in 1987 and supplemented by extracts from the correspondence and stenographed conversations between Heidegger and Boss (Heidegger, 2001a).

doctors about the philosophy that underpins their activities, which is represented above all by the name of *Descartes*. This seventeenth-century philosopher's work instigated the 'dictatorship of mind' that devalues everything that exists—even the human being—as measurable and calculable objects. The whole of medicine also bows to this, which is why its key concepts of 'health' and 'illness' are now only understood in technical terms. Against the backdrop of this critique, Heidegger undertakes to inform the doctors present concerning a 'daseins-appropriate' concept of health and illness. The goal is therefore not to gain a new understanding of psychopathological phenomena, but rather to overcome the scientific paradigm that generally dominates in medicine and psychology (including psychoanalysis) in favour of a new thinking.

According to Boss, daseinsanalysis was the precursor of a future movement that would revolutionise the whole of medicine and psychology, but it was nevertheless the first (and provisionally the only) scientific and therapeutic discipline that concretely implemented Heidegger's ground-breaking philosophical discoveries. In the view of its supporters, this gave it a unique significance and distinguished it from all other medical-psychological and psychotherapeutic approaches, which according to Boss despite their many differences were all united in remaining rooted in Cartesian philosophy. What Boss regarded as radically new and different was not only the Heideggerian conception of the human being that lay at the basis of daseinsanalysis, but also the phenomenological method that was being applied and the concept of a 'human-appropriate' theory of illness, which combined to give rise to a specifically daseinsanalytic form of psychotherapy.

2.2 The 'leap' from possessive subjectivism

When Boss first met Heidegger, more than twenty years had elapsed since the publication of *Being and Time* in 1927. Heidegger had since moved a long way from his philosophical position at that time and he therefore introduced Boss to the thought about 'being' that he had developed in the 1930s and 1940s. While *Being and Time* merely envisaged a revision—albeit fundamental—of the modern concept of the subject, his thinking then sought its elimination because he regarded it as responsible for the actual catastrophe of modernity. He regarded the modern-day philosophy of the subject as disastrous for its reduction of the world to the status of a totality of mere objects that was then surrendered to scientific calculation and technological exploitation by the fundamentally 'possessive' subject. According to Heidegger, the prerequisite for any 'salvation' would therefore be to overcome the modern thinking that proceeded from the subject and subjectivity. Boss's daseinsanalysis seeks to introduce this necessary change in thinking into medicine and psychology. Certainly—as Boss emphasises—there is no clear pathway from the old thinking to the new but only a 'leap'. What is required is a leap into a de-subjectivised disposition towards the world (Boss, 1994, p. 164, p. 292) that no longer takes possession of what it encounters as objects at its disposal but allows it to be what it is and keeps it as such. Because daseinsanalysis has made the leap from the possessive subjectivism of modernity, it represents the first implementation of Edmund Husserl's phenomenological injunction to be 'guided by the *facts themselves*' (1931, p. 82) instead of subordinating them to inapposite prejudices.

A new language

Breaking out of the subject–object model requires more than adopting Heidegger's terminology. What is required is a new regulation of language concerning syntax and verb forms, as well as the choice of words. These rules are certainly not explicitly formulated anywhere by Boss, but they are consistently applied in his writings. To summarise briefly: subject and object literally change places in the sentence. One model is Heidegger's example in which rather than 'I imagine a tree', first of all 'the tree presents itself to us' (1971, pp. 41–44).[13] Boss uses similar formulations that banish the experiencing and acting human being that previously occupied the subject position to the position of the object in the sentence. He loses the actively influencing position and becomes the one

---

[13]   The German verb 'sich vorstellen' means both to imagine and to present oneself (*Translator's note*).

affected or the recipient of the activity that proceeds from 'things'. Accordingly, verbs with an active meaning are reformulated in a passive and medial way. Any verb that denotes a creative individual achievement is stringently avoided. This includes the following: to decide, choose, act, wish, fantasise and want; to recognise, understand and argue. Even the verb 'to experience' (*erleben*) joins the blacklist as too subjectivist, although it actually expresses something that happens to us. Although this attempt to eliminate the subject through a regulation of language often strikes the reader as convoluted, it nevertheless becomes evident with hindsight that Boss introduced postmodern thought into medicine and psychology long before the postmodern 'death of the subject' and certainly long before the invention of the label 'postmodernism'.

2.3 Phenomenological dream interpretation

Boss worked out a theory of daseinsanalytic dream interpretation in two books (1957, 1977), which he demonstrated with many examples, mainly in the second book. He associates with this a consistent rejection of Freud's dream interpretation. As an alternative, he offers a procedure that is indebted to the phenomenological method and therefore—in Freudian terms—dwells strictly on the 'manifest dream content'. Yet for him this is not only a different method of accessing dreams but, furthermore, a redefinition of the dream itself, which he no longer conceives in the usual way as a product of psychic activity under the conditions of the sleeping state, but as a special mode of existence. What we call a 'dream' in reifying linguistic terms should properly be designated as 'oneiric being-in-the-world'. This is why Boss, whose first book about dreams still bore the title *Der Traum und seine Auslegung*[14] increasingly replaces the substantive 'dream' with the verb 'to dream'—not in the active form 'ich habe geträumt' (I dreamt) but in the passive form, 'es träumte mir' (it dreamt to me).[15] Accordingly, his second book about dreams is entitled *Es träumte mir vergangene Nacht...*

---

[14] Published in English as *The Analysis of Dreams* (Boss, 1957).

[15] This passive form is a more common construction in German than in English and this book's title is translated as *I Dreamt Last Night...* (Boss, 1977)—*Translator's note.*

What occurs in dreams or, better, 'in an oneiric mode' is not fundamentally distinct for Boss from waking life: whether awake or dreaming, we are 'addressed' by events in the world to which we 'correspond' according to our possibilities. The implications of this for a daseinsanalytic interpretation are that the 'supposedly complex problem of "dream interpretation"' can be reduced to 'two simple questions' (1977, p. 26):

1. 'For what phenomena the dreamer's existence is so open'?

2. '*How* the dreamer conducts himself toward whatever is revealed to him'? (p. 24).

To answer these two questions, the manifest dream content suffices; recourse to an unconscious or a latent dream content is just as superfluous as the associations that retrospectively occur to the dreamer. The interpretation of the dream reported by a 28-year-old single man who, as Boss notes in advance, is suffering from 'a sense of loneliness and of the meaninglessness of life', said to be illustrated by the following:

'Last night I dreamed that I was sleeping. I woke up in my dream, and looked out the window of my parents' house. Two hostile armies were in the fields. They began to fight. They were getting closer to the house, and I was afraid they might get in, so I ran around closing all the doors, then ran into my mother's bedroom. She was lying in bed. I climbed in. Suddenly everything was peaceful and quiet. The shooting outside stopped. I could sleep again' (p. 67).[16]

According to Boss, it is necessary first to consider to what the dreamer is open. The answer emerges from what appears to him when he looks out of the window: he sees soldiers from two hostile armies appearing. 'Outside' in the world a battle is therefore taking place—albeit one in which he is not taking part, since he remains in his parents' house. There are many possible responses to this situation. Therefore the second thing to consider is the dreamer's reaction to what is appearing. In dreaming he feels threatened by what is happening outside in front of him but not driven to active self-

---

[16] This dream is further discussed in Part II, Chapter 7 and interpreted in terms of a hidden ontological meaning.

defence or even to participate in the battle, but only induced to flee to his mother's bed. He discovers that he escapes the danger in this way and that all is 'well' again.

At first sight, this interpretation does nothing more than retell the dream content while adhering rigorously to the dream report. This can also satisfy the daseinsanalytic phenomenology orientated by the *essence* of things because it supposes that everything that occurs in dreaming and that the dreamer actively undertakes expresses this person's condition of being at that time. Therefore every detail of the dream is also to be taken seriously so that its meaning can be examined in terms of its essence. Someone who is capable of seeing what is essentially signified by 'war' on the one hand, 'parents' house' and 'mother' on the other hand—Boss refers here to the intrinsic view required of the daseinsanalyst—is able to gain an insight into the dreamer's psychic condition at that time from the dream report alone, independently of any other knowledge of his individual life situation. It can thus be inferred from this dream that the dreamer 'even in his waking life, [he] went around as a daydreamer, filled at all times with a pervasive feeling of anxiety toward the outside world of strange adults, whom he could see only as destructive combatants' (p. 69). According to Boss, the dream therefore enables a diagnostic judgement to be made concerning a person's psychological maturity. The therapeutic benefit of this form of dream interpretation consists for Boss in the fact that the patient does not have to subject himself to interpretations that are completely unverifiable from the dream events but can himself recognise in how open or closed a way he still exists and how inhibited his behaviour remains.

2.4 A 'daseins-appropriate' pathology

In the *Existential Foundations of Medicine and Psychology*, Boss puts forward 'a general daseinsanalytic phenomenology of illness'. Of course, the discussion here is intentionally of *being* ill rather than illness. In other respects, his pathology—unlike those of Binswanger and Freud—remains focused on the concept of being ill that is now interpreted privatively as 'a lack of health' (1994, p. 197ff) in accordance with Heidegger's explanations in the Zollikon seminars

(2001a, p. 46f.). No distinction can be made here between purely somatic and psychic or psychosomatic illnesses and an unexpected recognition that what is new in this pathology consists precisely in eliminating this distinction and regarding every form of being ill as an 'infringement' of openness and freedom. This includes the will to overcome body–mind dualism, for which Descartes is again blamed. In traditional parlance according to Boss, all human experience and behaviour, whether healthy or ill, should be termed 'psychosomatic' because the body is not an independently existing reality but still only the 'bodying forth' of human modes of behaviour.[17]

Something new in this pathology is a grid based around the human being's four 'fundamental characteristics': bodyhood, spatiality and temporality, attunement or mood and the fundamental characteristics of openness and freedom of dasein. Boss certainly assigns various pathological phenomena to one or other essential characteristic, such as claustrophobia and agoraphobia to spatiality, depression to attunement and schizophrenia to openness, but he simultaneously relativises these classifications by emphasising that ultimately all the fundamental characteristics are always concerned. With this he seeks to make clear that the daseinsanalyst is concerned not with the classification and diagnostic labelling of an illness but with the precise phenomenological description of whatever 'impairments' are hindering someone from existing in a truly open and free way.

2.5 Daseinsanalytic psychotherapy as a 'leap into freedom'[18]

The guiding objective of daseinsanalytic psychotherapy emerges from its definition of the essence of human dasein as 'openness and freedom' on the one hand, and on the other hand from the understanding of mental suffering as a falling behind in our own possibilities for open and free behaviour towards the world. The goal of a daseinsanalytic psychotherapy thus fundamentally consists

---

[17] Cf. the section on 'Human bodyhood' in the *Existential Foundations* (1994, pp. 100–106).

[18] The expression forms the title of a book by Gion Condrau (Vienna, Europa Verlag, 1972), Medard Boss's most important student and director of the Daseinsanalytic Institute for Psychotherapy and Psychosomatics, the Medard Boss Foundation (1971–2000).

in giving the patient space to make up for the development that
has so far been missed or prevented. For this the psychoanalytic
setting is maintained: the analysand generally lies on the couch in
a daseinsanalytic psychotherapy and is instructed to follow his 'free
associations'. Psychoanalysis equally remains the model in relation
to the frequency of the sessions and the duration of an analysis. It is
no surprise that Boss argues for retaining the couch, as well as the
fundamental rule of free association, since both can be understood as a
rejection of the subject fixated on control and as practice in adopting
the new attitude of 'it speaks to me'.

Boss declares the question 'after all why not?' to be the actual
centrepiece of daseinsanalytic psychotherapy. It forms the counterpart
to the psychoanalytic 'why question' that it is supposed to replace
(1994, p. 279f). The difference between the two forms of question
is that the question 'why' is directed at an increase in knowledge,
whereas the 'after all why not?' question is not a question at all in the
strict sense of seeking an answer, but is supposed to encourage the
analysand to open himself up more and dare to do things that have
so far been anxiously avoided—in short: to become freer.

The daseinsanalytic therapist regards himself as the ally of the
patient's dormant maturational potential that has been blocked from
developing by a deficient childhood upbringing. Accordingly, the
relationship between therapist and patient becomes the actual place
in which something new can occur and the analysand can test out
possibilities that have so far been avoided in life. In this sense Boss
vehemently opposes Freud's interpretation of what occurs in the
analytic relationship as 'transference'. Boss considers transference
interpretations, particularly when these concern positive feelings
towards the analyst, not only to be false but also to be therapeutically
harmful because they misjudge and devalue the new phenomenon
of the patient's first experience of growing love for another human
being instead of acknowledging and fostering it (1994, pp. 271–2).
Another difference from a psychoanalytic psychotherapy is that the
patient's so-called 'acting out' in Boss's therapy is no longer negatively
interpreted in Freudian terms as a relic of his early childhood past
that is to be transferred into 'memory' but positively as a first
testing of new relational possibilities. This is why Boss instructs the

daseinsanalytic psychotherapist not only to treat acting out with tolerance and respect, however childish a form it may assume, but even to foster it, in the confidence that with the therapist's help new, more mature solutions will develop from it.

Daseinsanalysis
Daseinsanalysis
Daseinsanalysis
Daseinsanalysis
Daseinsanalysis
Daseinsanalysis

|

Philosophico-anthropological foundations

Daseinsanalysis
Daseinsanalysis
Daseinsanalysis
Daseinsanalysis
Daseinsanalysis
Daseinsanalysis

Introduction

Every form of psychotherapy is based on fundamental philosophical premises, including when it explicitly refers only to psychological (and at most also sociological, ethnological or biological) theories about the human being. For daseinsanalysis, the reference to philosophy is central. From a historical perspective, it is—as has been shown—philosophical considerations that led to its founding by Ludwig Binswanger and Medard Boss. The name *Daseinsanalyse* is taken directly from the philosophy of Martin Heidegger, who gave this term to the philosophical anthropology he put forward in *Being and Time*.

This introduction to Heidegger's philosophy purposely focuses on the anthropological elements that form the basis of the systematic account of daseinsanalysis. I shall lay particular emphasis on a definition of the human subject's being that has been overlooked by Boss and Binswanger namely that philosophising is an intrinsic part of human being, rather than something retrospective that is only accrued from life experience, and it is certainly far from being the sole preserve of experts trained in it. This further reinforces the position of philosophy: whereas with Binswanger and Boss it was only significant insofar as it guided daseinsanalytic reflection *about* the human being, the daseinsanalyst now also encounters it in his 'object', the psychically suffering human being. This introduction is therefore concerned with two philosophies: first, with Heidegger's existential-philosophical definition of the human being and, second, with the philosophising that according to Heidegger is always in process when people exist.

1

The human being: dasein, being-in-the-world and existence

The three terms in the above heading stand in Martin Heidegger's *Being and Time* for the human being—to be more precise: for the essence of human being. Although in principle they are interchangeable, each term stresses one particular aspect. Since 1927, the publication year of *Being and Time*, someone using these terms indicates that he is thinking in the Heideggerian tradition or at least is referring to his philosophy.

By introducing new philosophical terminology, Heidegger seeks to show that his philosophical thought concerning the human being rests on a radically new foundation. The new expressions do not merely form a supplement to the traditional concepts with which the philosophical definition of the human being previously occurred but replace them altogether. They therefore occupy the positions in the philosophical tradition that used to be held by concepts such as 'subject', 'reason', 'self-consciousness' or 'person'.

Because these three terms contain the quintessence of Heidegger's view of the human being, their interpretation provides a good way into his thinking. Yet deciding with which term to begin is no arbitrary matter. Heidegger himself terms his project *daseinsanalytics* rather than *existential analytics*, which might seem to indicate that 'dasein' is the foremost subject of discussion. This would, however, be a premature conclusion because the correct understanding of 'dasein', as well as 'being-in-the-world', essentially depends on interpreting the term 'being' as it appears here as 'existence'. If this is not done, then we are right back in the dangerous waters of the old theory of being (ontology) as objective presence, which is precisely what Heidegger considers needs to be overcome.

1.1 Existence

The concept of 'existence' is already common in pre-Heideggerian philosophy and is used to indicate that something actually manifests before us, it exists in reality and represents something more than a fantasy. Its antonym is 'essence', which stands for what constitutes the essential nature of a thing or a person. These two concepts are entirely separate, for even if we know whether something exists, we may still know nothing about its essence. Conversely, a definition of essence (for example in relation to God) implies nothing about whether it exists in reality. Heidegger goes against this intellectual tradition in the definition of human being when he makes the provocative declaration that: 'The *"essence" of Da-sein lies in its existence*'.[19] So unheard of is this proposition that it has also generally remained unheard. Its meaning can be understood only if we recognise that while Heidegger is using the old concept of 'existence', he is according it a completely different meaning.

The essential step in the critical transformation of the old ontology consists in restricting the reference to existence and existing to human beings. From this point forward, the term 'existence' is used exclusively for the description of *human* being: only the human being 'exists'. 'Existence' stands in contrast to 'objective presence' or 'occurrence'. Things or living organisms are objectively present or even—like the tools made by human beings—at hand, but they have no existence, whereas the human being is never only objectively present or at hand but, precisely, 'exists'. The special characteristic of existing as opposed to mere presence-at-hand consists in the fact that it is only the human being who not merely is, , but has 'to be': 'The "essence" of this being lies in its to be' (*BT*, p. 39). For Heidegger the human being's particular nature therefore lies in the 'to be', which

---

[19] *Being and Time*, trans. Joan Stambaugh SUNY Press, New York, 1996, p. 40 (henceforth *BT*).

fundamentally distinguishes him not only from inanimate objects but also from non-human living organisms. It is only the human being's life that becomes a *task* that is set before him as long as he is alive, because it is only his life that does not live itself but must be taken over and 'led' or rather 'completed'. We must recognise here that the reference to a task is meant in a *fundamental* way rather than normatively in the sense of a duty to be fulfilled: the human being can do no other than assume this task in some way or other, and he does so even if he does not take life into his own hands in order to lead it in a purposive way but lives entirely non-autonomously, allowing himself to be led by others or even to drift aimlessly along.

What is revolutionary about this existential definition of the human being? While philosophical debates had previously revolved around whether the human being was essentially mind or nature, free or conditioned, his being was nevertheless conceived as objective presence, and therefore the mind, the drives or freedom were also understood as objectively present (or not objectively present) *characteristics* or *capacities* inherent in the human person's being. Heidegger exercises his veto against this thinking in 'categories of objective presence'. In so doing, he demands a radical change in thinking, for what is more familiar to us than describing the human being with reference to (innate or acquired) characteristics and capacities?

Let us try to illustrate with two examples what it means to conceive of the human being including everything that the individual concretely is, has and does 'existentially' rather than 'categorially'— not from the perspective of qualities or capacities but as '*a particular mode of being*' (p. 41):

1. All human beings are born into one specific gender: either as a man or a woman. According to Heidegger, however, I am not merely a woman by nature but have 'to be' my womanhood. The fact of being a woman never attaches to me merely as a given characteristic, but is something I have to take over and accomplish. This applies to all inherited abilities: rather than every person simply having a specific constitution, a specific appearance and specific talents, constitution, appearance

and talents are modes of being that everyone has to accomplish in his own way.

2. All human beings intrinsically have certain fundamental needs. Yet the human being is not simply hungry or tired in the same way as an animal because neither hunger or tiredness dictate to him how to deal with these needs. Although no one can manage without food or sleep, there is always a choice whether to satisfy our hunger now or not until later and to what extent and in what way, indeed what importance we generally want to accord to food in our way of life; similarly we always have to make a decision about when, how often and how strongly to give in to our need for sleep. No one can therefore avoid developing his own relationship to food and sleep. The fact that there are manifold variants of the human—both cultural and individual—response to being hungry or tired demonstrates that the human being also has 'to be' these basic needs.

Based on the definition of the human being as existence, Heidegger works out an existential ontology that sets out the specific structure of the human constitution of being and explains its individual structural elements, the so-called *existentials*. These replace the definitions of the human being's nature (so-called categories) in the old ontology based around 'objective presence'. Let us consider the example of space and time. Heidegger shows that the human being does not merely manifest in space and in time, neither is he merely subordinate to the laws of space and time, but exists spatially for example by approaching or moving away from something, and he exists temporally by conducting himself in some way towards his beginning and his end. Spatiality and temporality are therefore 'existentials'.[20]

---

[20] Cf. *Being and Time*, §§22–24 on the spatiality of dasein and §§ 61ff on temporality.

An existential concept of individuality

Heidegger certainly avoids the concept of the individual, but through the concept of existence he gains a completely radical understanding of individuality, according to which the human being exists only as an individual and not as a collective and he can also never lose his individuality. To 'exist' is only ever something the individual can do, which is why Dasein is *always my own* (*ibid.*). The existential formulation of individuality as 'always-being-my-own-being' does not concentrate on how I am individually formed in contrast to others but implies that I have to live my life myself without any possibility of delegation. For even if I extinguish my individuality and try to merge into another person or into a collective, it is nevertheless still I who orientate my life in that particular way and no other. In this lies a radical 'singularity' from which I cannot escape and that nevertheless does not contradict the fact of being-with in relation to other human beings.

An existential concept of freedom

If life is given to the human being to live ('to be'), then the conduct of his own life always already entails a choice; for he has always already decided in some way or other (usually completely unreflectingly) *how* he lives his life. Jean-Paul Sartre adopted the concept of freedom determined in Heidegger's understanding of existence and made it the centrepiece of his magnum opus *Being and Nothingness*. For him too this is an existential rather than a categorial concept of freedom. Existential freedom is not a 'good' that we possess and about which we are to be concerned because we may also lose it, but a fact of our existence, which is why Sartre provocatively states that the human being is '*condemned to freedom*' (2003, p. 506, p. 574). To illustrate this, he gives the example of the slave who has no prospect of freeing himself from his slavery and yet possesses a freedom that can neither be lost nor relinquished (p. 436). It consists in the fact that his being a slave does not determine *how* he lives this fact or the attitude he takes towards it: abject or defiant, resigned to his fate or despairing and so on. The slave epitomises the human being here. However far someone's life may be determined by birth and origins or restricted by severe blows of fate, he nevertheless remains 'free' in the existential sense in that it is left to him how he integrates what is immutable into his life and what he makes of it, whether he views it positively or negatively, in denial or self-confrontation. Because this freedom can neither be lost nor relinquished, we are never merely blameless victims of circumstances but always also agents who are *responsible* for our free position (p. 576).

1.2 Being-in-the-world

This expression is clearly a substantivisation of the statement that the human being is 'in the world'. Even this statement only applies to the human being: all other beings certainly have the 'innerworldly' quality but not that of 'being-in-the-world'. In other words: only the human being does not simply manifest in the world but exists 'in a worldly way', which means that unlike all other beings, the human being is *related* to the world. In the 1929 lectures, Heidegger distinguishes between the human being, the animal and the inanimate object on the basis that the human being is 'world-forming', the animal is 'poor in world' and the stone is 'worldless' (2001b, p. 176ff).

Let us see what is new in Heidegger's definition of the human being as being-in-the-world.

First, the term repudiates the widespread notion of the human being as a primarily worldless subject that has to forge his accession to the world only in retrospect. He is not a pure subject separated from the world but is always and never anything other than 'being-in-the-world'. This means that he has to deal with things practically and theoretically without first stepping out from his inner world into the external world. Furthermore, the factical subject does not exist in isolation; the human being is only there as 'being-with', which means among other human beings, approached by them and related to them. This even circumvents the opposition between subjectivity and intersubjectivity.

Second, the expression 'being-in-the-world' repudiates the widespread notion that the human being relates only to objects or to other subjects in his life, and asserts another more fundamental relationship, namely the *relationship to the world as world* that is the human being's preserve. But what does 'world' mean? First, any association of the world with 'the earth' and 'living on earth' must be avoided: 'the world' is not to be understood geographically; neither does the word denote the totality of everything that there is on the earth and that happens on it. If we want to say positively what 'world' means, we come across a double meaning of this concept and with it also a double meaning of 'being-in'.

In an initial sense, 'world' means the comprehensive context of significance or meaning in which a human being lives and from which he perceives, thinks and acts. With reference to Hans-Georg Gadamer, 'world' in this sense can also be understood as a *horizon of understanding* (2004, p. 301ff). The individual largely shares his own horizon of understanding with the other human beings of his time and environment, which is why understanding between people also operates relatively well within this common world.[21] This concept of the world could be termed 'hermeneutic' because it establishes the 'world' inhabited by human beings as one that is always already interpreted. Everything that encounters the human being is a part of this world and derives its meaning from it, which again means that to the human being everything including himself is comprehensible only through his 'being-in' this world. It follows from this that understanding between human beings becomes more difficult, as the differences increase between the historical and cultural 'worlds' they inhabit, and that a meaning can be only ascertained for the initially entirely alien, indeed apparently nonsensical statements from other worlds—if at all—with a great expenditure of interpretive work. 'Being-in-the-world' therefore means in this first sense being 'at-home' in a (historically, culturally and socio-economically conditioned) interpretation of the world (cf. *BT*, p. 176). Metaphorically speaking, for the human being the interpreted world has the meaning of an 'at-home' that he inhabits and in which everything that happens is 'familiar' to him (cf. *BT*, p. 51). These metaphors are not intended to suggest, however, that this is also

---

[21] This concept of the world was adopted by Binswanger to form the basis of his daseinsanalytic theory of the world-project (cf. Historical Part, Chapter 1.1).

already a positive being-domiciled and secure; rather, this living in the world is less a matter of homeliness than of a habit that also includes existing in habitual misery or in habitual outsider status.

In a *second* sense that is opposed to the first, 'world' stands for the opposite of everything that has meaning and significance, which can no longer be understood in any positive way. In order to distinguish this 'world' from the interpreted world, it is termed 'the *world as world*', 'the world as such' and 'the world ... in its worldliness' (cf. *BT*, p. 175) or even 'the nothingness of the world' (*BT*, p. 255). The 'nothingness' relates here to 'meaning' or 'significance' and is intended to imply that this 'world' lies beyond all ascription of meaning. It can most accurately just be described as a horizon of openness in which what is appears merely in its *sheer factuality*, its *bare 'that it is'*. This 'world' encompasses and gives rise to all possible world-horizons in which human beings comprehendingly operate. With his discovery, Heidegger moves on to that ultimate ground from which the human being exists—admittedly one that now proves to be an *abyss*.[22] For how can the human being dwell in the 'nullity of the world'?

Heidegger defines the dwelling in the 'nothingness of the world' as 'not-being-at-home' (*BT*, p. 176) and thus denies that it allows any possibility of living in this world at all. This already follows from the human being's inability to orientate himself comprehendingly in this world, for not only is everything that surrounds the human being meaningless, but he himself 'has the character of complete insignificance' (*BT*, p. 174).[23] Because this world provides nothing to understand, there is no viable orientation or foothold, and it cannot be inhabited. It is therefore not simply a matter of an alien world that is unfamiliar to me but a world in which even the 'alien–familiar' opposition has become obsolete. Therefore 'in' this world the human being finds himself not even in a state of 'fear' but of '*Angst*';[24] it no

---

[22] The contrast is more marked in German with the cognate terms *Grund* (ground) and *Abgrund* (abyss) (*Translator's note*).

[23] In his Freiburg inaugural address of 1929, Heidegger establishes this 'being-in' as 'being held out into the nothing'; cf. *What is Metaphysics?* (Heidegger, 1988, p. 91).

[24] Heidegger's theory of *Angst* (*BT*, § 40) and his distinction between the concepts of fear and anxiety are presented in more detail in Part II, Chapter 4.

longer contains anything concrete that could frighten him; rather, it feels generally '*uncanny*' to him (*BT*, p. 176).

With the thesis that 'being-in-the-world' always also means being thrown into the 'nothingness of the world', Heidegger rejects the dominant notion that human existing is fundamentally held secure in meaning-contexts. He thereby turns the tables: someone who suffers from a sense of meaninglessness or complains of a loss of meaning does not simply yet have to find the meaning and has not temporarily lost it, but is being confronted with the truth that we indeed mostly dwell in meaning-contexts without really being secure in meaning because all meaning is fragile and 'behind' all meaning 'bare being' always lurks in its facticity that is devoid of all meaning. The human subject thus emerges here as the being that is certainly reliant on a meaningful orientation but at the same time is driven in the experience of anxiety into the more fundamental dimension of the naked 'that there are beings' and 'that I am and have to be'. It is not critical here how many human beings have ever factically experienced 'anxiety' (as opposed to mere 'fear'); although authentic anxiety is 'rare', in principle it can intrude at any time, without any special cause being required (cf. *BT*, p. 177f).

If human 'being-in-the-world' is inherently oppositional, indeed even contradictory, then its two modes can neither stand together without reference to each other nor coexist in harmony. Rather, 'being-at-home' in the interpreted world is always *threatened* by the (more fundamental) 'being-*not*-at-home' and the human being strives to protect himself from this threat. This gives rise to a *third* meaning of 'being-in-the-world', namely *falling prey to the world* (*BT*, p. 164). 'Falling' does not denote any pathological dependency (psychic enslavement) here but means the constant movement that leads *away from* being-not-at-home and *into* an interpreted and therefore inhabitable world. In falling prey to the world, the human being gives in to the basic need to be domiciled in a familiar world. Nonetheless, this also involves a *movement of flight*: in falling prey, the human being flees the anxiety-inducing truth of being thrown into the nothingness of the world. This is, however, a flight from himself that can never truly succeed. The factical subject therefore has an intrinsic tendency to self-deception, which is why—

in Heidegger's words—he lives 'equiprimordially in truth and in untruth' (*BT*, p. 210).

Now Heidegger also gives 'falling prey' another more specific meaning when he refers to the intrinsic human tendency to deny the difference between himself and non-human beings and also to conceive of himself as an objectively present being (cf. *BT*, p. 122). With this, Heidegger establishes the dominant tendency not only in philosophy but even more so in the contemporary human sciences to objectify the human being and interprets this in terms of a quasi-natural tendency towards reifying self-interpretation.

1.3 Dasein

Even the definition of the human being as 'dasein' is the substantivisation of a statement that this time reads: 'The human being is there'.[25] It can already be concluded from the above explanations that this does not involve any indication concerning the human being's spatial presence. Instead, the statement must be read from the start to mean that the human being '*exists the there*', which means: has to be. But what does the 'there' mean? It denotes the fundamental fact that the human being does not live his life 'blindly' but 'with his eyes open' and thus always somehow 'with consciousness', whereby Heidegger always refers to 'disclosedness' rather than consciousness. The definition of the human being as 'dasein' thus takes an old philosophical statement of essence concerning the human being that he is the creature endowed with reason and consciousness, and expresses it existentially: '*Da-sein is its disclosure*' (*BT*, p. 125). Just as in traditional philosophy human consciousness always implied consciousness of itself, the 'there' is also reflexive, which is to say that the *Dasein* is ' *"there" for itself* '(*BT*, p. 125) and it exists as 'self-disclosedness'.

Now in post-Cartesian philosophy 'self-consciousness' is considered to be a distinction of the human subject. What is new in Heidegger's definition of the human being as 'dasein' is its existential interpretation. Both the question of *how* the human being

---

[25] 'Da sein', as two separate words, literally meaning 'to be there' (*Translator's note*).

is disclosed to himself and the question of *in what* this form of self-knowledge actually consists receive answers that are based on new distinctions; these are the distinctions between 'understanding' and 'attunement', on the one hand, and between 'ontical' and 'ontological' self-disclosedness on the other. Both distinctions are central to daseinsanalysis as a psychotherapeutic movement and therefore require a brief explanation.

Understanding and attunement

What is new is that Heidegger postulates not only understanding but also attunement as a genuine source of knowledge. Here the term 'understanding' is used much more broadly and fundamentally than usual; it stands not for a specific (humanities-based) method, nor even for theoretical knowledge divorced from practice but for human life-experience in general, which is itself permeated with 'understanding'. Colloquial language provides ample evidence of this when for example someone is said to 'understand something', meaning that the person can do something well. What applies to any form of activity can also be said of the conduct of life in general: fundamentally, the human being only ever lives so that he can (somehow!) deal skilfully with life.[26] 'Perception' and 'thought', which for Kant still represented the human being's two fundamental cognitive faculties, are grounded in understanding gained from life experience and derived from it. Like Kant, however, Heidegger insists that there are two forms of knowledge that are equiprimordial and thus also equally valid; only here these are no longer perception and thought but understanding and attunement. The term 'attunement' stands for what is colloquially called 'mood', and these interact: 'Attunement always has its understanding ... Understanding is always attuned' (*BT*, p. 134).

To accord a world- and self-disclosing power to moods is objectionable from the traditional philosophical standpoint. There are certainly philosophical considerations of the meaning of emotionality

---

[26] The reader is reminded of the above explanations concerning the 'world' as a 'horizon of understanding' and 'being-in-the-world' as 'inhabiting' a collectively interpreted world.

in the realm of aesthetics and morality; yet in the domain of theoretical knowledge the so-called affects and passions were regarded as mere, and even disruptive, secondary phenomena that had to be screened out if possible. According to Heidegger, moods are significant for the recognition of the world and the self in three distinct ways:

a) 'Pure beholding, even if it penetrated into the innermost core of the being of something objectively present, would never be able to discover anything like what is threatening' (*BT*, p. 130). Only the attunement of fear rather than its mere perception enables me to state that a danger is confronting me because only the emotional experience of being afraid can convey to me that I am threatened. This applies not only to things that are dangerous but likewise to what is pleasant, sublime, distasteful, splendid or regrettable. These qualities of things, circumstances or even human beings are only directly accessible to us in the corresponding feelings—which, however, in no way means that feelings cannot also deceive us in each case; for example, it is possible to fear a danger where none exists and so on.

b) In contrast to (intentionally directed) feelings, moods by definition have 'no object' to which to relate. This is shown in the example of joy as a feeling as opposed to cheerfulness as a mood: whereas I may be joyful about something or made joyful by an event that has taken place, cheerfulness is not directed at anything—we feel generally cheerful, that means: in a good mood, light-hearted and lively, cheery, optimistic, often without being able to say what has put us in this mood. Its cognitive achievement therefore relates to nothing concrete but to the world and our own being-in-the-world: 'Indeed, we must *ontologically* in principle leave the primary discovery of the world to "mere mood"' (*BT*, p. 130). What this means is that we realise best from experience that the moods in which we find ourselves are far from being intrapsychic states alone but always concern the whole world. Each prevailing mood in fact always makes everything around us appear in a particular light. When someone is cheerful, the whole world shows him a friendly face, and everyone appears cheerful and good-hearted; in a dejected mood, however, the world too strikes us as drab and forbidding. Precisely because mood casts a particular light over everything that is and occurs, it blunts the differences between what is and thus the world manifests itself as that in which everything operates. While in the previous chapter we characterised the 'world' as horizon of *understanding*, this now proves to require some amplification: the world is also and even primarily a *horizon of mood*.

c) Yet there is more to this: for Heidegger even self-knowledge is originally a matter of moods: 'In attunement, Da-sein is always already brought before itself, it has always already found itself, not as perceiving oneself to be there, but as one finds one's self in attunement' (*BT*, p. 128). This high evaluation of moods as a 'site' of original self-knowledge does not lead, however, to any cult of feeling in Heidegger because moods can also be deceptive: '"Mere mood" discloses the there more primordially, but it also *closes* it *off* more stubbornly than any *not*-perceiving' (*BT*, p. 128).

The ambiguity of the human self-relationship

From ancient times, 'ontology' was considered a basic philosophical discipline that enquired into the 'being of beings'; from this could be derived specialist ontologies that addressed, for example, the being of living nature in contrast to the being of the human subject. In this sense, Heidegger's daseinsanalytics is also an ontological undertaking to the extent that it enquires into the specific being of the human subject. What is radically innovative about the daseinsanalytic ontology is that it does not merely ascribe a specific being to the human subject but makes this 'being' the concern of every single human being. Heidegger in fact sees it as the crucial point about human being that the human subject does not simply (like all other beings) possess a specific constitution of being but *that he conducts himself towards it*.

Therefore he can provocatively state: 'The ontic distinction of Da-sein lies in the fact that it *is* ontological' (*BT*, p. 10).[27] With this, every human being is recognised as an ontologist, that means—implicitly knowing about his own being and adopting a position towards it. The widespread notion that only the philosopher freely decides to turn his attention at leisure to the question of being is thus repudiated in favour of the thesis that every human being exists philosophically in an elemental way and that it would not even be possible explicitly to posit the philosophical basic question as to the being of beings if every single human being did not always already have an implicit, *pre*-ontological knowledge of being.

For Heidegger, the discovery that the human being has a knowledge of his own being was solely of philosophical rather than psychological interest. It served the development of his own ontology and is therefore developed only in a basic, even cursory way in *Being and Time*. Turning this knowledge to good account for daseinsanalytic psychology psychopathology and psychotherapy requires some further, extrapolating explanations.

---

27 In contrast to 'ontological', the term 'ontical' (or 'ontic') always denotes the concrete entity; 'ontical' is therefore also the human being as a concretely existing creature that can be empirically apprehended and described. The distinction between 'ontical' and 'ontological' corresponds to that between 'existentiell' and 'existential'.

2

Existence as attuned understanding of our own being

2.1 The pre-ontological inclusion

I f according to Heidegger the human being is distinguished by having a relationship to his being, how is this relationship with his being to be understood? For this we are best guided by the term *pre-ontological inclusion*, although it only appears once in *Being and Time* for the purpose of characterising human understanding: 'Every ontic understanding "includes" certain things, even if only *pre*-ontologically' (*BT*, p. 288). From this it follows first that the knowledge belonging to human being about its own being is *inherent* in the specific ('ontical') understanding of any given fact. If we also accept that 'understanding' in the Heideggerian sense encompasses all human experience and behaviour, this implies that the entire concrete conduct of everyday life has a philosophical dimension. Second, it becomes clear that (pre-)ontological knowledge is *included* in concrete experience and behaviour, which means it generally remains unnoticed (unconscious), and represents a mere background knowledge.

It first emerges that the pre-ontological inclusion is actually indispensable for the concrete-everyday understanding of something. For instance, we would not be able to ascertain from a quick glance at the clock what the time is and how much time we have left for some work we have begun, if the ontological fact were not also already disclosed to us at the same time that everything we do is subject to time and that time passes inexorably. Neither would it be possible for us to interpret the feeling of hunger as an indication that we need food if we did not at the same time have available an ontological pre-understanding, however vague and diffuse, of our bodily nature and bodily needs. It would be equally impossible for us to interpret a pain in the stomach as the sign of a possible illness (instead of only feeling a vague discomfort) if we did not at the same time know about our susceptibility to disease and so also the fragility of our bodily existence. Neither would we be in a position to decide 'in favour of something' and thus at the same time 'against something' if we did not secretly see that we cannot circumvent repeatedly deciding in some way or another and thus renouncing something and at the same time bearing responsibility for it.

Ascertaining that our concrete understanding (and actions!) are always grounded in a basic ontological understanding without which they would not come about at all is, however, only half the truth of the matter. The other half consists in the fact that the human being is also *endangered* by this. This generally only latent endangerment becomes acute if the pre-ontological background knowledge moves into the foreground and imposes itself directly. This is possible in principle at any time because the comprehending dealing with concrete facts *in itself* points to the ontological conditions of our existence. The fact that this indication generally remains screened out is not in any way self-explanatory but instead requires its own justification.

The fact that we always secretly feel threatened by this background knowledge is clear for example from the way we begin and end almost every encounter with other people, however fleeting, with good wishes. When we wish each other a good day, what secretly underlies this wish is the (anxiety-inducing) knowledge that no one can know what good or bad things the day will bring and that, however calm and ordinary everything seems, we are fundamentally subject to possible disaster at any time. Likewise, when we say 'bless you' to each other it is because we secretly know how precarious good health is and that any one of us can be struck out of the blue by a life-threatening illness. Again, when we wish each other success or good luck for an undertaking, it is because we secretly know that everything we start can also fail and often depends on conditions over which we have no influence. Indeed we generally do not think explicitly about the 'ontological' meaning of these wishes and generally only use them in the sense of polite gestures. Nonetheless, ontologically they have the function of incantatory formulae to keep at bay the knowledge of our own being that is difficult to tolerate.

The example provided by these wishes points to the supposition that the 'pre-ontological inclusion' inherent in every experience and action mostly remains included (that means: in the background) only because we *actively* blind ourselves to it or banish it into the background. We acquire the habit of paying attention only to the concrete meaning-content of something and only attending to what is concretely in front of us. So wishing the neighbour a good day still only has the meaning of greeting him in a friendly way; sudden stomach pains are attributed only to ordinary ailments in order at most to take the further step of having them investigated by a doctor; alternatives between which we have to decide are only weighed up for their pros and cons. This generates the impression that the human being generally understands the world aphilosophically and is only alerted to the fundamental conditions of his own being on exceptional occasions or on account of a personal theoretical interest in them.

2.2 Experiences of being in everyday life

That the work of repudiation that keeps the knowledge of being obscured is inherently fragile is indicated by what are relatively frequent incidents of inappropriate experience and behaviour that very suddenly emerge for no apparent reason. It happens now and then that on account of a small thing we are 'scared to death'; that because of a minor disappointment we 'fall into a pit of despair'; that because of a small mishap we really wish 'the ground would swallow us up'; that we approach a simple task as if it were an 'unscalable mountain'. In such cases, we are much more deeply affected than would be justified by the matter in question but we are also inclined to dismiss such incidents as pure nonsense and quickly forget them again. They are in fact enigmatic as long as we seek the explanation only in the concrete context; they become comprehensible only when we work from the premise that the 'pre-ontological inclusion' has therefore irrupted at some point into everyday life. For whatever reasons, we have then heard what we are given to understand about human being by an intrinsically harmless and highly familiar occurrence; we have had an 'experience of being'. Under these circumstances, a stomach pain can unexpectedly induce panic because it points beyond itself to our own fragility and thus presages the ontological certainty of death; similarly, an overdue decision, even if it concerns something utterly trivial, can make us feel completely at a loss and helpless because it presents us with the situation of 'choice' in all its gravity.

It is therefore not surprising that everything gets out of proportion as soon as our own experience and behaviour fall under the sway of the usually obscured knowledge of our own being. For this overloads the concrete incident with meaning and gives it a weight that it does not otherwise have. Usually we manage to file away such imponderable experiences of being as momentary derailments of our mental life and to get everything back in proportion. We regain our footing and are relieved to discover that once again we have made a mountain out of a mole-hill. Everyone is familiar with such overreactions to a harmless event; everyone also has his individual hypersensitivities in particular areas. If these neuralgic points are struck, we lose our composure more quickly than usual, are stubborn, repeatedly react against better knowledge in the same stereotypical and inappropriate way. It comes down in every instance to how strongly this ontological experience thrusts into the foreground but also, conversely, how well the quasi-natural defence operates, for the more the latter fails, and the more frequently, the less successfully we can deal appropriately with what is concretely in front of us.[28]

2.3 The originary ontico–ontological conflict

It must therefore be supposed that the average everyday conduct of life is based on a constant screening out of a latent fundamental knowledge that does not need to be actualised for dealing with

---

[28] This forms the starting-point for an existentially-ontologically based theory of mental suffering, which is developed in Part III.

concrete day-to-day living, in fact can even become a hindrance. What is screened out in this way for the purposes of a well-functioning everyday life is nonetheless true. Because this truth is suppressed in the normal course of daily life, Heidegger describes everydayness as a being '*in "untruth"*' (*BT*, p. 204). However, this is only partly correct because after all it is only this resistance to ontological truth that makes it possible to perceive the concrete reality appropriately and to operate appropriately in it. Since there is also a truth to factical reality, we should probably instead refer to an incompatibility of two truths that are mutually exclusive for practical daily living. The course of everyday life opens up only the alternative possibilities of being deceived as to ontological truth or opening up to it at the cost of disrupting the ordinary course of daily life.

Heidegger did not recognise this originary conflict as such because he worked from the premise that the human being always exists either 'inauthentically' or 'authentically', in general though 'inauthentically'; that is, screens out the pre-ontological inclusion by 'falling prey to the "world"'.[29] The state of inauthenticity is overcome only by a human being's explicit willingness to attend to that which he otherwise purposely disregards, thus by a free decision to confront the truth of being and to take on the anxiety that is bound up with it. If, however, we take seriously Heidegger's statement that '*Angst* can arise in the most harmless situations' (*BT*, p. 177), then there is definitely a *third* between authenticity and inauthenticity—namely, being confronted entirely unprepared and involuntarily with the truth of being and being overtaxed by it.

Whenever the ontological inclusion of a concrete experience or behaviour imposes itself and thrusts forward, we are—at least for the moment—displaced from the meaningful universe and confronted with the pure facticity of 'that I am and have to be'.

---

[29] The construction 'Man' in the German original (rendered as 'they' here) is a substantivisation of the pronoun 'man' ('one' or 'they') that denotes all the convictions, conventions and rules of living (the 'world') that 'one' shares by belonging to a particular society or even a group. So 'falling prey to the world' in Heidegger—in contrast to Medard Boss—is not an individual failing that indicates a lack of psychological maturity but an 'existential': it is intrinsic to the human being initially and generally to have fallen prey to the 'world'. To emphasise the positive element of this existential, I shall frequently be referring to 'participation in common sense' rather than 'having fallen prey to the world'.

This displacement can only be experienced by the human being as horrifying.[30] There are two expressions with which Heidegger seeks to capture in words the horrifying aspect of such experiences of being: on one occasion, he refers to the 'inexorability of an enigma', as which the 'the that of its there ... stares at it [Dasein]' (p. 128); on the other occasion to the 'barren mercilessness' in which its 'pure That' (p. 315) is revealed to *dasein*.

Let us consider for substantiation the two examples of the feeling of hunger and the decision: if the ontological inclusion of the entirely normal and everyday feeling of hunger thrusts into the foreground, then I am faced with the sheer fact that this need pursues me as long as I live, that it urgently demands satisfaction regardless of whatever I would like to do myself and whether I am actually in any position to satisfy the hunger. I am thus confronted with my irresoluble neediness and dependence and indeed as a 'bare' fact that is not further justifiable and is at the same time inaccessible. If the ontological inclusion of an impending decision thrusts into the foreground, I am confronted with two other, equally inaccessible conditions of being. First, there is the fact that I am paradoxically compelled by the decision to enforce a renunciation on myself, regardless of what decision I make, because with any free choice I am depriving myself of other possibilities that are open to me. Second, I realise that I can never have enough knowledge to be sure that the decision is also the right one. I must recognise that I am ultimately 'going out on a limb' with every decision, which is why it is always possible that it will later prove to be the wrong one, but that a wrong decision nevertheless is and remains my decision, for which I must answer and take responsibility for the consequences. It is also the case here that renunciation and responsibility are revealed in their 'naked that it is' as basic conditions that constitute my life.

Here we have encountered the crucial point. The ontological inclusion reveals our own being in its pure facticity, without yet being swathed in reassuring interpretations. With this it attacks the focus of everyday dealing with life and what Husserl even designated as the

---

[30] The hyphenated form of the German 'Ent-setzt-Werden' ('entsetzt' meaning 'horrified') emphasises the roots of 'entsetzen' in a literal displacement that is not conveyed by the English word (*Translator's note*).

human being's 'natural disposition': to operate unquestioningly and naïvely in the belief in a secured meaning of the being of the world and, supported by this belief, to be purposively orientated towards the concretely impending concerns within the world.

2.4 Collective forms of self-protection

What Heidegger generally terms 'falling prey to the world' serves to protect us from the incursion of overtaxing experiences of being in everyday life. I would like to distinguish between three interdependent forms of self-protection: everyday activity (busy-ness), common sense and the cultural establishment of meaning.

Everyday activity

Being taken up with everyday activity is often felt to be soulless and deadening. Moreover, everyday life consists not only in habits and routine but also worries and misgivings. To break out of everyday life is therefore a wish that exists in many people's imaginations. We refer however to 'everyday culture' in a way that expresses the eminently positive, even unrenounceable aspect of this mode of life, which consists among other things in the way everyday life leads us away from ourselves in a specific sense and censors self-perception. The more we allow ourselves to be taken up with concrete demands, the less inclined we are to 'philosophise' and thus to attend to the pre-ontological inclusion. The oft-cited everyday stress thus has a 'being-reassuring' effect; it is easy to observe that to many people stress comes at times that are not inconvenient, in fact even that they seek it out and also structure their leisure time in such a way that they are taken up with constant duties and demands for achievement, for instance in sports activities. What gives better protection though than mere activity is real engagement, the readiness to strive for something 'body and soul'. The greater the interest and the corresponding application to a task, the lesser the danger of being confronted with the abysses of human existence.

Common sense

The German expression 'gesunder Menschenverstand' (literally: sound human reason or understanding) is used in a similar way to the English term 'common sense'. It is no less eloquent than the English, yet it indicates that the basic concurrence of thinking and feeling allows and protects not only the conduct of daily life but along with it also the individual's psychic health. This is achieved by common sense because it contains rules concerning a worldly-wise approach to intrusive experiences of being. 'Everyday Da-sein derives the pre-ontological interpretation of its being from the nearest kind of being of the they' (*BT*, p. 121). The 'they' in the common-sense meaning contains a rich store of expressions and witticisms, maxims and sayings for every life situation. Here are a few examples: 'Don't make a mountain out of a molehill', 'Things are never as bad as they seem', 'That's life', 'Time will tell', 'Make the best of it', 'Pride comes before a fall', 'Lies have short legs', 'Where there's a will, there's a way', 'Time heals all wounds', 'Man proposes; God disposes'. These and similar sayings circulate as pieces of worldly wisdom that hand down long-preserved experiences on which we can thus depend. Someone who has common sense lives by sayings of this kind.

It is already clear from this small selection of expressions that common sense warns us not to let ourselves be upset by momentary incursions into everyday life and assures us that what appears meaningless at one moment will also reveal its meaning in time and what is not in order now will fall into place. However, the power of common sense should not be overestimated. Individual people share it to widely varying degrees. Heidegger did not consider this because as a philosopher he did not take into account that the human being does not live in 'the they' from the outset but as a child slowly grows into the world view held by adults. The course that this individual process takes depends on many factors, not least on the individual himself, who identifies with common sense views or rejects them on the basis of a particular sensitivity. Furthermore, the maxims of common sense are valid primarily for everyday life but offer inadequate protection when people—whether as individuals or as part of a population—are so strongly affected by unusual ('traumatic') events that their belief in meaning is shattered. Protection from this is given as necessary by the elaborated interpretations that are provided by every culture in some form or other.

Culturally established meaning

Every culture provides collective interpretations that refer explicitly to basic existential experiences. They are generally religious or quasi-religious in nature and claim (with the exception of Buddhism) a transcendental authority 'beyond the world' as the founder and preserver of meaning. Transcendental (metaphysical) interpretations are sought in particular when all innerworldly meaning has been thrown into question by catastrophic events. They generally have a long tradition. Common sense finds its necessary amplification in this traditional knowledge of meaning. Its constancy thus also stems from the fact that it is rooted in ancient traditions. However, modernity has brought a radical change here. A more or less hermetic and generally binding world view has been superseded by a multiplicity of meanings on offer. This has opened up a previously unimaginable scope for the individual to shape his own life. This emancipation of the modern subject has, however, a disadvantage if we consider that along with the binding nature of traditional interpretations of the world, their immunising effect against experiences of being has also been lost. Under the conditions of modernity, ontological inclusions also now press faster and more effectively, more confusingly and disturbingly into everyday life. Many people feel a lack here that they seek to remedy by turning to new doctrines of salvation. The typically modern or postmodern stock of meanings on offer from every cultural environment is, however, so inherently contradictory that it can only have a weak immunising effect, and generally only for a short period. With the disintegration of traditional knowledge of meaning that is in progress, common sense too has lost some of its constancy and profundity. It is increasingly expressed today in ephemeral views that are fashionable at a particular moment and give information about what is 'in' at the time. This points to the conclusion that the modern subject is more disposed towards mental suffering because he has to manage without the protective measures that traditionally protected him from overwhelming and therefore pathogenic experiences of being. His everyday life is no longer 'being-reassured', and this applies not only to the everyday lives of adults but equally and probably even more to those of children, who are particularly dependent on learning to deal with experiences of being. The consequences are that entirely trivial disappointments and insults can instigate uncontrollable psychic processes. What this means will form the subject of the next chapter. The philosophical part has merely prepared the ground for an adequate understanding of mental suffering by revealing its anthropological foundations.

Daseinsanalysis
Daseinsanalysis
Daseinsanalysis
Daseinsanalysis
Daseinsanalysis
Daseinsanalysis

II

Philosophico-psychological aspects

Daseinsanalysis
Daseinsanalysis
Daseinsanalysis

Introduction

I t is slightly misleading to present 'philosophico-psychological aspects' as the second part; however, philosophy is again accorded an important function here in the psychological domain, instead of being regarded only as the basis for the daseinsanalytic psychology that can now be anticipated. It is right to ask whether two different questions are not being confused here, instead of the two disciplines and their intellectual approaches being precisely and neatly distinguished. It follows, however, from the insight gained in the last chapter that everything 'ontical'—that is, a person's concrete modes of experience and behaviour—includes a 'pre-ontological' engagement with his own being that daseinsanalysis also remains reliant on philosophy for its psychological investigations. Because everything mental therefore has a philosophical dimension, a daseinsanalytic psychology even if it seeks to be nothing but psychology can only abandon philosophy at the cost of inappropriately curtailing its object, human psychic life.

What will follow are not propositions of a daseinsanalytic psychology, but an introduction to daseinsanalytic thought based on the psychological subjects of particular importance for daseinsanalytic psychopathology and psychotherapy. These include (1) the human being's bodiliness, including the question of the relationship between body and mind, (2) the human being's temporality and historicity, including the question of a daseinsanalytic understanding of child development and (3) human sociality, including the question of a daseinsanalytic definition of the Other. They also include the three emotions that have the status of (philosophical) basic moods in the existential perspective: (4) anxiety, (5) shame and (6) guilt. It should become apparent here that these subjects are not simply objects of psychological research but a field of basic existentiell questions and experiences that confront every human being in some form or other.

These subjects are also addressed in Freud's psychoanalysis, albeit on the basis of theoretical suppositions drawn from nineteenth-century mechanical and energic conceptions. This factor long misled daseinsanalysis into throwing out the baby with the bathwater and rejecting not only the theoretical packaging but also the content as 'non-phenomenological'. It is much more productive, however, to adopt a positive phenomenological attitude to psychoanalytic theories and to draw out the significant insights that they contain. This happens here, for example, when (1) the psychoanalytic theory of the drives is incorporated into an existential understanding of the body and (2) the genetic-developmental psychology perspective is incorporated into an existential understanding of 'being towards the beginning' as well as (3) being-with. This concludes with existential interpretations of (6) 'the unconscious' and (7) dreams, which form the prerequisites for a daseinsanalytic approach to psychopathological phenomena.

1

The body

Daseinsanalysis has striven from the outset for an adequate understanding of the body. Starting from Heidegger's definition of human existing as being-in-the-world, *Ludwig Binswanger* and *Medard Boss* have shown that the human body too, contrary to the dominant notion both in everyday life and in the sciences, is not 'objectively present' but 'exists', and therefore also contrary to appearances is not a bodily thing that we somehow have but is part of the conduct of being-in-the-world. For them the gain in knowledge consists primarily in being able to dissolve the age-old prejudice of a body–mind dualism that is connected with the concept of the body and mind as two objectively present essential beings, which makes the question of how the two belong together obsolete as a mere pseudo-question. This resulted in a new approach to hysterical conversion symptoms and psychosomatic illnesses.

A close reading of the analyses of human bodiliness by Binswanger and Boss shows the same one-sidedness in both. To overcome the idea of the body as merely an objectively present bodily thing, both avoid any reference to 'the body', either generically or to the living human body. Whereas Binswanger instead refers to various 'modes of bodiliness' (1992–1994, Vol. 2, *loc. cit.*, p. 40ff.; p. 422ff.), Boss almost only ever uses the verb 'to body forth' in place of the substantive, the body (1994, *loc. cit.*, p. 100ff.). By this he seeks to express that what we are accustomed to thinking of as an independently existing unity is nothing but the bodily element that always belongs to individual modes of behaviour. Thus the body is detached in both authors; with Binswanger it becomes a 'mode of existence' that changes according to every relationship to the world, in Boss a 'bodying forth' of the specific modes of behaviour carried out by the individual dasein in each case. Both the visible body with its at least temporarily invariant forms, masses and weights and the body as an organism, which mostly functions spontaneously because it obeys its own biological laws, now emerge as the result of a reifying perspective that has completely lost sight of the true nature of the body.

Allowances must be made for Binswanger and Boss, since it is extraordinarily difficult to define the bodiliness of the body—its 'nature'—in positive terms without reifying it or at least elevating it to an agency that governs mental life. Furthermore, in *Being and Time* Heidegger never even once mentions either the human body or the fact that dasein always exists either as a woman or a man. The human being appears here as a pure neuter, devoid of a body or a sex. Because this omission can hardly be dismissed as a mere accident, the suspicion quickly arises that the body's naturalness is something that completely eludes Heidegger's concept of existence.

The following considerations are designed to show that his concept of existence certainly also provides an approach to the bodily-natural side of human being. From it two statements can in fact be inferred: 1. that as *existing* beings we neither simply 'have' a body nor simply 'are' this body, but that *we have to be* it; 2. that our bodily being is also *disclosed* to us, and indeed in understanding as well as in moods.

1.1 The task of being a body

We conceive the body existentially when with Heidegger we cease to ask: '*What* is the body?' and instead ask 'How *is* the body?'. The human body is such that everyone has 'to be' his bodily being, and that means: has to assume it as his task.[31] This already implies something crucial, namely that our bodily being imposes obligations on us, whether

---

[31] The term 'Leibsein als Aufgabe' (The task of being a body) is drawn from the title of Böhme's (2003) book on this subject.

we like it or not. It can only do this, however, insofar as it is neither produced by us nor is simply intrinsic to our behaviour. Therefore the fact that our own body becomes a task—far from contradicting the notion that we are *thrown* into it and are thus also *subjected* to bodily processes—confirms it. The body only becomes a task for us because it represents the largely inaccessible *nature* that we ourselves are and have to be (Böhme, 2003, *loc. cit.*, p. 101).

It thus emerges that the body has to be interpreted neither as an 'objectively present thing' nor as a 'tool at hand' for its autonomy to be recognised. For it appears by becoming a task for us—for instance in the form of bodily needs that declare themselves imperatively, which we have to satisfy within a certain freedom of scope for deferral and degree. No one is free to decline this task, however much he or she may rebel against it. But what about our dealings with the body's functioning according to its own laws as an organism? Is it even possible in the domain of the internal organs or the autonomous musculature, where everything occurs automatically, which is why particularly on good days we hardly notice it at all, to refer to a task we are set by the body? Absolutely, and indeed because we know that we are dependent on these autonomous bodily processes, which represent a 'black box' for us, without any possibility of transparency, let alone control. To learn to tolerate this knowledge is probably the most difficult aspect of the task that we are set by bodily being.

The dream of the natural life

Because we are not simply bodily, but have to be our body, there is also no 'return to nature' for the human being. Any possible path 'back to nature' is blocked for us not primarily by culture but by the very fact that we stand in a relationship to our bodily being and cannot escape from this relationship. Because we have to be our body, the unity with the body is already broken and cannot be restored. The idea of a natural state to be regained is widespread above all in regard to sexuality. Precisely because Christian-western culture was so hostile to the body and sexuality, it was long believed that the emancipation from cultural prejudices might point the way back to a purely natural relationship to sexuality free both of inculcated inhibitions and of guilt. Neither does nature prescribe to us how to live our being a woman or a man. In this connection too, it is illusory to believe that we have only to overcome cultural prejudices to discover the supposedly original, nature-appropriate image of woman and man that we might then realise for ourselves. It is much more the case that culture with its respective notions of typical male and female being leaps into the void in orientation left by nature.

Delegation of the task to the body

The fact that our bodily being is given to us to live in no way means that we also recognise and take on this task as such. Precisely the experience of its sovereignty also conceals the temptation to delegate the existential task to the body and declare it to be the authentic and true subject to which we entrust the conduct of our own lives. This has only become possible, however, since the negative mystification of the body that dominated western tradition under the influence of Platonism and Christianity gave way to what tends to be a positive mystification. Instead of the body being regarded as in previous times as the epitome of everything base and animalistic, it has now become the *yardstick* of the natural and thus the good life. Bodily needs are now considered—precisely because they declare themselves spontaneously—to be inherently justified. By identifying with them, we imagine that we are freed from our responsibility for the way we conduct our lives. Thus instead of recognising bodily being as a task, we short-circuit bodily needs as instructions on which to act; instead of taking over responsibility for satisfying our bodily needs by adopting them as something to be carried out, we delegate the responsibility to the body, which is assumed to know what is right and good for us as individuals.

Psychosomatic suffering can also be understood as the delegation of our own being as a subject to the body. Here the body vicariously assumes the task of representing an existentiell problematic and suffering from it. The cost of the bodily suffering is offset by the advantage of no longer being directly confronted with a problematic by which we feel overwhelmed. In place of feelings that are difficult to bear, such as anxiety, powerlessness, anger and guilt, as well as a sense of hopelessness, anonymous physical complaints appear that according to orthodox medicine have nothing to do with me as a person and are therefore easier to bear. In addition, as a physically ill patient we have a legitimate claim to treatment and consideration, and can delegate the healing to the skills of medicine and the body's so-called self-healing powers.

1.2 Bodily experiences as experiences of being

Bodily being can only be given to the human being to carry out because he has some knowledge of his bodiliness. Heidegger's discovery that we know ourselves not only through understanding but also in our *moods* proves to be especially productive in relation to the body. As already mentioned, the understanding of the body and its implicit evaluation have radically changed in our culture—from a hostility to the body to what tends to be an idealisation of the body. This change is due not only to the general decline of the Christian tradition but also to increased prosperity and the major advances of medicine, which can treat previously incurable diseases, ease pain and postpone old age and death. It would therefore also be premature to refer sweepingly to a change to a strictly positive relationship to our body. For what is affirmed, even deified, today is not the body as it is given to us by nature but the eternally youthful body that is considered beautiful according to the prevailing criteria. This also manifests a bitter struggle against our bodily nature. What is lacking today is an understanding of the body that directs us also to affirm the imperfect, damaged, ill and ageing body.

Three basic experiences of bodily being

The fact of being bodily is revealed to us more directly through bodily *sensations* than through understanding. By the term 'bodily sensation', I am referring generally to all affective and mood-type experiences that we have in and with the body.[32] I am restricting myself here to

---

[32] Hermann Schmitz (1998) has made the major contribution of examining and differentiating bodily sensations from a phenomenological perspective.

the important question for daseinsanalysis as to the moods in which we (have to) experience both directly and undisguisedly *that we are and have to be bodily*. It may initially be surprising that three negative moods are adduced for this, namely pain, nausea and shame. What these have in common is that they not only declare themselves but also impose themselves and persist against our will. It is different with positive bodily feelings, both pleasurable physical sensations and generally the state of physical well-being. We are no way simply passively subjected to those but experience them only on condition that we accede to them. Acceding to them, however, already contains an active factor of affirmation. Not so with pain, nausea and shame: we are overwhelmed by these, although we want to escape them. And in them our body comes to our notice in a negative way and thus enables us to experience it in its otherness and alien nature. In them we experience bodily being as a 'burden' from which there can be no true release because we inescapably are and have to be the body.

Pain

In physical pain we are often literally thrown back on to our bodily being. While previously we may have entirely forgotten that we exist in a bodily way because we have thrown ourselves into something 'body and soul', the body now compels our attention as a hurting body. This is achieved by pain because it tears apart the previous unity with the body. In his interpretation of a poem by Georg Trakl, Heidegger even equates pain with tearing: 'But what is pain? Pain rends. It is the rift' (1971, p. 204). In pain, the body emerges in its bodiliness, as the Other to myself, alien to me and yet my body, which I am and have to be. Every pain has its 'pre-ontological inclusion'; even a fleeting pain indicates to me the painful ontological truth that the body is fundamentally vulnerable, susceptible to disease and—in short—mortal.

   This helps to explain why many people want to avoid pain at any cost; this makes it all the more mysterious, however, when instead pain is sought through actively self-inflicted injuries. If we are not merely to dismiss this as a pathological symptom that can be described and psychiatrically diagnosed but not understood, the question that must be asked is what these people are seeking in pain. This brings to the fore a second aspect of pain, which Heidegger called a 'gathering': 'Pain indeed tears asunder ... yet so that at the same time it draws everything to itself, gathers it to itself' (1971, p. 204). Pain involves a retreat from worldly relationships, throwing the sufferer back on himself and thus conveying the certainty of his own existence. Pain thus helps to provide a fundamental self-reassurance. Precisely the person who has difficulty filtering external stimuli and therefore gets lost in what streams into him from outside regains an illusion of autonomy—albeit temporary—in the identification with bodily pain.

Nausea

In addition to pain, nausea is the elemental experience that confronts us directly with our own bodily being. Nausea can be triggered by blood, excrement or wounds but also by the perception of the inexorable process of bodily ageing. To this it can be objected that nausea—unlike pain—represents an acquired defence reaction against our own nature; the more civilised human beings are, the more strongly developed is their sensation of nausea. The only question is whether nausea can be subsumed as a 'reaction-formation' in Freud's sense.[33] Although the degree of nauseous sensations, like their respective causes, is culturally determined, this certainly does not mean that only culture produces nausea. This is opposed above all by the Sartrean view of nausea as the fundamental experience in which the human being undergoes the emotional realisation that his body is not merely an instrument and also not only a bodily expression of his person but sheer 'flesh' that is subject to the process of decay and will one day become nothing more than flesh, namely a corpse (cf. Sartre, 1965; 2003, *loc. cit.* p. 362, p. 366ff). This means that every feeling of nausea, whatever its object, indicates the pure fleshliness and thus fragility of our own body. If nausea is understood as the primal experience of our own bodily being, it becomes a plausible hypothesis that all the efforts invested in the stylisation, adornment

---

[33] Freud terms the reactions that oppose a repressed drive wish 'reaction-formations' (1913a, pp. 333–8). These include nausea, which replaces the child's originally enjoyable preoccupation with his excrement.

and beautification of the body constitute attempts to escape the experience of nausea.[34]

Shame

Like nausea, shame too initially seems not to be a primal experience but an acquired one, yet the young child experiences neither. And however often they may relate to our physical appearance, the causes of shaming experiences are actually much more varied and also concern our actions and even thoughts that remain invisible. This, however, does nothing to alter the fact that whatever the concrete cause may be, any experience of shame confronts me with the fact of my bodiliness. For feeling ashamed always comprises the desire to become invisible, to be swallowed up by the ground or vanish into thin air. In feeling ashamed, we always simultaneously experience the unrealisability of this wish, along with our powerlessness against being condemned as a body to be visible for other people.[35]

1.3 Suffering from bodiliness

Because we are not simply bodily, but have a relationship to being so, our body and the fact that we exist in a bodily way can cause us mental suffering. This suffering is to be distinguished both from suffering from a physical disease and from psychosomatic suffering. Whereas psychosomatic symptoms express a mental suffering, here the body itself becomes the object of mental suffering. Why? No one has chosen his body and yet he has to live in it throughout his life and to present himself with it. Despite advances in medicine and cosmetic surgery, innate physical characteristics even today are only rectifiable to a small degree, which is why every individual faces the task of identifying with the body that is given to him and in this way making it his own body. Many people find this difficult but they nevertheless have to tolerate having been born in this and no other—stronger, healthier, more beautiful—body.

---

[34] This argument is put forward by Winfried Menninghausen (1999).

[35] A detailed daseinsanalytic interpretation of shame will follow in Part II, Chapter 5.

Suffering from our bodies can take many forms but always implies a revolt against the unjust fate of having one or another set of bodily characteristics.[36] Ludwig Binswanger's case of *Ellen West*, to which we have already referred, is one tragic example.[37] At the age of eighteen, Ellen—who had a naturally strong and robust constitution—felt a desire to be physically delicate and ethereal. The desire took an increasingly strong hold on her, so that her whole life was governed by one viewpoint, which was how she could become and stay thinner (by fasting or taking too many laxatives). When she looked in the mirror, she hated her body and beat it with her fists. The notes in her diary contain the plea: 'Create me once again but create me differently!'[38] There she also expresses acutely clear-sightedly the insolubility of her problem: 'I am perishing in the struggle against my nature. Fate wanted to have me fat and strong, but I want to be thin and delicate' (May et al., 1994, pp. 264–5). This battle ended in suicide, as her only means of freeing herself from her hated body.

Just as widespread as the suffering from the imperfection of our own bodies is the suffering from bodily existence itself and thus being subjugated to laws of nature. Suffering from this also means here rebelling against the insurmountable restrictions that it imposes on our own possibilities. So, for example, someone can revolt against the everyday experience of *tiredness*, which makes him realise that his powers are limited and he is dependent on sleep whether he likes it or not and can struggle with every possible means against the need for sleep. Even the currently widespread *anorexia* belongs in this category, since it contains the refusal to yield to the bodily dictate of the need to consume food. The stronger the desire to be sovereign over our own bodies, the more offensive are all bodily manifestations that expose this desire as an illusion. This includes in particular any indication that our body is subject to an ageing process and furthermore is always susceptible to disease—in short: that it and thus we ourselves are destined to die. The ensuing suffering can take the form of *hypochondriac fears* about our own state of health, which

---

[36] On the daseinsanalytic concept of suffering compare Chapters 1 and 2, Part III.

[37] Cf. Historical Part, Chapter 1.4.

[38] The case of Ellen West, in May et al., 1994, p. 297.

leads to constantly monitoring our own bodily processes and also having them medically investigated, when even the doctor's assurance that everything is in order does nothing to allay our anxieties.

2

Beginning and end

Sigmund Freud as thinker of the beginning

For Freud and psychoanalysis, it is beyond doubt that the human being can and should be understood in terms of his beginning—his early childhood history—because the human subject is constituted in the early stages of life, which set the course for later life. This is why the main focus of psychoanalysis to this day is directed at early childhood development and its consequences. Accordingly, its thought operates fundamentally in the temporal horizon of past and present, with the present understood as the product or outcome of the past. No autonomous role is accorded to the future because it merely contains—both positively and negatively—the germination of the seed that was sown in the period of the beginning. This also applies to the widespread fear of the future and death, which according to Freud is merely 'analogous to the fear of castration' (1926a, p. 130). He sees no reason to accord to knowledge of death a reflexive effect on life because the determining factors are not to be sought in consciousness but in the unconscious, which 'does not know its own death' and therefore 'does not believe in its own death; it behaves as if it were immortal' (1915a, p. 296).

Martin Heidegger as thinker of the end

In total contrast to Freud, Heidegger conceived the human being not in terms of the beginning but of the end. For him, dasein is 'being-towards-death' from the outset: 'Factical Da-sein exists as born, and, born, it is already dying in the sense of being-toward-death' (*BT*, p. 343). The fact that the human being is born into a specific situation is only mentioned abstractly in relation to the concept of 'thrownness' and there is not even a single reference to the fact that every human being goes through a period of childhood, with its physical and mental development. As being-towards-death, the human being exists essentially *prospectively*. This does not mean, however, that Heidegger does not also understand the past as a temporal dimension—it is just that it is essentially determined by the future. He thereby corrects the prevailing idea that only what precedes something can have an influence on what occurs later, rather than the other way round. Certainly nothing that happens later can alter the brute facts of the past, but our own relationship to the past probably changes in and with the future, being reinterpreted and re-evaluated in the light of subsequent events.

In the following explanations, I shall attempt to connect Freud's and Heidegger's insights in order to interpret the significance of beginning and end daseinsanalytically as the two basic elements of the human *self-relationship*. The human being always behaves in some way towards his beginning (that has happened) and towards his end (in the future), including when he is apparently taken up entirely with the prevailing present. This means that the two do not constitute mere events but always simultaneously have the quality of a task: everyone has to *exist* his beginning as well as his end throughout his life. And the way in which he shapes his life depends fundamentally on the attitude he adopts towards both, even if this attitude consists in an apparently unconcerned disregard of them.

In accordance with the daseinsanalytic approach, the *ontological dimension* of the relationship to our own beginning, as well as to our own end, moves into the foreground. For behind all the variations of the concrete beginning and end (whether it has begun badly or well and whether death will be easy or difficult and so on) stands the pure facticity that I began at all and that death inevitably approaches me.

2.1 Being-towards-beginning

The facticity of the beginning

When we consider our own beginning, we generally think of the specific events that we know about from stories, written documents, photographs and so on. At the very least, we wonder how our own arrival was experienced by other people, by parents and siblings, or whether we were wanted or not. Indeed, generally we also set out for the period of the beginning a story that is certainly not based on our own memories but on other people's accounts and our own suppositions. Even this story has its pre-ontological inclusions. These do not involve concrete events at the time but three basic facts that apply to every human being's beginning and that are difficult to accept in their stark reality:

a) the fact that I did not myself begin but simply *was begun*, and indeed that I was born from another human being, the mother, without even witnessing the event by which I was brought into the world. When I finally begin to realise consciously that I exist, the beginning is already a considerable way behind me and I am dependent on inadequate information from other people who were present if I want to know anything about my beginning.

b) the fact *that* I simply was begun without it having been possible to give this any deeper explanatory meaning. The more I can discover about the concrete circumstances of my conception and birth, the clearer it becomes to me how random procreation and birth were, how very differently things could also have happened, that I therefore owe my existence to chance and could just as easily not exist.

c) the fact that the details of *how* I was begun are equally contingent (random): the question of why I was produced by precisely this man and no other, and by no other woman, and why I was born into these circumstances and into this period of world history remains unanswered.

Traditional interpretations of the beginning

The difficulty of tolerating this confrontation as a human being with the pure facticity of our own beginning can be indirectly construed from the vast cultural endeavours to place every birth into what is mostly a transcendentally attested context of meaning and thereby assure everyone that the accident of his birth has a positive meaning; that his existing is intended and thus desired in the plan of creation. This is regardless of whether he is a child who was wanted by his parents or not; higher powers attend his beginning and have preserved him from dangers; the special circumstances of his beginning, however bad they may appear, accord with a higher plan and therefore have a good, albeit hidden meaning. The function of such interpretations is obvious: the individual is to be protected from the shocking experience of the sheer contingency of his own beginning and the often flagrant injustice of an individual fate.

Suffering from our beginning

Someone who *suffers* from a fact experiences it as negative and detrimental, and therefore cannot come to terms with it.[39] Someone who suffers from his own beginning in life generally only suffers from *how* it began for him and with him, rather than from its having begun at all. This idea also forms the basis for the psychoanalytic theory of neurosis in its premise that neurotic suffering can be traced back to real or even fantasised events and actions at the time. However, if we consider that everything that has concretely happened to us and that we have done ourselves has its own pre-ontological inclusions, then with neurotic suffering from our own childhood history we must also pay heed to the ontological dimension. It is concerned not with the how but the pure 'that it is' of our own beginning, the fact of being born at all, as well as the fundamental contingency and heteronomy of every beginning. Our own beginning is owed to chance even if we were wanted as a child. However, if we owe our lives to pure chance, are we not lacking the *legitimation* to champion our own life, if necessary to defend it against others? Someone with

---

[39] The daseinsanalytic concept of suffering will be presented in Chapter 1, Part III.

a sensitivity to this factical 'lack of entitlement' of his own dasein easily ends up waiting because he finds it difficult to carry on living without a basis in rights and henceforth to claim his own place in the world in all good conscience. Conversely, however, there can also be no *obligation* given the contingency of our own beginning, to assume this particular beginning as our own. Why should we pursue what has begun in a purely externally determined way without our consent? Why accept that this beginning will influence our whole life—without an opportunity ever to be free of it? Why live this beginning when there is no one there who is assigning me this task?

Revolts against our own beginning

As in all suffering, in suffering from our own beginning there also lies the desire for deliverance from what has been suffered. This wish is certainly not realisable in reality, but probably is so in imagination. We are free to construct a better beginning in our imagination and thereby find the restitution that is prevented for us by real life. Freud classifies such fantasies among the products of the disappointment that the child normally experiences in his initially idealised parents (Freud, 1909). Such fantasies can be extended into an entire imaginary world, into which the adult individual also retreats in daydreams. They relate though in the neurotic person only to the concrete *how*, turn the banal or even damaging beginning into a special one that attracts admiration. This leaves untouched *that* I was begun and that I originate from bodily parents. A far more radical revolt against our own beginning pertains when its contingency and heteronomy are totally denied. We find this denial in psychotic delusional certainties of a beginning that no longer makes reference to any form of bodily descent from human parents but postulates either a divine origin or self-creation (Racamier, 1992).

2.2 Being-towards-end
The facticity of the end

As already established in the introduction, Freud's recognition of the determining influence of the beginning on future life requires some amplification. Not only is the relationship towards our own end just as significant for the shaping of life, but the attitudes towards the end and the beginning are interdependent. This is why due consideration should now be given to the aspect of the human being's relationship to himself that Heidegger termed and analysed as a 'being-toward-death' (*BT*, §§ 227–231). Let us first consider what the beginning and end of every human being have in common: both are independent of his will and both are natural processes that the human being shares with all living creatures. Also, death is as certain as birth—albeit with the significant difference that death still lies before us, and thus belongs to our future. This constitutes the unique characteristic of death: that it is absolutely certain, although it has not yet occurred. The only other things to be regarded as certain are those that have already happened. The future death is the only exception to the rule that nothing the future will bring is certain. Our reflections must proceed from this unique characteristic, for it introduces a *paradox* into the relationship with our own future.

We are bound by *hope* and *fear* to what lies ahead because we do not know what the future will bring. Precisely because we are in the dark about this, the future can become a vast screen on to which we can project our wishes that have so far remained unfulfilled. We can picture it as the time-span in which great happiness still awaits us. This hope helps many people to tolerate a difficult present. The future is simultaneously the time that lies open to us to exert our own influence and shape. Still having a future thus always also means that we still have the opportunity to realise our own plans. That too is a source of hope and fear, for no one can know whether his actions will lead to success or whether he will fail in them.

Do we also fear the future because it will bring our death? The question indicates that some special considerations apply where death is concerned. For generally we fear what *can* threaten but does not necessarily do so, which is why fear always resonates with hope that danger may pass us by or prove to be something we can successfully avoid. Death is the only danger that will strike us with total certainty despite all precautionary measures. This, however, does not entirely account for the unique nature of this danger. In general, we can to some extent locate future dangers temporally and spatially, and can say where they are likely to come from and when they may possibly occur. Even that does not apply to our own death. This has the characteristic of being something that cannot be influenced either in terms of *when* or *how*: it can intrude totally unexpectedly and strike us in a way that we would never have imagined. That makes death an incomparable danger—a danger in fact that not only awaits us within the timescale of the future, but threatens our very future. If it were only the case that our life some day would have an end instead of continuing endlessly, the facticity of death would be something entirely endurable, indeed the knowledge of its approach would even be a relief because it holds the promise of an eventual release from the worries and requirements of life. Above all, it would then be possible to distinguish between life and death, to see death as the counterpart to life and to adopt an attitude either towards life or towards death. This, however, proves to be an illusion because death can strike at any time—suddenly and unexpectedly—and this is why it is an intrinsic part of life.

The relationship to our own future is therefore always simultaneously a relationship to our own death as a constant possibility, which makes it appear uncertain whether we still have any future at all ahead of us or not. With this we encounter the paradox already indicated: someone who wants to plan his life must be able to reckon with a specific time-span, although it is totally uncertain whether in fact one is available to him. How can we strive for a future life, when it is not only uncertain *what* the future will bring but *whether* we even have a future? The relationship to death is generally influenced by the desire for it to come when life is inherently rounded off and has thus become 'whole'. If this desire is fulfilled, then death is the *conclusion* of life; if not, it is the *discontinuation*. Whether death will come when life has become as it were mature for it and we have brought our lives to a good end, or whether it will intrude into life for no reason and senselessly and break it off, no one can know. Experience shows that death comes regardless of whether the dying person is ready or not, whether he is satiated with life or still hungry for it, whether he has fulfilled his important life tasks or not. Even our own end, like our beginning, is generally *contingent* and *externally determined*—although with the significant exception that I can also actively bring about death because it lies *before* me by killing myself. Someone who grasps this opportunity thereby gains power over the how and when of his own death—albeit only at the cost of depriving himself of the opportunity of a future that remains open.

Anxiety about death and fear of death

Someone who is constantly aware that his own death or that of those closest to him could happen immediately at any moment certainly lives more truthfully than the majority, who generally reassure themselves that while death will certainly come one day it will not yet, but he has great difficulty getting through everyday life. Everyday life can only function when we manage to screen out the irrefutable fact of the death that is possible at any time.[40] Common sense assists in this. It supplies reassuring arguments by indicating for example the empirically proven fact of an average life expectancy and argues for an adherence to what is probable. Someone with common sense also has confidence that he can have an influence over the when and how of his own death by for instance living healthily and avoiding dangerous situations and activities.

Not all human beings by a long way are convinced by such reassuring arguments. This makes them susceptible to the numerous daily indications of death. For in fact almost everything we perceive and do can be understood as a presage of death: the wilted leaf on the ground, as well as the repeated occurrence of nightfall or the annually recurring birthday, a sense of physical nausea or news of accidents and crimes and so on. In order not to have to live in constant fear of death, other reassuring strategies are thus required. They are rarely conscious, but they manifest themselves in a conduct of life that also becomes conspicuous in everyday life. Someone for example who organises his life entirely around health and fitness, who walks along only narrow and straightforward paths, who constantly conserves his own strength, indirectly shows that he lives in constant fear of death and will spare no pains to avoid being caught unawares by death. According to Heidegger, *fear* of death is to be distinguished from *anxiety* about death. It requires courage to allow this anxiety to

---

[40] Cf. Heidegger's analysis of 'everyday being-toward-the-end' as a '*constant tranquillization about death*' (*BT*, pp. 233ff).

emerge (cf. *BT*, p. 235). For whereas fear is always coupled with the illusory hope of somehow still escaping the danger, anxiety confronts us with the naked truth that death can come at any time and is beyond our control. Anxiety therefore always implies the need to recognise this truth and live our own life with regard to the ever-present possibility of death.

Yet not only does anxiety about death disclose to us the 'certain uncertainty' of death; in it we also discover the truth about death itself. Now this may be surprising because either religion or biology is generally held responsible for this. Heidegger insists, however, that anxiety alone gives us undisguised information as to what death consists in. The two key terms here are its *not-to-be-bypassed possibility* and its *non-relational potentiality*.

Death as a barrier

Over a lifetime many things come to an end: stages of life end, projects are completed, relationships break up and so on. There are endings that are foreseeable and others that come out of the blue; some that we fear and others for which we long. What is crucial is that all these endings are characterised by a *boundary*. A boundary is defined by the fact that something continues beyond it and something else begins. The boundary is therefore always simultaneously a transition, even if what is approaching is entirely unknown. With reference to life, this means that everything that ends during life marks a boundary beyond which something new begins. In describing death as 'impassable', Heidegger defines this end not as a boundary but as a *barrier*. Death is a barrier rather than a boundary because it brings an end to the entire conduct of a human life. That death is a barrier rather than a boundary makes it something that we absolutely cannot imagine. For as a barrier death is also 'non-relational'. It is certainly part of life and yet it tears us out of it and is therefore no longer connected with other possibilities. All imagining is, however, a connecting. Because death has no connection with any other possibilities of life, it is incomprehensible and so the fact that it is nevertheless part of our life surpasses our powers of imagination. Nevertheless we have a knowledge of the facticity of our own death—namely in anxiety.

Only the mood of anxiety is capable of disclosing to us what must remain closed to our perception and thought: to grasp our own death as *our own* and at the same time as *unimaginably alien*.[41]

Religious interpretations of death

The sting can be drawn from death by defining it as a boundary instead of a barrier and thus as a mere transition into a new mode of being. This is generally undertaken by religions. From an existential viewpoint, they always have the function of allaying anxiety. Whether their notions of an after-life remain vague or are entirely concretely depicted, whether they are predominantly positive in nature or instead threaten a judgement on the other side and punishment to be endured, is less important than the assurance that life does in fact continue, that the end only applies to the life on this side and thus coincides with the beginning of a life beyond it. Anxiety is in any case alleviated by the fact that death appears as something that is actually bypassable and relational because it is an integral part of a comprehensive meaning-context.

2.3 A daseinsanalytic interpretation of the repetition compulsion and the death drive

Sigmund Freud's theory of a *repetition compulsion* that prevails in neurosis and its derived hypothesis of a *death drive*[42] confirm his status as the thinker of the beginning that we accorded him in the introduction. I should next like to show that a better understanding of both can be gained by incorporating the future dimension and interpreting both the repetition compulsion and the death drive as a defence against anxiety about the future and about the death that lies in the future.

---

[41] Here we encounter for the second time an inextinguishable alienness in our self-relationship; the first time it concerned our own body as our intrinsic nature that we have 'to be'; cf. Chapter 1, Part II.

[42] Freud introduced the repetition compulsion in 'Remembering, repeating and working-through', 1914, p. 151ff. and the death drive in *Beyond the Pleasure Principle*, 1920, p. 50ff.

Repetition of the past as a denial of the future

Freud defined the repetition compulsion as an unconscious process that forces the subject to keep re-enacting negative past experiences that have not been overcome. It is clear that this involves a fixation on painful childhood experiences. However, as soon as we also consider that people suffer not only from the beginning that has occurred but also from the end that is to come, the repetition compulsion can also be related to the future. Anyone who lives the present entirely in the service of repeating the past is living diverted from the future in a way that enables him to screen out his approaching death. If the re-enactment of the past in the present were more than a sterile repetition, the future dimension would inevitably open up, along with awareness of our own mortality. That life will come to an end may seem trivial, even unreal, to someone who looks back in rebellion against his difficult start in life. Always repeating the same thing thus proves from this viewpoint to be an (inevitably unsuccessful) attempt to stop time and deny its passage. If human existing is understood as a 'being-towards-death', then the repetition compulsion relates not only to the past but also to the future, and also has the meaning of escaping death. We might even say it is the relationship to the beginning that is supposed to provide a release from the relationship to the end.

The death drive as a rejection of being-towards-death

More productive than the still unresolved debate within psychoanalysis as to the correctness of the hypothesis of the death drive Freud introduced in 1920 is the question of an inner connection between exactly what Freud means by the term 'death drive' and Heidegger's definition of human being as 'being-towards-death'. At first sight, the two seem to be referring to opposite things: whereas Freud's death drive is inherent in all living things, being-towards-death is a specific human fact; whereas the death drive takes us back to that primal beginning from which all life emerged, Heidegger's being-towards-death is a relationship that propels us forwards to a future death. Freud thus has a different death in view: not the specific human death but death as the transition of all living things into what is inanimate; death not as the inconceivably and unimaginably different unknown that stands before the human being and makes him anxious but as the absolute peace towards which it drives him back. If we conceive daseinsanalytically what Freud biologically termed the drive as a human wish (only the human being can wish) then the death drive can be understood as a desire arising from the human being-towards-death to return to before our own beginning, in order to be able to fulfil the 'primal fantasy' (Freud) of a life free of tensions and contradictions, without uncertainty and possible failure and thus without any danger of the ending that is possible at any time.[43] This is a fantasy that is not only illusory but, as Freud rightly recognised, constitutes the greatest threat to humanity's survival because the insistence on its fulfilment can lead to self-destruction.

---

[43] For an existential interpretation of Freud's theory of the death drive, see Holzhey-Kunz, 2001, loc. cit., Ch. II.6, p. 99ff.

3

The Other

3.1 The daseinsanalytic definition of dasein as being-with-one-another

Daseinsanalysis has always set great store by conceiving the human being not as an individual psyche and indeed in no sense as a 'psychic apparatus' (Freud) but being guided by Heidegger's dictum that human dasein 'in itself is essentially being-with' (*BT*, p. 120). Ludwig Binswanger's principal work *Grundformen und Erkenntnis menschlichen Daseins*[44] contains an extremely important analysis of 'being-with-one-another'. Although this is not immediately apparent from the title, this is only because for Binswanger being -with is not simply one of several characteristics of the human being, but that which defines him from his very foundations, which is why the basic forms of human Dasein can be nothing other than basic forms of being-with-one-another. Even the individual posited by modernity still represents a form of being-with-one-another, albeit a deeply deficient one, since the relationship to his fellow human being has dwindled to a minimum here. For Binswanger this gives rise to the methodological approach to understanding a human being's individuality: it is necessary to discover the basic form of being-with-one-another in which his life predominantly occurs. In this sense,

---

[44] Basic forms and knowledge of human dasein (1992–1994, Vol. 2) Cf. the explanations in the Historical Part, Chapter 1.

Binswanger summarises his patient Ellen West's dasein as follows: 'Instead of the authentic I–Thou relationship of the being-with-one-another, instead of being sheltered in the eternal moment of love, we find the *Mitwelt* consisting of merely togetherness of one with the others—specifically, in the form of the ... unceasing urge to dominate and lead others' (May *et al.*, 1994, p. 273).

However, Binswanger's work is not limited to the phenomenological analysis of the basic forms of being-with-one-another. Rather, to this is added a further, equally important analysis of the connection between being-with-one-another and knowledge. At its basis lies the interesting thought that all forms of knowing are rooted in corresponding forms of being-with-one-another. This also applies in particular to the methodological procedure of the human sciences based on the natural scientific ideal, since they claim to provide objective knowledge concerning the human being. This form of knowledge is rooted in the form of being-with-one-another in which the other person is perceived as a mere 'thing', which involves a high degree of reductionism. For Binswanger, however, it is less a matter of criticism than of the question as to which basic form of being-with-one-another must be the source of the knowledge that does not turn the human being into a thing but is able to comprehend him as a *human being*. His answer can easily be guessed from the preceding explanations in the Historical Part: this can only be *love* as the highest form of human being-with-one-another, for it is only on this foundation that the human being to be acknowledged is recognised as a 'you' and as a 'partner in dasein'. Binswanger's knowledge of dasein is therefore conceptualised intrinsically as a 'loving' form of knowledge. This does not mean, however, that the daseinsanalytic investigator must love all his patients but it merely has the methodological meaning of perceiving the 'whole human being', instead of regarding him as a pathological case and focusing only on his deficiencies.

If we compare Binswanger's daseinsanalysis with Freud's psychoanalysis in this regard, the comparative progress is strikingly obvious: it has overcome both the reification of human mental life into a 'psychic apparatus'—dominant at least in psychoanalytic theory—and the idea of a 'primary narcissism' that according to

Freud is only abandoned by the child because unfulfilled drive needs force him to turn to the other person and to perceive and use him as a possible 'object' of his own need for satisfaction.

3.2 Recent developments in psychoanalysis

Since Freud, psychoanalysis has developed some new theories concerning the infant's post-natal situation that contradict Freud's hypothesis of primary narcissism. I shall refer here to two representative proponents, *Michael Balint* and *Jean Laplanche*, because their conflicting theories bring to light a problematic that is relevant to the existential definition of the interpersonal relationship to be presented here.[45] Even in 1937, Balint stated in a lecture that 'a very early, most likely the earliest, phase of the extra-uterine mental life is not narcissistic but directed towards objects', involving a purely passive form of love in which the infant wants to be '*loved and satisfied*' by the mother, '*without being under any obligation to give anything in return*' (1949, p. 269). This moves what Heidegger conceived anthropologically as original being-with on to the psychological plane and relates it to the beginning of life. The human being does not enter into a relationship with his fellow human being only at a later stage, but is related to the mother from the outset; the clinically observable narcissism is not something primary but 'always a protection against the bad or only reluctant object' (*ibid.*). Laplanche (1992) also works from the premise of a primary relatedness between mother and child and even declares it to be the basic anthropological situation insofar as he regards all subsequent forms of relationship as determined by this original form. However, he turns Balint's view of the initial mother–child relationship on its head: whereas with Balint the baby is at the centre, and wants entirely egoistically to be loved, with Laplanche the mother is at the centre. She wants something from the infant that he cannot find his way into at all because—according to the hypothesis—she as an adult person whether she likes it or not also directs sexual messages at her child that must be entirely enigmatic to him. Thus here, rather

---

[45] I shall not be addressing empirical infant research or attachment research here, because I am dealing only with the fundamental question of the importance accorded by psychoanalysis to the interpersonal relationship and to the real Other.

than the mother revolving around the child as in Balint, the child revolves around the mother in the desperate endeavour somehow to decipher the incomprehensible messages.

With his theory, Laplanche wants to bring about 'a Copernican revolution' in psychoanalytic thought, which consists in recognising the significance of the *real Other* for the child subject. This is in fact a radical change, since the psychoanalyst was hitherto committed to the intrapsychic perspective, so that any reference to real parental figures was considered to be a descent into social psychology. With Laplanche, the Other is not only relieved of its status as a mere intrapsychic representative, but is even accorded the status of something more than a part of the prevailing interaction—specifically, an *Other* who remains ultimately mysterious and alien in his otherness.

If we turn away from Laplanche back to Binswanger's theory of being-with-one-another, it becomes clear that the daseinsanalytic objections have actually been invalidated by the further development of psychoanalysis, but without any rapprochement between the two positions having taken place. The difference is two-fold. It concerns *first* the role of the fellow human being. Laplanche characterises him as 'other' in order to make clear that he is not taken up by being part of a relationship that incorporates two (or several) people in the same way. This avoids the currently widespread view of the interpersonal encounter as an *interactional* occurrence. It is not interaction that is primary but the Other who produces the interaction merely by being there and wanting something from me. Relationship is therefore not from the outset a game between me and others but primarily a game that the Other has with me, into which I must enter whether I like it or not as the person to whom it is addressed. The way in which the Other consequently surpasses me is not a lack to be overcome but the underlying basis of all possible reciprocity. With Binswanger, by contrast, who works from the premise of an original being-with-one-another, the love in which a harmonious 'we' is formed with another appears as if self-evidently as the authentic and highest form of interpersonal relationship, of which every other form of relationship can be understood as a deficient variation. The *second* difference concerns the approach to the subject of relationship, for as we know the answers always depend on how the question is framed. Whereas Binswanger's question concerns which basic forms of being-with-one-another there actually are and which of these is to be considered the true and highest form, both Balint and Laplanche proceed from the desire that is directed at the Other and ask what the child desires from the mother or, conversely, what the mother desires from the child.

3.3 An existential understanding of being-with-others

The digression on Balint and Laplanche and the comparison with Binswanger have drawn our attention to the fact that these are not merely different theories concerning the specific nature of interpersonal relationships but that a different question is being posed from the outset. So we would do well here first to clarify how we want to enquire into the interpersonal relationship. From the preliminary work accomplished in the philosophical part, it is already clear that in order to gain an *existential* understanding we should be wary of questions such as 'What is a relationship?', 'What are the characteristics of human being-with-one-another?', or 'What is the Other?' and instead ask what it means that everyone *exists* together with others and also that our fellow human being does not simply occur in the world, but *exists* on his own account.[46] This forces into the foreground what remains overlooked in the traditional question of being: that being-with-one-another has the quality of something that is conducted—and that this conduct has a dual nature that is simultaneously ontical and ontological.

Being-with-one-another as a task

It follows from the concept of existence that being-with must also be understood as a *having-to-be-with*. Just as each person's own bodily being becomes a task for him (cf. Chapter 1, Part II), and he also has to take over and live his own beginning that always already lies behind him (cf. Chapter 2, Part II), so being with others also represents a constant task. This has key significance for the definition

---

[46] Cf. Chapter 1.1: The human being: dasein, being-in-the-world, existence.

of the relationship of the self to the Other because it implies a rejection of the usual polemical opposition between subjectivity and intersubjectivity. It is wrong to seek to offset the definition of dasein as an original being-with against its definition as an individual. The fact that the individual always already exists in relationships means neither that others are taking away from him the task of leading his own life nor that they are discharging him from relating to others himself and living and being responsible for these relationships. But it is precisely in this that the individual's inextinguishable subjectivity in all intersubjectivity consists. He is not simply integrated into relationships but somehow knows about his relatedness to others and therefore cannot avoid also adopting a position of some kind towards this basic fact.

The ontico–ontological ambiguity of being-with-one-another

Heidegger's discovery that 'every ontic understanding "includes" certain things, even if only *pre*-ontologically' (*BT*, p. 288) also leads towards an existential understanding of being-with-one-another. Let us begin with what mainly stands in the foreground and with which we are chiefly concerned: the concrete ('ontical') dealing with the Other. Insofar as this is considered at all and does not simply proceed as if automatically according to the usual patterns, it is always guided by the following questions: what does this specific Other mean to me, what do I feel for him, what do I think of him, how do I evaluate him, what use am I to him, what do I want from him, and what can I realistically expect from him and so on; and likewise: what do I mean to this specific Other, what does he feel for me, what does he think of me, how does he evaluate me, what does he want from me and so on? According to each answer, the relationship to the Other is formed, whether it becomes close or remains detached, whether it is based on trust or characterised by distrust, whether I am negative or encouraging, whether I envy or admire him, whether I emulate him or want nothing to do with him, whether I want to foster him or damage him, whether I deliberately ignore him or do not even perceive him.

However, because we exist both ontically *and* ontologically, it is always about more than just the concrete dealing with this specific human being. In the relationship to the Other as a specific person also lies a relationship to the Other as the Other—thus to that otherness of the Other that has nothing to do with his concrete individuality or his particular cultural origins. Now in *Being and Time*, Heidegger provided the prerequisites for an ontological definition of the Other as an Other, but did not proceed to an explicit development of this theme. This was first achieved by Jean-Paul Sartre in *Being and Nothingness*.[47]

3.4 'Conflict is the original meaning of being-for-others'

Underlying the question of *how* this specific Other encounters me is the irreducible fact *that* he encounters me, and behind the question of *how* I am to behave towards him stands the equally irreducible fact *that* I am inevitably exposed to him and have to present myself to him in some way. Sartre has both these ontological facts in mind when he declares the mere existence of the Other to be an 'insuperable scandal' (*BN*, p. 481). The scandal consists in the fact that the Other is another human being and therefore is not an object for me but like me is a free subject on his own account. As such he therefore does not appear because I want him to do so but at his own discretion: he *appears*. This sounds banal but it is far from neutral because the fact that the Other appears also already means that he is fundamentally beyond my direction and control. It is true that people with whom we have to deal mostly behave in accordance with our expectations and therefore also predictably—but it is never certain, since the Other as a subject in principle has the freedom to behave entirely differently from what is expected. Worse still: because he is a subject himself, he can for his own part turn me into an object—the object of his gaze and thus his judgement. In this lies an anxiety-inducing power of the Other, the power to see me and judge me as he pleases, and to create his own image of me. So the mere fact that the Other can freely direct his gaze at me—even if he is my friend or my subordinate—is scandalous. I can certainly try to exert an influence on the Other's gaze and to

---

[47] Jean-Paul Sartre: *Being and Nothingness. An Essay on Phenomenological Ontology*. Trans. Hazel Barnes. London, Routledge, 2003, Part Three, 'Being-for-Others', loc. cit. p. 243ff (henceforth, *BN*).

manipulate it. This extends to sophisticated self-enactments for the Other and to desperate efforts to appear to be something more than I am. But whether this succeeds, and if so for how long, is not at my discretion. Furthermore, the Other is able to see me fundamentally from a standpoint that I can never hold myself. This gives the Other *per se* a power over me, even if he is far below me socially—the power that derives purely from the fact that as an Other he sees me in a way that I cannot see myself. The Other therefore always knows more about me than I can know about myself and therefore possesses 'a secret, the secret of what I am' (*BN*, p. 386).

How though does that *conflict* come about which according to Sartre determines even 'the original meaning of being-for-others' (*BN*, p. 386)? The relationship to the Other is fundamentally conflictual because I suffer not only from the Other's freedom but also from my own freedom. This is why I need the Other, although he makes me anxious. He is to remove the burden of responsibility for my own life or at least to share it with me. This is why I turn to him and seek out his gaze, which is to confirm to me that I am good and in this way I become dependent on him. There is therefore an irresoluble contradiction inherent in the relationship to the Other: I want to flee the Other's freedom and at the same time to flee towards him; I want to escape it and at the same time I require it in order to be rid of the use of my own freedom. Correspondingly contradictory are the expectations of the Other: the Other is to give up his otherness and yet remain an Other; I myself want to deprive him of his otherness in order to be safe from him, and at the same time I want to grant it to him in order to be saved by him from myself.

3.5 Apparent solutions to the irresoluble dilemma

The pre-modern notion of being children of God

The religious notion that all human beings (or at least all believers) are children of God can be interpreted as an attempt to make the Other appear more familiar than he is and at the same time to relativise his significance. If we are all God's children, then we are brothers and sisters. This contains the reassurance that we are all ultimately alike, although so much alienness and misunderstanding prevails between us, and that manifestations of other human beings that are incomprehensible to me are understood by God, who sees into all hearts, indeed are even willed by him. Someone who can subscribe to this idea is freed from the pressure always to understand the Other and to anticipate his future reactions as far as possible. The 'children of God' concept places us, however, in a relationship with a unique Other who is not beside us but above us. This is why this relationship is inalienable and steadfast—it remains the preserve of every human being, even if all human beings have become alien to him, and he perceives or imagines himself to be abandoned by everyone, indeed surrounded only by enemies. All attributes that would have to attach to an interpersonal relationship for us to feel secure in it as individuals—steadfast loyalty, recognition of our own worth and being lovingly cared for—characterise God's relationship with the human being. The religious relationship to the 'Heavenly Father' therefore relativises the insecurity that infuses all interpersonal relationships and thus makes them more tolerable.

Romantic love

If modern people in a secular world can no longer count on supernatural aid to resolve ontological relational conflicts, they rely on the concept of an ideal interpersonal form of relationship that withstands this conflict or can itself resolve it. This is the modern view of love. This means that the formerly supernatural expectations are now transferred to the earthly lover. Love enters the field of vision here in a completely different way from in Binswanger who enquired into its essential nature. Now it is a matter of the two questions that we have already encountered in Balint and Laplanche: what does the lover desire? What is the function of love? Sartre states briefly and succinctly that the lover wants nothing other than to be loved himself (cf. *BN*, p. 388). Being loved by the Other promises release from a threefold anxiety: first, from the anxiety about having to exist as an individual, for if the Other loves me, he enters into a communion with me in which I myself become part of the 'we' and am merged in it; second, from the anxiety about the inconceivability of the Other, for if the Other loves me then he voluntarily surrenders his power over me, voluntarily puts fetters on his freedom, no longer compares me with others but looks only at me, which is why I can then feel secure in his gaze; third, from the anxiety that I am superfluous as a product of chance in this world, for if the Other loves me, then I am irreplaceable for him, and am therefore really valued for myself, instead of merely being used to carry out a role or perform a task and being tolerated only on that basis.

These expectations of deliverance prove over the short or long term to be unrealisable, and so the lover can only fail. Someone who clings to illusory expectations seeks to blame the actual partner for this failure and invests his hopes in a new love relationship. However, the disillusionment also often leads to seeking another solution, since love brings too much pain. The great alternative to romantic love is represented today by 'partnership'.

Partnership

In contrast to irrational love, partnership is based on the rational principle of 'do ut des'—'I give that you may give'. In order to realise it, the reciprocal claims, rights and duties are *negotiated*. This should proceed fairly; neither should prevail over the Other and both should stick to the agreed rules and be ready to make compromises. The ideal here is the functional, cooperative team in which both can find fulfilment. The obligation to rationality also extends to the dissolution of the partnership, which should proceed equally reasonably and fairly. If we now ask what one person expects from the Other in partnership, then it suddenly becomes obvious that here the resolution of conflict in reciprocal predictability is sought. The Other is supposed to be able to operate in principle only by adhering to the agreed rules. When that succeeds, the danger that proceeds from his freedom is eliminated. As long as both keep to directing at the partner only expectations that are rationally founded and correspond to the common agreements, each party is protected from disappointments, as well as from the criticism of having failed.

The unique characteristic of systemic couple therapy is that it defines couple relationships as partnerships and therefore offers strategies and techniques for making a dysfunctional partnership functional again (Retzer, 2002; Holzhey-Kunz, 2005). From a daseinsanalytic perspective, this consistently overlooks the ontological dimension of the couple's reciprocal expectations. This makes it possible to treat the suffering from partnership conflicts as a technically soluble matter. The fact that this suffering is only in the foreground and is fuelled by another form of suffering, namely from the fundamental unrealisability of expectations of the partner, which are mostly concealed but all the more virulent in the background, cannot therefore even be glimpsed. The practice of fair dealings with each other only conceals, however, the secret rebellion against the fact that only fairness can be expected from the partner rather than love and so each party remains alone.

Violence

Having made clear that every close relationship, albeit mainly covertly, is beset with fundamental anxieties and (unrealisable) wishes that arise from these, the high propensity for violence in interpersonal relationships becomes comprehensible without any reference being required to an innate aggressive drive in the psychoanalytic sense. The use of violence also always has an ontological meaning and seeks by force to resolve the irresoluble conflict in the relationship to the Other by attempting to eliminate his otherness. For this reason, every close relationship has an inherent potential for violence that is unleashed when peaceful means of overcoming anxiety and fulfilling wishes seem to be ineffective.

4

Anxiety and desire

No one goes through life without anxiety and no one is perfectly happy. Furthermore, the wishes people nurture are as diverse as the anxieties that pursue them. This heading does not refer though to anxieties and wishes in the plural, but puts them both in the singular. Importantly, the singular does not stand in the usual way for what is common to the various kinds of anxieties and wishes and can therefore be considered to be the essence of anxiety or wishing. Instead the reference is to a particular anxiety and a particular wish characterised by belonging not to the (ontical) level of the concrete conduct of life but to the (ontological) level of the relationship to our own being. There are three questions to elucidate: the relationship of the (one) anxiety to the many anxieties and fears, similarly the relationship of the (one) desire to the many wishes and needs and the relationship between anxiety and desire.

4.1 Anxiety and anxieties

We have already encountered anxiety in earlier chapters, for instance in relation to the existential definition of 'being-towards-the-end' (Chapter 2, Part II) that led to the differentiation of anxiety about death from fear of death. Now it is a matter of establishing the distinction between (singular) anxiety and (plural) fears and guarding against some common misunderstandings. We should start with the proviso that both anxiety and fear are specifically human phenomena, even if there can be no doubt that more highly-developed animals react to danger with an experience similar to fear. But to say that animals feel anxiety or fear in relation to a danger is only correct in a figurative sense. Certainly, animals can also be observed to show fight or flight responses in threatening situations and to exhibit the typical physiological counterparts to anxiety such as trembling and heart palpitations, a specific physical posture, increased alertness and the production of specific noises. Yet this is a matter of external observation and that is where it ends. We cannot actually know what danger means for an animal because for us dangers only ever exist within an interpreted world and these are therefore also verbally interpretable and communicable. But what does danger mean to an animal that cannot tell itself and others: 'I'm afraid of something' or 'I'm feeling frightened'?

The distinction between *anxiety* and *fear* was introduced into philosophy by Søren Kierkegaard (1980, p. 42) and taken up by Heidegger.[48] It is artificial in that it cannot refer to the colloquial use of the two words, since in colloquial language the two words 'anxiety' and 'fear' are used more or less synonymously. A distinction is certainly frequently made now between fear and anxiety in psychological and psychiatric papers, which define fear as object-related and anxiety as objectless. Accordingly, reference is made to anxiety when someone cannot say what he actually fears, and also no actual cause can be found for it, and/or the objects of fear are interchangeable (so-called free-floating anxiety).

To understand the existential meaning of anxiety, it is not enough merely to distinguish this from fear. Equally important is its difference from *fearfulness* and *anxiousness*, which designate a general emotional state (daseinsanalytically a 'mood') and therefore also appear without a concrete reason and sometimes persists over a long period. Fearfulness and anxiousness are interchangeable terms for the mood in which *the world as a whole* appears threatening to someone and accordingly he feels *generally* threatened. Someone who is anxious senses possible

---

[48] In *Being and Time*, § 30: Fear as a mode of attunement; § 40: The fundamental attunement of *Angst* as an eminent disclosedness of Da-sein.

dangers everywhere, whereas it is possible to be afraid of a concrete danger without being an anxious person. Nevertheless, the object-directed feeling of fear and the mood of fearfulness are akin and are radically distinct from the mood of anxiety in Heidegger's sense.

In what does the difference consist? The mood of anxiousness takes its place *alongside* the moods of cheerfulness, sadness, exuberance, hopelessness and so on. In all these moods, the world that someone inhabits is cast in a particular light: in an anxious mood, everything appears potentially dangerous, and there is a tendency to exaggerate concretely existing dangers or to perceive dangers where none exist. In a cheerful mood, the same thing appears not only free of danger but even friendly and inviting and we live with the sense that the world is peaceful and nothing could go wrong. *Anxiety* cannot be placed in this category, for in it the world becomes *uncanny* because everything loses its previously familiar meaning and instead assumes 'the character of complete insignificance' (cf. *BT*, p. 174). In anxiety nothing is 'relevant' any more, even the fact of whether there are dangers in the world or not. In anxiety, the world instead collapses as a familiar *meaningful whole* and what opens up instead is the '*nothingness of the world*' (*BT*, p. 255).[49] It is tempting to refer in psychiatric terms to a 'loss of world'. In anxiety there is nothing left by which to orientate ourselves, from which to understand ourselves, on to which to hold. The difference from the mood of anxiousness is therefore huge, for although everything may appear threatening to the anxious person, this threatening quality nevertheless proceeds specifically from important, significant circumstances or things that paradoxically still give an orientation even as dangerous; in anxiety, however, we experience ourselves as being torn out of all meaningful reference-points and pushed out into the 'not-at-home'. It is precisely this experience that is expressed in the colloquial expression that 'in Angst one has an "uncanny" feeling' (cf. *BT*, p. 176). It is not uncanny specifically to me as this individual person but to me as a person in general because in anxiety—in contrast to anxiousness—I myself as this specific person am also meaningless.

---

[49] Cf. here the explanations of the dual meaning of 'world' in Chapter I.1.

A pathological or an ontological experience?

How should anxiety be classified? Does it constitute an experience at all or is it only a philosophical construct? At first, it seems obvious to assign it to the domain of abnormal or pathological experiences, since it is reminiscent of typically psychotic anxieties about loss of the world and the self, as well as anxieties induced by traumatic experiences. These traumatic experiences are known to be characterised by the fact that they can no longer be integrated into the previous familiar world but instead destroy everything that previously had a meaning. This, however, would mean stripping the experience of anxiety of any truth content. In contrast, Kierkegaard and Heidegger define anxiety as that *basic ontological experience* in which the truth about our own constitution of being manifests itself to us. This accords it a high status and elevates it to a philosophical mood. Because it is a human characteristic to know about our being, anxiety can in principle intrude at any time. In anxiety, meaning-interpretations are revealed as what they are, namely as interpretations that are supposed to protect the individual human being from the confrontation with the naked truth of the 'that he is and has to be'.

4.2 The return of anxiety in fear

In Heidegger, there are two statements about anxiety that appear difficult to reconcile: one is that anxiety 'can arise in the most harmless situations' (*BT*, p. 177), and the Other is that authentic anxiety is 'rare' (*BT*, p. 177). This ceases to be a contradiction, however, if we assume that anxiety appears in two different forms, as 'authentic' anxiety that is seldom experienced and as 'inauthentic' anxiety, which is frequent.

How does inauthentic anxiety manifest itself? It mainly appears as *fear*. 'Fear is *Angst* which has fallen prey to the "world". It is inauthentic and concealed from itself as such' (*BT*, p. 177). Thus fear can as it were replace anxiety. Yet this does not happen simply as a matter of course but results from the fact that the human being initially and generally flees anxiety. We are all inclined to deny the nameless anxiety and when it nevertheless obtrudes to reinterpret it as concrete fear of innerworldly dangers. For whereas nothing can be done to combat that nameless threat that is indicated to us by anxiety, it is possible to respond to innerworldly dangers with understanding and actions. If anxiety is expressed as fear, it can be talked about; it becomes unexpectedly comprehensible and potentially surmountable. This means that concrete fears, as well as a general mood of fearfulness, are fundamentally easier to tolerate than anxiety.

The thesis that anxiety returns in the form of fear should not be taken to mean that every fear is to be conceived as a return of repressed anxiety. There are enough real dangers that justifiably fill us with fear and towards which feeling fear is a sign of a functional sense of reality. So we must distinguish between real and unreal or rationally based and irrational fear. In unreal or irrational fear, we may suspect anxiety that is returning in a distorted form. For someone who on the basis of a special *sensitivity*[50] constantly encounters the uncanniness of existing in normal everyday life often reinterprets it as an (imaginary) innerworldly threat and thus acquires the illusion that it is due to specific circumstances and therefore also surmountable through suitable precautions. For this he certainly pays the price of a partial misjudgement of concrete reality. But even when the fear is inherently justifiable, such as for instance the individual fear of unemployment or the collective fear of terrorist attacks, the corresponding degree of fear, and its frequently observable increase beyond all measurable proportions, betrays the fact that latent anxiety about 'not-being-at-home' ontologically is also finding symbolic expression in it.

With all anxieties that strike us as absurd in the ontical-real context, whether they are object-related or objectless, psychiatry steps in with the diagnosis of an 'anxiety disorder'. This explanation, just like the reinterpretation of anxiety as fear, serves the purpose of reassurance about being. By contrast, the existential understanding of anxiety as a basic mood provides a *hermeneutic guide* that makes it possible to understand pathological anxieties as concealed suffering from not-being-at-home. If we interpret the many forms of irrational, inauthentic anxieties as a distorted return of authentic anxiety, then we accord them a truth as well. They bring to expression in an encoded way the fundamental threat that is inherent in human

---

[50] Cf. Chapter 2, Part III on this daseinsanalytic concept of sensitivity.

being, which besets especially sensitive people more than others. When these people do not simply talk themselves out of their unreal anxieties, this is also because there is a real threat that corresponds to these anxieties, even if they cannot give them their true name but confuse the threat that is inherent in their own being with concrete innerworldly dangers.

What in fact does 'authentic' anxiety feel like? Is it something that can be experienced at all or does it only ever emerge indirectly as fear? Important, firstly, is Heidegger's conception that while authentic anxiety is rare, it is not impossible. This is precisely where Sartre (2003, *loc. cit.* p. 585f) diverges from Heidegger. For him, the human being is fundamentally in flight from anxiety, driven by the '*désir d'être*', the desire to free himself from the uncanniness of dasein and to become healthy and whole in his being. For Heidegger, however, the human being has at least in principle the freedom to *take on* anxiety (cf. *BT*, p. 285, p. 296). The criterion for authentic anxiety is therefore the readiness to withstand it, which is synonymous with *affirming* the truth it contains. There are no criteria, however, for when this is actually the case. In my view it is also not so much a case of separating out pure experiences of anxiety but very much about holding to its fundamental possibilities. For if authentic anxiety comprises the capacity and readiness to withstand it, then it cannot be identified with psychotic anxieties about the loss of world and the self. Specifically in psychosis, the fear of anxiety is overpowering. Furthermore, Heidegger leaves no doubt that the '*courage to have* Angst' (*BT*, p. 235) also changes the concrete conduct of life because it provides an illusionless and therefore free view of our own possibilities of being. Someone who is ready to confront anxiety is *free of* those irrational anxieties that are the form in which denied anxiety usually returns and therefore becomes *free for* an autonomous conduct of life.

4.3 Is the desire an existential?

In the daseinsanalytic theory of Binswanger and Boss, wishes play only a subordinate role—in total contrast to psychoanalysis, which fundamentally interprets the human being from the viewpoint of his (conflicting) wishes. Accordingly, both have made vehement critiques of the false absolutisation of the wish in psychoanalysis (Binswanger (1955 [1947], Vol. 1, *loc. cit.*, p. 173f; Boss, 1994, *loc. cit.*, p. 174f., p. 182)[51] and agreed in emphasising that wishing represents only one of many behavioural possibilities. Heidegger too seems to accord only secondary importance to the wish, which he disqualifies by calling it the 'mere wish' (cf. *BT*, p. 180ff.). Nevertheless, it can easily be shown that central importance attaches to wishing not as a word but certainly as a thing in Heidegger's philosophical definition of the human being—namely in the wish to free ourselves of anxiety. Heidegger considers not the many wishes that operate at the ontical level of the concrete conduct of life but the desire in the singular, which is directed at our own being. This desire is manifested for Heidegger in *falling prey*, which means fleeing the uncanniness of our own being (*BT*, pp. 164–168).

Common to all wishing is the sense of a lack that we then seek to eliminate. We wish only when we experience and judge something as a lack. The human being with no wishes either lacks nothing or does not suffer from the lack but accepts it. The lacks in the plural from which people suffer that in wishing they would like to remedy should be distinguished from the lack in the singular that Heidegger terms 'existential nullity' (*BT*, p. 263) and Sartre terms 'lack of being' (*BN*, p. 586). All human beings are affected by this—and most human beings also strive to eliminate it. When Heidegger states that the human being is initially and generally in flight from anxiety, this means that he is driven by the wish to free himself from the nothingness of his own being. This means that the human relationship to his own being generally takes the form of the wish—to be more precise an illusory wish, since it is fundamentally unrealisable because it seeks to change that which is immutable.

4.4 The return of the desire in wishes

It seems obvious that—like the anxiety that is transformed into fear—the desire for release from anxiety also becomes concrete and assumes the form of wishes that are directed at something specific. The most

---

[51] Cf. also Martin Heidegger (2001a, *loc. cit.*, p. 172).

direct transformation of the ontological desire is religious in nature; it manifests itself as the wish to be protected by a god or gods or to be guided by Providence. Accordingly, religious interpretations of the world and the human being generally also contain the assurance that anxiety belongs only to the earthly and not the divine world.[52] The desire for flawless conditions of being is also virulent, however, in wishes for material goods, power and social recognition, and it then makes their fulfilment appear inordinately important. The insatiability that is so often encountered in these matters is therefore to be interpreted ontologically as an indication that it is less about the fulfilment of the concrete wishes than the illusory hope of eliminating anxiety in this way.

The fact that concrete wishes often contain the ontological desire and are therefore seeking more than they claim is shown by the disillusionment, even disappointment, that so often sets in when something for which we have long wished or at least long awaited or worked for—a house, a partner, a child, professional breakthrough and so on—has finally occurred. We then realise that it was actually something else for which we were striving, but without realising that this 'something else' is illusory in nature. Because we recoil from admitting to ourselves the reason for the disappointment, we set new goals for our wishes, which again secretly promise more than they can deliver.

4.5 Desire and violence

The readiness to resort to violence to fulfil our own wishes is great and a whole range of economic, social and psychic reasons can be given for this in each individual case. Here we are concerned only with the ontological dimension of violence. Is the temptation to violence inherent in the desire itself? To affirm this is not to postulate an innate destructive drive as Freud does but it does situate the readiness for aggression in the human condition instead of merely inferring it from concrete circumstances. We have already encountered

---

[52]   This is illustrated by Christ's words in St. John's gospel: 'In the world ye shall have tribulation: but be of good cheer; I have overcome the world'.

the disappointment that is inherent in every wish-fulfilment, because it never brings what we have secretly hoped of it—namely complete satisfaction or perfect happiness. Here lies an unavoidable potential for frustration and therefore also aggression, which is all the greater, the more we insist on the fulfilment of what is unrealisable.

This helps to explain why people not only fear violence but are also fascinated by it. Suddenly violence seems to make possible what otherwise remains unattainable—namely to overcome the 'lack of being'. The fascination that violence exerts over many people is connected with the idea that flawless conditions of being can be enforced if we only baulk at no cost and recoil from nothing. Violence thereby fascinates in two forms: as violence that is exercised and as violence that is suffered, which if need be is even voluntarily undergone.[53]

4.6 The relationship between anxiety and desire

When contemporary daseinsanalysis—against the objections of its founders Binswanger and Boss—accords desiring the status of an existential, is it returning to the psychoanalytic conception that the human being is fundamentally a wishing creature? There remains one key difference. For Freud, wishes are ultimately rooted in the human being's biological nature, and therefore each and every one of them stems from drive wishes, even if these are partly so strongly transformed and directed at other goals that their derivation has become unrecognisable. Daseinsanalytically, however, every wish, even if it is a drive wish that stems directly from a physical experience of lack, has a pre-ontological inclusion, which means it incorporates the desire for release from anxiety. Therefore wishing is indeed fundamental for daseinsanalysis but not the ultimate thing that sets the course for everything else. Because wishing is also related to anxiety, this is not a matter of being blindly driven but a particular way of conducting ourselves with respect to anxiety. This is the difference that meant that Freud had to declare 'psychic freedom'

---

[53] The connection between desire and violence and the fascination of violence has been investigated primarily by René Girard (1977).

to be an 'illusion' (1916–17, p. 49), whereas for daseinsanalysis the human being always has the freedom either to flee from anxiety into the desire or to take on the anxiety-inducing truth about his own being, even if he only rarely embraces this freedom.

5

Shame and guilt

The existential approach of daseinsanalysis can deepen our understanding of the phenomena of shame and guilt because it can uncover the deeper dimension that—like anxiety in fear—also mostly remains concealed in concrete feelings of shame and guilt. That means that experiences of shame and guilt also have a dual meaning. On the one hand, they belong to a specific—cultural, social and also individual—context in terms of which they can also generally be understood; on the other, they belong to the ontological dimension of human existing and therefore represent *experiences of being*.

By designating shame and guilt as experiences of being, both phenomena are to be accorded an exceptional status that consists in not only indicating our own being *in some way* but—as with anxiety—disclosing it in a primordial and overt way. This ontological shame and ontological guilt can therefore also only be referred to in the singular, although colloquial language in both these cases has no word to differentiate shame in the singular from shame experiences in the plural and, accordingly, guilt in the singular from the many feelings of guilt, as is possible in the case of anxiety and fear.

A separate chapter will be devoted to shame and guilt because they form a triad with the existentially understood anxiety and define the uncanniness of our own being experienced in authentic anxiety in two respects. This does not imply any devaluation of other basic emotions, such as hatred, envy, distrust and despair. These too are highly significant for understanding human existing, but nevertheless do not fall into the same category as anxiety, shame and guilt. For these are not pure experiences of being, but emotional responses to it. That hatred, envy and so on are responsive in nature is already indicated by the fact that each of them can be assigned a positive correlate: love to hatred, gratitude to envy, trust to mistrust and hope to despair. A daseinsanalytic interpretation of these emotions therefore presupposes an existential interpretation of the three basic attunements to which they respond. The following explanations of the dual meaning of shame and guilt are orientated by Heidegger's distinction between fear and anxiety: fear of a specific, identifiable danger that threatens us in a specific way and anxiety about the uncanniness of our own being.

5.1 The two-fold meaning of shame

Sartre provides the following formulation for the complex phenomenon of shame: '*I am ashamed of myself* as I appear *to the Other*' (BN, p. 246). This defines what always happens when someone feels ashamed, however completely differently the content (of what we are ashamed), the circumstances (why we are ashamed) and the other people (before whom we are ashamed) may be determined in each individual case. In this definition, the ontological meaning of shame certainly still remains concealed. It conforms to another formulation that is not in fact elaborated by Sartre but that directs his analysis of shame. This is: '*I am ashamed of the fact that I appear to the Other*'. This appears to be a minor change—with 'as' replaced by 'that'. Two simple but fundamental definitions of being are therefore revealed to me in ontological shame: that I appear to the Other at all and that I am seen by the other person.

The ontical meaning of shame

Let us begin by considering the first formulation, which captures the essential nature of all concrete experiences of shame: *who* sees me *how*. Someone who feels ashamed feels negatively exposed, whether it is more negatively than he would like to represent himself or more negatively than falls within the prevailing rules. It is always a matter of a lack becoming visible in the broadest sense, which reduces our own worth or standing in other people's eyes and that we would therefore like to conceal. In shame, I feel exposed and at the same time demeaned because I must discover that something about me has become obvious to others that I myself would never have wanted to reveal and that is not intended for them to see. Demeaning is the powerlessness of not being able to escape the situation, of being trapped in it, although in the sense of shame we are fully concentrating on flight and the fulfilment of the wish to be able to hide away and conceal ourselves.

Of what do we actually feel ashamed? There are three separate domains at which shame is directed. First, we are ashamed of things about which we can do nothing ourselves. These include the figure with which we have been born if it does not correspond to the ideal of beauty, whereby physical defects that cannot be concealed are particularly conducive to shame; they also include social origin, coming from impoverished circumstances or a 'disreputable' family. Second, we feel ashamed of inadequate abilities or our lack of skill, for instance not having passed an exam, being a bad dancer or not having mastered a foreign language. And third, we feel ashamed of our deficiencies of character, ashamed of having failed morally.

Before whom are we ashamed? Whether we are in fact ashamed of a deficiency that becomes visible, and how strongly, depends on the person to whom we are being exposed with this deficiency. Not every exposure before another person is experienced as shaming. It makes a difference whether the person concerned is important or unimportant to us, whether he is someone in authority on whose judgement a great deal depends for us, whether we consider him as someone who is well-disposed towards us or as someone who will use his knowledge of our weaknesses against us.

This already implies a great deal about *why* being ashamed is so intolerable and what we find so bad and therefore fear about situations of shame. We fear being given a condescending smile at or even laughed at by others for physical defects that we can do nothing about; we fear being negatively judged or even despised for our lacking abilities; and we fear being rejected as an entire person and ostracised from the community for our moral failure. We therefore fear the power that accrues to the Other through the exposure of our weaknesses and we find the feeling of shame so intolerable because it demonstrates to us our own powerlessness in relation to others.

Shame, ashamedness, shamelessness

Shame about *how* I appear to others—like fear—is always an interpreted shame: I generally know why I feel ashamed in front of this particular fellow human being. Feelings of shame, like fear, belong to the concrete everyday world that I share with other people. And just as a general anxiousness or acute panic in which I feel generally threatened can be distinguished from the fear of a specific danger, so a general *ashamedness* in which I constantly somehow feel ashamed or liable to be shamed by anyone can be distinguished from a concrete shaming through the exposure of a specific lack before particular people. I can try on the basis of a general ashamedness to make myself as invisible as possible, can avoid going out of the house any more, in order not to have to live constantly in fear of somehow making a negative impression. And just as contrary to the mood of fearfulness there is also fearlessness, there is also shamelessness: people who seem to be ashamed of nothing, who enjoy broadcasting countless intimate details, who shamelessly flaunt themselves or are equally shamelessly concerned only with their own advantage.

The ontological meaning of shame

Whereas ontical-concrete shame always involves my appearing to specific others in a detrimental way, ontological shame concerns the sheer fact that I appear at all and therefore always stand in the Other's view—that, as Sartre put it, I exist 'for the Other'. Here the Other is not a specific person, to whose ridicule or even contempt I am subjected when I reveal a weakness but any human being whose power derives from the mere fact that he is a subject and free to look at me from his own vantage-point, and who condemns me to powerlessness through the sheer fact that I am being looked at by him.

We can refer back here to the explanations in Chapter 3, Part II concerning the otherness of the Other and note that in the ontological experience of shame we are confronted with the fact that the Other is there and that our life happens under the Other's view; that the Other is free in that it is up to him whether he dignifies us with a glance at all and if so how he looks at us and what he discovers in us. Neither mere looking nor thinking—the two traditional sources of knowledge since Kant—enable us to infer what it means for each of us to lead our lives under the gaze of the Other. In shame, however, we experience ourselves—as Sartre starkly expressed it—as 'thrown, abandoned at the heart of the Other's freedom' (*BN*, p. 271).

This elucidates the *connection between ontological shame and anxiety*. Shame is anxiety about being exposed to the Other's gaze; it is anxiety about the factical powerlessness of standing in the Other's gaze without having any control over it and without being able to know whether and how he sees me; it is also anxiety about the insight that being exposed to the Other's gaze is in no way alterable. Shame is therefore a specialised form of anxiety. Whereas anxiety reveals to me that I am exposed to the *nothingness of the world*, in shame I discover that from the nothingness of the world *the Other as Other* appears and looks at me.

With what does the Other's gaze afflict me if not with my concrete deficiencies? With the fact that I am visible to the Other at all, which means that living always means *making an appearance*. However, that is not all. For if the Other's gaze is no longer directed at the how but at the pure 'that it is' of my visibility and therefore my exposedness, it determines all the more who I fundamentally am and have to be—namely a *free subject*. The Other's gaze throws me back on my own subjectivity and thereby destroys the illusion that my own being-a-subject can be escaped by fleeing to the Other or to others, adapting to him, uniting with him or them, in order thus to exist *like* the others or even *as* an Other. This is why shame is at the same time the purest self-experience, namely the experience that I lead my own life in the Other's view in a way that cannot be delegated and for which I have to be responsible. Psychoanalysis, which is predominantly concerned with the history of the subject's emergence in childhood, is therefore also right to emphasise the great significance of the development of shame for the constitution of subjectivity (Seidler, 1995, p. 126ff).

On the relationship between shame and desire

Any feeling of shame entails an intrinsic *desire* to escape from the shaming situation: we wish to sink into the ground or even vanish into thin air to escape the Other's gaze. It is not that we first feel ashamed and then want to flee the shaming situation in order to get rid of the feeling of shame as well; rather, the feeling of shame itself is the effort to flee that is doomed to failure: in feeling ashamed, we are filled with the ardent and also unsuccessful desire to become invisible. By demonstrating to me the unrealisability of the desire, the experience of shame forces on me the truth that I have to lead my own life under the Other's gaze.

The return of ontological shame in ontical experiences of shame

If authentic anxiety is said to be 'rare' (Heidegger), this is equally true of *authentic shame*, in which we not only involuntarily suffer the fact of being seen by the Other but also recognise and endure it. For the most part, we are not ready for this recognition but adhere to the desire to escape the Other's gaze or to break its power over us. Then we deal with ontological shame as we do with anxiety: we reinterpret it as a mere ontical shaming against which something can be done—whether we are constantly striving only to show no weakness, to behave as correctly as possible or in an entirely unnoticeable way, or whether we focus on an impeccable self-representation. The more sensitive someone is to the ontological meaning of shame, the more susceptible he is to concrete experiences of shame and the more inclined he is to sense a potential shaming in everything and perceive all others as potential agents of shame.

Now the individual attitude to shame is strongly culturally determined. Today in my view a rather disturbing *change in the relationship to shame* is emerging. Having feelings of shame is becoming increasingly obsolete and the suffering they cause is accordingly being assessed to be a pathological symptom. Media broadcasts in which people reveal themselves by voluntarily placing intimate details into the anonymous public domain propagate the courage for shameless sincerity and vilify the previously normal sense of shame as an erroneous inhibition acquired from a mendacious society. More disturbing than voluntary self-revelations is the *pressure for inflated self-representation in the workplace*. What would once have been denigratingly characterised as 'bluff' is now regarded as the indispensable know-how of successful career-building. The general economisation of life forces everyone today to become his own salesman and to advertise himself like a product on sale. Anyone who has inhibitions about representing himself as fundamentally better than he is, who is ashamed to ascribe or impute to himself capacities that he knows belong to the so-called 'person specification' for a particular job has hardly any chance of being considered in the general struggle for job vacancies. Gone is the hope that ultimately our own achievements will count and our true abilities will be appreciated, and correspondingly outdated is the tendency to hide our own light under a bushel, which used to be extolled as a virtue.

Running in parallel with this development is the psychiatrisation of feelings of shame that are generated by the economic pressure for inflated self-representation. What used to be shyness has become 'social phobia'. This new psychiatric diagnostic evaluation turns the incapacity for shameless self-representation into a disorder requiring treatment. Collectively denied shame therefore returns under the label of social phobia. From a daseinsanalytic perspective, psychiatry plays an ambiguous role here. On the one hand, it affords some protection to people who have too much shame to become marketing experts on their own behalf by diagnosing their incapacity as a pathological reaction for which by definition nothing can be done. On the other hand, through this very pathologisation of shame reactions it proclaims the requisite self-enactment as a worthwhile capacity that the psychologically healthy human being should have at his disposal.

5.2 The two-fold meaning of guilt

According to the daseinsanalytic conception, guilt operates not only at the level of moral lapses but also at the level of the relationship to our own being. There is therefore a distinction to be drawn between moral and pre-moral ontological guilt. With regard to the *experience* of guilt, this means that guilt feelings are not only related to an actual or an imagined moral failure but also to a guilt that belongs to the human being as such.

Now moral guilt is considered to be essentially redeemable. We can regret committing sins, take the deserved punishment on ourselves, and beyond this hope for forgiveness. By contrast, the guilt that we heap on ourselves not for an inappropriate action but for the sheer fact of existence is in no way to be redeemed. Sartre is referring to this form of guilt when he declares that: 'the peculiar character of human reality is that it is without excuse' (*BN*, p. 575).

It might seem that the concept of an ontological guilt could be equated with the Judaeo–Christian theory of original sin, since this is also a guilt that has burdened all human beings since the act of disobedience to God carried out by Adam and Eve. Such an equation must, however, be avoided. From an existential viewpoint, the doctrine of original sin places at our disposal a religious interpretation of the incomprehensible ontological guilt that—precisely because it gives a reason for the inexplicable—has a liberating and reassuring effect on being. Furthermore, with the reinterpretation as original sin the chance of a redemption appears on the horizon and the only matter of dispute becomes whether the redemption from the original guilt can be achieved through good works or is granted by God's grace alone.

The two-fold ontological meaning of guilt

The guilt that we must bear even when we lead a thoroughly moral way of life is again of a dual nature: it consists on the one hand in the fact that we must claim a right to life purely through the fact of being alive, and on the other in the fact that it is not remotely possible to lead a guiltless life.

Compelled to self-authorisation

To exist means to be there instead of not be there. To be there as a human being at all, however, means to assume a place in the world that cannot simultaneously be held by any other person. This is why for sensitive people the question arises of the legitimacy of claiming this place. This cannot be answered without bringing religious interpretations into play. It leads instead to the insight that there is no valid reason why I am there instead of not being there, and therefore that I cannot make recourse to anything that might justify my claim to life. This means, however, that *only I myself can be the agency that authorises my life*. Here we encounter the most unfathomable element of human being-a-subject: the baseless self-authorisation that can only be experienced as guilt. The feeling of guilt confronts me with the *presumption* that is contained in my sheer existence. If, as explained, existential anxiety confronts us with being 'condemned to freedom' (Sartre), then the feeling of guilt reveals to us that this freedom is rooted in a primal act that is not to be justified and yet constantly has to be renewed, in which we authorise ourselves to live.

Compelled to make choices

Living my own life means taking it over myself and leading it, which again means having to take decisions. However, any decision can always make us guilty, even just because no one at the moment of decision can be entirely certain of knowing whether, as the saying goes, the time for the decision is yet ripe, and whether he has given adequate consideration to the pros and cons. And even if this seems to be the case according to our subjective assessment, indeed even when we make a decision on the basis of purely altruistic considerations and set aside self-interest, we still cannot yet know for certain what will result from such a well-founded decision and what negative consequences it may have. For these unforeseeable consequences we certainly cannot be morally afflicted, but we remain their author. This is why every decision is burdened with *possible guilt* of an extent that no one can predict.

As well as potential guilt, every decision also implies a *factical guilt*. We make ourselves guilty with every decision, even if it has a moral basis and brings no negative consequences. This is because every decision in favour of one possibility simultaneously includes a decision against another and therefore, expressed over-trenchantly, always means an 'extermination' of the possibilities that are not chosen. We make ourselves guilty towards these other possibilities that are blocked from realisation by the decision. Even a morally legitimised decision is therefore the basis for the guilt at having decided against other possibilities. This also involves a self-authorisation, which everyone arrogates to himself with every decision—has to arrogate to himself, and inevitably makes himself guilty by it.

The return of ontological guilt in moral guilt feelings

The willingness to take over my own life is generally based on the capacity to screen out ontological guilt and to live as if my own existence were unquestionably justified. For only on the basis of the belief that I am essentially entitled to a place in this world is it possible to judge appropriately in daily life what I may and may not do, what is permitted to me and thus to what I am and am not entitled, to what I have a right and by what I make myself morally guilty. Someone who cannot screen out the lack of justification for his own existence will inevitably seek other means of freeing himself of this (pre-moral) sense of guilt. Just as the basic attunement of anxiety can turn into a general anxiousness about possible dangers, so the basic attunement of guilt can turn into a constant sense of being able to become guilty about everything and towards everyone or to have already incurred guilt. This conversion also imposes a heavy burden on everyday life. Nonetheless, it is easier to bear than ontological guilt because we believe we can take precautionary measures to avoid becoming guilty at all. One example of this is people who cannot help apologising for everything they do, even though no one is denying them the right to do anything. This comes across as inappropriate and can only be understood in terms of these people being especially sensitive to the unavoidable guiltiness of their own being and therefore constantly trying in vain to free themselves of it by seeking absolution for anything and everything from other people. We just as frequently encounter people who try to shirk every decision, however minor, and therefore endlessly postpone all decisions or delegate them to other people. What manifests itself as a pathological incapacity to make decisions is rooted in such a person's special sensitivity to the guiltiness inherent in every decision and the ensuing illusory hope of being able to remain guiltless by abstaining from decisions altogether.

6

An existential interpretation of the unconscious

What is the daseinsanalytic approach to the unconscious? It is already clear that daseinsanalysis does not use the *concept* of the unconscious since its counterpart, consciousness, does not feature in its terminology. So it is not yet possible to conclude from this a negative attitude towards the unconscious as a fact. Yet as it is a matter here—as the word already implies—of the kind of fact that is not directly revealed but can only be inferred from specific phenomena, we must distinguish between that which compelled Freud to suppose the existence of an unconscious and the metapsychological conceptualisation of this supposition as a compartment of the psychic apparatus. It follows that daseinsanalysis cannot take on the latter from its understanding of the human being as existence, which does not permit that form of reification of psychic life into a objectively present interior with various domains. Daseinsanalysis can therefore only accept Freud's discovery if it simultaneously interprets it existentially.

Neither Ludwig Binswanger nor Medard Boss made reference to an unconscious for their understanding of human experience and behaviour. One important reason for this was their indebtedness to the phenomenological method, which does not permit any recourse to merely hypothetical suppositions. Nevertheless, neither of them simply denied Freud's hypothesis. For Binswanger, the recourse to the unconscious simply did not go far enough because he was convinced that a human being's individuality was determined not by unconscious psychic material but by the 'world-project' that underlay the whole of mental life. Boss, on the other hand, accorded an essential truth to Freud's metapsychological theory of the unconscious despite its speculative nature, on the basis that Freud had in fact intuited an entirely different, much more fundamental 'hiddenness', but had totally misinterpreted this intuition (Boss, 1994, *loc. cit.*, p. 135f).

The answer to the question of how daseinsanalysis views the unconscious determines not only the question of its proximity to psychoanalysis but also whether it can establish a *comprehending* (hermeneutic) rather than just a descriptive and explanatory approach to mental suffering and dreams. This is because both psychopathological symptoms and dreams become only partly comprehensible as long as we limit ourselves to what is directly shown. A meaning to the phenomena that manifestly appear meaningless can only be discovered through the supposition of an unconscious.

It is inaccurate to refer to Freud as the discoverer of the unconscious. What he actually discovered was that neurotic symptoms have a meaning. He attained the insight that neurotic symptoms, however senseless they may appear and however disturbing their manifestations, are not in fact pathologically generated phenomena of deficiency but meaningful forms of reaction with a hidden meaning.[54] It was this discovery that made it necessary to postulate an unconscious. As a result of this postulate, Freud became the founder of a *hermeneutic psychopathology* that *interprets* both neurotic and psychotic symptoms with recourse to an unconscious instead of only describing and explaining them as senseless products of a pathological psyche (or brain).

Daseinsanalysis therefore confronts the choice between becoming reconciled with the idea of an unconscious or instead being satisfied with a mere description of the manifestly incomprehensible symptoms of neurotic and psychotic suffering. Only if it assumes the task of elaborating an existential concept of the unconscious is it in a position also to offer an alternative to psychoanalytic interpretation, which consists in interpreting mental suffering as a 'suffering from our own being' (cf. Chapter 2, Part III). The following proposal for an existential

---

[54] This subject will be discussed in more detail in the next chapter.

interpretation of the unconscious can draw support from both Sartre and Heidegger because in both philosophical definitions of human existence the phenomenon of 'fundamental self-concealment' has a central significance.

6.1 The unconscious as self-deception

We have already established in various ways that matters are not decided by finding a specific answer to a question but by enquiring into a subject in one way or another. The usual question would be: 'What is the unconscious?' This would already be to admit, however, that the unconscious is a objectively present reality, with its own specific characteristics. Freud however merely discovered initially that his hysterical female patients were unaware of many of their motivations. The unconscious was therefore a *characteristic* of certain wishes and fantasies, as well as specific actions. Only the question of how this characteristic could be explained then led to the hypostatisation of the unconscious as a compartment of the psyche inhabited by repressed wishes and fantasies, and to the premise of its unknown and unpredictable effects on conscious mental life. The unconscious therefore stands at first merely for the fact that the human being only knows himself in part, whereas he believes that he knows himself completely. In Freud's famous metaphor, the ego imagines itself to be 'master in its own house' although in reality it 'must content itself with scanty information of what is going on unconsciously in its mind' (1916–17, p. 285). But someone who believes that he knows himself completely and knows why he thinks and acts in one way and not another, although he only knows himself partly and often acts on motives of which he is entirely unaware, is *caught in self-deception.*

Now there is a special feature to these self-deceptions. Hardly anyone disputes that these occur, but they can only ever ascertain them in other people, not in themselves. This makes it clear that the unconscious consists not merely in a not-knowing but in not knowing that I do not know and therefore believing that I know everything about myself. The unconscious therefore stands for a twofold not-knowing and therefore for the erroneous conviction of knowing myself, being subjectively sincere and concealing nothing. This is precisely why it is especially mortifying to have to recognise that we are caught in self-deceptions. We therefore ascertain that the unconscious initially only stands for the observation that people deceive themselves about themselves. Yet this observation presents a great, almost insoluble enigma—namely as to how self-deception can come about. What is initially conceivable is only ever the deception of others, which consists in deliberately deceiving another person or being deceived by him. The former succeeds because another person can never see through all my thoughts and intentions. The latter, because for my part I am also incapable of penetrating the façade of what the deceiver is staging for me. A self-deception, however, seems impossible because after all I know my own intentions, and thus necessarily see through the game. How therefore can I deceive myself and at the same time mistake the deception for genuine currency? How can I at the same time be the person who is insincere with myself and imagine myself in all seriousness to be subjectively sincere? Or to put it yet another way, how can I be both perpetrator and victim in relation to deception?

Freud surrendered to this enigma; his spatialisation of the unconscious into a compartment of the psyche is the consequence of this surrender. As soon as the unconscious is envisaged as an intrapsychic domain that is inaccessible because it is sealed off by a censor, we have 'the same relation to everything that occurs inside this space as we have to a psychical process in another person, except that it is in fact one of our own' (1933, p. 70). Now deceiver and deceived are no longer the same person, but are divided into two intrapsychic areas in which it is simultaneously certain who is deceiving whom or who is being deceived by whom: the Other or rather the unconscious deceives me and I am deceived by my unconscious. This is possible according to Freud because the unconscious functions within my mental life like 'a state within a state' (1939, p. 76), which itself cannot be influenced but can have powerful effects on the other parts of the psyche.

6.2 *Mauvaise foi* as the conduct of self-deception

It is Jean-Paul Sartre's great achievement to have demonstrated with his micro-analysis of *mauvaise foi* (bad faith) that and how it is possible to deceive oneself and at the same time to allow oneself to be deceived by oneself (*BN, loc. cit.*, p. 70ff). Sartre even provocatively stated that he rejected Freud's postulate of the unconscious (*BN*, p. 591). This statement is not, however, to be taken at face value, since what he rejected was only its reification as an objectively present entity. Sartre begins by distinguishing *mauvaise foi* from the *lie*. Whereas I cannot lie to myself because the lie 'collapses beneath my look' through the knowledge that it is a lie, I can easily deceive myself about myself through *mauvaise foi* because unlike the lie this is not a transparent but an evanescent phenomenon: 'The decision to be in bad faith does not dare to speak its name; it believes itself and does not believe itself in bad faith' (*BN*, p. 91). Bad faith thrives on ambivalence. We do not *suffer* it but neither do we choose it unconsciously; instead one '*puts oneself in bad faith* as one goes to sleep and one is in bad faith as one dreams' (*BN*, p. 91). We therefore leave everything in obscurity. We refrain from believing in order to believe after all and we believe in order not to believe, so all our own convictions are always simultaneously non-convictions. Sartre also indicates the specific steps by which the insincere act is reinforced. We decide to believe something although there is 'no evidence' for it, then surrender to 'impulses to trust', and afterwards decide to continue believing it, and go on to behave as if we were certain that we believed it. *Mauvaise foi* is more here than a series of individual behaviour patterns; it is an *attitude*, a *way of life*, in short: 'a type of being in the world'. Having once got used to this way of living, it is difficult to find a way out of it (*BN*, p. 92f).

What is achieved by this analysis? Nothing more and nothing less than an existential understanding of the unconscious. By demonstrating how self-deception is possible without having to make any recourse to a reifying partition of the psyche, Sartre simultaneously shows that the so-called unconscious is nothing other than a particular way of behaving towards oneself. The unconscious is therefore not an objectively present entity inside me but the constant conduct of the concatenation of deceiving-myself and letting-myself-be-deceived-by-myself. This renders obsolete the stark oppositions between 'conscious' and 'unconscious', as well as 'autonomous' and 'heteronomous', which cannot be attested by concrete phenomena but constitute artefacts that arise from the reification of the unconscious. In reality, something is seldom entirely beyond my awareness, and my actions are also hardly ever directed by motives of which I am entirely unaware, but I know something and yet do not know it, deliberately think past it, am more or less purposely inattentive and so on, which gives rise to a diffuse and obscure half-knowledge.

By conceiving of the unconscious as a process of self-deception, Sartre redefines the relationship between ego and unconscious. With Freud, this is an entirely one-sided relationship in which the ego is accorded the passive role since it is denied access to the unconscious areas of its inner life and it does not even notice that it is influenced by effects that proceed from the unconscious. It *suffers* the self-deception and is unfreely *caught* in it. But if the unconscious consists in deceiving itself about itself, the ego regains an active role that consists in *making oneself passive* by *allowing* oneself to be deceived. The ego is now no longer a mere pseudo-subject that believes itself to be autonomous, while it falls under the dictates of unconscious parts inside it, but an active subject that operates its own deception. This in turn is only possible because the subject of *mauvaise foi* is an *insincere subject* that as such is full of cunning towards itself, dupes itself, *wants* to pull the wool over its eyes and at the same time persuades itself that it is being completely honest with itself.

6.3 Ontical and ontological self-deception

If we work daseinsanalytically from the premise that the unconscious consists in the conduct of self-deception, there are two questions to explain, which cannot be treated separately: one is the question as to *what* I deceive myself *about* when I deceive myself about myself, and the other is what kind of *interest* I could have in deceiving myself about myself. So far we have only discussed self-deception in abstract terms. But as soon as it has become clear that we are not simply victims of self-deceptions but actively operate these processes, we must have a reason for doing so. This is the point at which to introduce the daseinsanalytic distinction between the ontical and the ontological self-relationship with reference also to the unconscious. The distinction therefore needs to be drawn between the interest in deceiving myself about myself as this person X and the interest in deluding myself about my own being in the sense of the pure 'that I am and have to be'. For the former (ontical) interest, we find information in Freud; for the latter we find it in Heidegger.

In summary, and thus abridged, in Freud it is the child in the oedipal situation who reaches for methods of self-deception or has to do so because his wish for love—in the son's case directed at the mother—which is connected with the wish to eliminate the father as a rival—brings the threat of the punishment of castration. Therefore the only possibility is to repress the wish. The repression of the wish can simulate the required renunciation. It allows not only others but also ourselves to be made to believe that we have renounced the forbidden wish, and are therefore good, obedient children who do not deserve to be punished. For *Heidegger* self-deception operates on the level of the relationship to our own being. As already explained, it is only in anxiety that the human being overtly knows how matters stand with his own being.[55] It follows from this that he has an elementary interest in deceiving himself about his own being and thus escaping anxiety. Although Heidegger never once uses the adjective 'unconscious', the subject of the flight into forgetting[56] and into the making unconscious of our own being is a key element of his existential definition of the human being as dasein. This matter has incidentally already been addressed in my earlier explanations under the term 'the screening out of pre-ontological inclusions', which also already made clear that this does not involve a single act but an ever-recurrent disregard of the anxiety-inducing truth about our own being, in order thus to keep it in forgetting.

Because Freud only knows the fear of threatening drive wishes but not the anxiety about our own being, for him the unconscious

---

[55] Cf. here Part I, Chapter 1 and Part II, Chapter 4.

[56] Cf. *BT*, p. 324: 'In order to be able to "really" get to work "lost" in the world of tools and to handle them, the self must forget itself'.

also consists in nothing other than the sum of these same drive excitations that are feared and therefore repressed by the ego. For Freud the unconscious can only wish. For Freud the locus of fear is not the unconscious but the ego. This conception can no longer be maintained if we distinguish between anxiety and fear and see the fear of anxiety as the actual motive for self-deception. For it follows from this that *the core of the unconscious is anxiety itself*—anxiety in the singular, which, unlike Freud's castration anxiety, is not externally induced but brings to expression the existential threat that is inherent in the being of dasein.

This brings us back to the *relationship between anxiety and desire*. For Freud, the unconscious can consist only in wish-excitations because he grounds the human desire in biology and regards the drive-wish as the ultimate motivation for all human experience and behaviour. For him, what is preserved in the unconscious is what the human being is by his nature, but must suppress in order to adapt to reality and cultural demands. From the psychoanalytic perspective, fear is therefore ultimately always a trepidation about the constantly endangered wish-fulfilment. But if daseinsanalytically we take anxiety (not fear!) into the unconscious, the question arises as to how unconscious anxiety and unconscious wishes interact.

For Freud, the unconscious is the domain in which all the laws that constitute reality are invalid: the unconscious knows neither time nor death, neither denial nor the contradiction between irreconcilable wishes, and it also knows nothing of the difference between good and evil (1915a, p. 289; 1933, pp. 74ff.). In unconscious mental life, wishes are therefore immortal and everything appears not only to be possible but also permitted. The absence of laws that restrict life is according to Freud an expression of the unrestrained dominance of the 'pleasure principle' in the unconscious. From the daseinsanalytic perspective, the reference to the pleasure principle illustrates the idea of a life without temporal restriction, without conflicts and without guilt and shame. Freud's unconscious governed by the pleasure principle therefore stands for the primal desire for a life free of anxiety, guilt and shame. This primal desire stems from anxiety and simultaneously envelops it, creating the impression that the unconscious can do nothing but desire.

Let us summarise the key elements of an existential concept of the unconscious: the unconscious is conceived as a constant conduct of self-deception in the Sartrean sense of *mauvaise foi*, which above all serves as protection from the traumatising confrontation with the incomprehensible and therefore uncanny fact of the 'that I am and have to be'; self-deception has the structure of wishing and pretends that unrealisable wishes are realisable or already fulfilled; the wishes relate to overcoming the nothingness of our own being and also the emancipation from anxiety, guilt and shame. Such a concept of the unconscious is indispensable in order also as a daseinsanalyst to acquire a comprehending (hermeneutic) approach instead of a merely descriptive approach to psychopathological phenomena, which will be discussed in the chapters of Part III.

7

Dreams

The account of daseinsanalytic dream interpretation leads on to daseinsanalytic psychopathology, but the dream presents similar problems to the symptoms of people who are suffering psychically. What occurs in the dream often appears muddled, incomprehensible and even completely nonsensical. In 1900, when Freud's groundbreaking *Interpretation of Dreams* appeared, the view also prevailed that dreams were senseless products of physiological stimuli during the state of sleep. To this Freud opposed his thesis of the *dream as a wish-fulfilment*, which has since formed the core of psychoanalytic dream interpretation. This not only postulates the fundamental meaningfulness of dreams, but also creates the bridge to psychopathology, since neurotic symptoms also represent concealed wish-fulfilments from a psychoanalytic perspective. According to Freud, the dream can be interpreted as a neurotic symptom because it has the character of a symptom: 'Dreams are themselves a neurotic symptom' (1916–17, p. 83). If the dream represents the neurotic symptom that everyone produces, then the traditional boundary between mental health and mental illness becomes blurred.

Medard Boss set out a daseinsanalytic interpretation of dreams that radically rejects Freud's interpretative approach. Instead of repeating his criticism of psychoanalytic dream theory, we will consider the difficulty that at first sight makes it impossible for a daseinsanalyst to share Freud's approach. If in fact the human being is understood as 'existence' or as 'being-in-the-world', the dream can no longer be interpreted as a *product* of mental life. Ludwig Binswanger recognised this in his 1930 essay 'Dream and existence' (Binswanger, 1986) and redefined the dream as a special *form of existence*. Since then dreaming has represented for daseinsanalysis a special way of 'being-in-the-world'. With it, however, Freud's distinction between the manifest dream content (the dream as remembered by the dreamer) and the latent (unconscious) dream thoughts can no longer be maintained. The questions remains of whether a dream can still be interpreted at all if it is defined as a special form of being-in-the-world. If we follow Boss, the answer to this must be negative. For him, the dream presents nothing to be interpreted, for everything the dream can tell us is plain to see. We need only look at what the dreamer encounters in the dream and how he behaves towards it in dreaming.[57] Is this rejection of interpretation in favour of a mere (phenomenological) description and evaluation of what is shown in the dream compelling?

In the meantime we now have available some works by Uta Jaenicke (1998, 1999, 2008) on a daseinsanalytic *interpretation* of oneiric being-in-the-world. It emerges from these that latent dream thoughts are not a prerequisite for enquiring into a hidden meaning of the dream. Indispensable, however, for this are on the one hand the so-called 'day residues' (elements from the experiences of the previous day) that occur to the dreamer about the dream and knowledge of the mood that prevailed in the dream. This daseinsanalytic interpretative approach works on the assumption that all dreams involve a form of wrestling with our own being.

Jaenicke's thesis of an *ontological meaning* of dreams appears highly speculative if we realise that the dreamer is mostly involved in entirely concrete, actual events that often follow each other unconnected. On what grounds, then, can daseinsanalysis claim that in the dream—unlike in the waking state—we are concerned first and foremost with the human condition? On what basis can it state that despite every appearance to the contrary the dream involves an ontological problematic that summons the dream and also determines the course of events in the dream?

---

[57] Cf. Medard Boss's account of dream interpretation in the Historical Part, Chapter 2.3, as well as the literature cited there.

7.1 Why we are especially sensitive in dreams

The answer can only be: because during sleep we have withdrawn from that shared waking world in which we are responsible for the task of leading our lives under set conditions and in interaction with others. The dream world is not a shared world, although we interact with other people in it. Binswanger describes it as an 'idios cosmos' (own world) because everything that happens in it relates to me alone and is entirely my concern. How other people behave in my dream reveals nothing about their individuality but merely shows my subjective view of them. In the dream world, objective laws to which all events and actions in the waking world are subordinate are also invalid. In dreaming we can exist again as the child of that time; in the dream, people who have long since died reappear, and we can fly unaided or stay under water without drowning and so on. The dream world is therefore freer of restrictions but at the same time more restricted than the waking world: in it on the one hand the impossible becomes possible, on the other hand there is no continuity, since we generally find ourselves in a completely different world in the very next dream.

What is the justification for conceptualising the dream as a specific form of existence? Freud explains the characteristic nature of dream events by the fact that the sleeping state removes the intrapsychic censor that in waking life keeps away from consciousness any wish that would disturb the relationship to reality (1916–17, p. 218). The sleeping state makes this censor superfluous, which is why the wishes in the dream can be lived out in a harmless way. Now daseinsanalysis too knows a censor that influences waking life; only it connects this not simply with conflictual childhood wishes but with the human relationship with being—more precisely, with the fact that the human being is dependent for a successful conduct of daily life on being able to screen out his philosophical knowledge of the nothingness of his own being.[58] Freud rightly argues that the censor that operates in waking life demands a great psychic effort, although it functions unnoticed. This effort is due to what is called 'mental health'. Sleep enables everyone to relax the censor and to abandon the

---

[58] Cf. here Methodological Part, Chapter 1.2, on experiences of being as intrinsically threatening to the human being.

effort. While sleeping we are in that form of existence in which the 'ontological inclusions' of ontical events and experiences emerge from their confinement and can unfold their effects unhindered. This helps to explain why the dream represents the only 'neurotic symptom' that 'also occurs in all healthy people' (Freud). Put in daseinsanalytic terms, this means that the dream represents the form of existence in which we all, whether mentally healthy or suffering, are gripped by the basic questions of our being and seek a solution to them.

Daseinsanalysis therefore puts forward the view that every dream is to be interpreted in terms of a hidden ontological meaning, including when a dream event seems so real that we are convinced at the moment of waking that what we have just dreamt belongs to the waking world, when its content merely seems to replicate what has happened in the day. *That* something or someone finds his way from the waking world into the dream world shows from a daseinsanalytic perspective that it is not only about this concrete fact or this person but a problematic of being that is represented in it. In dreaming, this problematic gains the upper hand and enforces an engagement with it that is free of the restrictive conditions of waking life. It is because in dreams we are open to what in waking life mainly remains concealed behind everyday concerns that the dream often appears so meaningless or crazy; it brings into the picture not the generally comprehensible ontical meaning of something but its ontological meaning as it is experienced by the dreamer at the time.

7.2 Dream events as a depiction of basic mood

If oneiric existing is governed by the ontological meaning of events and actions rather than the ontical-concrete meaning, special attention must be paid to emotionality because the conditions of being can only be experienced primarily through mood. From this it can be inferred that the dream events themselves illustrate the mood in which the dreamer, whether sleeping or awake, finds himself at the time and in which his own being is disclosed to him. So someone may dream that he has to take an exam, although in waking life nothing of the kind is approaching. The exam in the dream illustrates what the dreamer is also particularly sensitive towards at the time in waking life—namely the fact that living life always has the aspect of a test situation in which one has to prove oneself and may also fail. In waking life, the dreamer is usually not or at most only dimly aware that he has a sense of being examined and tested in general but in the dream this mood is now illustrated as an entirely concrete situation to which he must react in some way or another. This basic mood has to be distinguished from the feelings that the dreamer has in the dream: how the dreamer concretely feels and how he deals with it, whether he tackles the exam with great anxiety or shirks it out of anxiety, whether he is indifferent to how well he passes the exam or whether he is actually pleased to demonstrate his ability, whether he successfully passes it or fails, shows his emotional attitude at the time to the fact that life always has the aspect of an exam: it shows whether he experiences this fact of being as an opportunity or a danger, whether he feels equal to it or overwhelmed by it.

However, the daseinsanalytic focus on the mood as the main path of interpretation does not involve any devaluation of the dream image. So it makes an enormous difference whether someone dreams about a feather (or himself as a feather) swaying around in the wind or a bird (or himself as a bird) moving in the air. The bird can fly and also determines the direction and goal of the flight, whereas a lifeless feather is moved by the wind. Dreaming about being a bird therefore illustrates the basically denied but often deeply desired freedom to be able to fly, not only through the technological invention of the aeroplane but by oneself. However, someone who dreams he is a feather in the wind illustrates another equally fundamentally denied and simultaneously desired freedom, namely to be freed of the burden of his own being-as-a-subject and instead to live without goals and thus also blamelessly.

This leaves the question of why the daseinsanalytic dream interpretation expounded here follows not Boss but Freud and considers for interpretation the so-called 'day residues' (obvious connections with events of the previous day), as well as the dreamer's 'free associations' to his dream. Boss demanded an interpretation purely in terms of the dream because he was convinced that the dream spoke for itself and that including daily residues and associations would only lead away from the dream statement. This cannot be maintained if we understand the dream as a wrestling with our own being because then we must assume that the problematic of being that is lived in the dream is also virulent in the background in waking life and therefore arises also in possibly entirely trivial daily events in an unremarkable way. To interpret the ontological meaning of the dream we are therefore dependent on the dreamer's associations.

7.3 Dreaming as a wrestling with our own being

In conclusion, I would like to elucidate the procedure of an ontological dream interpretation with the dream that has already served to illustrate Medard Boss's phenomenological dream interpretation (1977, *loc. cit.* p. 67). The dream report is as follows:

'Last night I dreamed that I was sleeping. I woke up in my dream, and looked out the window of my parents' house. Two hostile armies were in the fields. They began to fight. They were getting closer to the house, and I was afraid they might get in, so I ran around closing all the doors, then ran into my mother's bedroom. She was lying in bed. I climbed in. Suddenly everything was peaceful and quiet. The shooting outside stopped. I could sleep again.'

The opening sequence in which the dreamer wakes, opens his eyes and looks out of the window seems, since it is everyday and therefore unremarkable, to require no further commentary. But it deserves our attention because it is part of a dream. If the man dreams of something as everyday as waking up, this is because he is oppressed by its ontological meaning, namely as a human being whether he likes it or not waking into the world and being-in-the-world and being confronted anew every morning with this fundamental truth of human existing. Also, what the dreamer discovers when he looks out of the window tells him something fundamental about the human condition. If Boss had asked about the experiences of the previous day, the dreamer would presumably have become aware that he was witness to a conflictual altercation that he had however, since he was not involved, quickly forgotten again. The dream the following night deals with the ontological inclusion of this event. This is far from neutral and, furthermore, directly concerns him because it makes it unambiguously obvious to him *that* it is part of life in the world also to be embroiled in combative struggles with other people; that also *his* life, which fundamentally is played out in the figurative sense outside the house and outside in the world, is no exception to this. In the dream, the primal fact that being together with other people always also involves being against each other is illustrated as the war taking place directly in front of the parents' house. As the dreamer perceives the war scene through his bedroom window, he encounters himself as a person who like all people is pushed into a 'not-at-home' of a world that is always also hostile. He experiences this in the dream as being as unavoidable as it is intolerable, so that he can only deny this truth, only reject the necessity of taking over his 'being-in-the-world'. So he quickly shuts all the doors, wants to see and hear no more, wants to go back to sleep and thus to the state of self-forgetting and supposed innocence. For this, however, it is not enough only to crawl into his own bed because, while on his own, he is still subjected to the noise of war despite the closed doors and windows. He is only able to screen out this noise, which reminds him of an extremely threatening basic condition of human existing, by hurrying back to his mother's bed and indeed specifically not in the oedipal sense to take his father's place but in the hope of being able to return to a foetal state in which there is no outside yet and therefore also not yet any anxiety. By returning to his mother's bed the dreamer says no; he metaphorically rejects the unreasonable demand to take up the challenge of life, he enacts the desire for a flawless, invulnerable life in the pure interior without any threatening others—and therefore without conflict or struggle. In the dream, the fundamentally unrealisable desire is fulfilled: the mother's bed is there for him and, on his successful return home to his mother, peace also sets in outside, the noise of warfare dies down, the world becomes peaceful again—the dreamer can sleep again reassured.

This ontological interpretation of the dream—unlike Boss's dream interpretation—contains no diagnostic judgement as to the dreamer's degree of psychological maturity. The dream permits no such judgement because according to the interpretation presented here it in no way portrays the dreamer's individual being-in-the-world but stages his actual wrestling with the human condition at the time. It therefore implies nothing about the level of freedom or maturity that the dreamer is able to exercise in waking life. An ontological understanding of the dream is based much more on the fact that we are all especially sensitive in dreams and are therefore especially prone to overwhelming experiences of being. This is why in dreams other people or we ourselves can be violent without seeming excessively anxious, distrustful or even aggressive in waking life, and this is why the wish to return to the mother's bed can appear and even be fulfilled, although in waking life the fact of being adult and thus separated from the mother seems to be broadly accepted. From the fairy-tale fulfilment of the wish in the dream it can only be recognised that the dreamer at that moment is *especially sensitive* to the anxiety-inducing fact of being placed as an individual into the not-at-home of the world and having to lead his own life and be responsible for it, which is why that primal desire for an at-home in which he can hide is actualised, a desire that is dormant in every human being and is symbolised here as the return to the mother's bed.

Daseinsanalysis
Daseinsanalysis
Daseinsanalysis
Daseinsanalysis
Daseinsanalysis
Daseinsanalysis

III

Mental suffering

Daseinsanalysis
Daseinsanalysis
Daseinsanalysis
Daseinsanalysis
Daseinsanalysis
Daseinsanalysis

Introduction

This section contains the programme for a *daseinsanalytic hermeneutics of psychopathological phenomena*. Accordingly, the term 'mental suffering' does not mean the same here as 'mental illness'. This requires some explanation because in colloquial usage the terms 'suffering' and 'illness' are more or less interchangeable, whereas in medicine and psychiatry reference is generally made to 'mental illnesses' or 'mental disorders' according to the World Health Organization classification. It is wrong to suppose that the terms 'illness' and 'disorder' are so neutral that they imply nothing about the characteristics of neurotic and psychotic phenomena. These terms presuppose that nothing other than (negative) deviations from mental health or mental non-disturbance are concerned. Where the concept of suffering is used instead of the concept of illness in the following chapters, it is precisely this assumption that is being denied, so that due consideration can be given to the hermeneutic question concerning the meaning and significance of these phenomena.

This is where daseinsanalysis starts to follow in Freud's footsteps, since psychoanalysis emerged with the discovery that hysterical symptoms do not constitute defective phenomena caused by illness but have a meaning.[59] Daseinsanalysis therefore shares the psychoanalytic

---

[59] Cf. the explanations in Chapter 1, Part III. Following Freud here also means rejecting the 'daseins-appropriate pathology' put forward by Boss (Cf. Historical Part, 2.4), which is based on the medical concept of illness and therefore classifies psychopathological phenomena as mere afflictions.

conviction as to the hidden meaningfulness of mental suffering, but takes a specifically daseinsanalytic approach that refers primarily to the human relationship to his own being and is therefore to be described as 'existential' or 'ontological'. The impetus for this comes from Sartre, who laconically observes that the madman ('*le fou*') merely 'in his own way realizes the human condition' (*BN*, p. 396n).

1

Mental illness or mental suffering?

T here is a general consensus today that mental suffering should be classified as an illness, without specifying whether this is understood to be disease of the psyche or the brain. The question as to whether it is illness or suffering complicates this consensus by probing whether it is accurate to subsume psychopathological phenomena under the concept of illness or whether they would be better subsumed under the concept of suffering. The question is incomprehensible without some clarification, since the two concepts are generally used interchangeably, except that the term 'illness' tends to be applied to the objective fact and 'suffering' to the accompanying subjective state of mind. The question raised here therefore only makes sense if 'illness' and 'suffering' denote two alternative views of what can be understood as psychopathological phenomena.

1.1 The difference between medical and psychoanalytic discourse

Freud begins the fifth lecture of the *Introductory Lectures on Psycho-Analysis* as follows: 'Ladies and Gentlemen,—It was discovered one day that the pathological symptoms of certain neurotic patients have a sense' (1916–17, p. 83). If—as Freud supposes—this truly concerns a 'discovery', the neurotic is suffering not simply from his neurotic disorder but in reality from something that comes to expression in this disorder in disguised form—in other words: he is suffering from a painful circumstance without knowing himself what he is actually suffering from. Similarly, his neurotic symptoms do not constitute mere manifestations of a disease of the mind or the brain, but have their own intrinsic 'meaning', even if the person affected does not understand this meaning himself and his symptomatic experience and behaviour appear absurd in everyday life and merely make themselves felt as a disorder.

This leads directly to a *non-medical concept of suffering* with which we are thoroughly familiar from colloquial language. For colloquially we never merely talk about someone suffering from an illness but also about suffering from famine, unemployment, loneliness or being lovesick and so on. What Freud adds to these many possible forms of suffering is the possibility of suffering from something without knowing what this is. Whereas the doctor seeks to diagnose an illness correctly by asking what someone is suffering from, the psychoanalyst seeks the hidden 'object' of this suffering. And whereas for the doctor the diagnosis of hysteria or obsessional neurosis follows from the incidence of some of its typical symptoms, for the psychoanalyst it emerges from the hidden object of the suffering. Freud gave a general answer to the question of what the neurotic is actually suffering from by stating that neurotics 'suffer from reminiscences' (1910, p. 16).[60] By reminiscences he meant painful childhood memories that are no longer conscious but continue to trouble the neurotic so that the suffering from them as it were replaces the memory. For the psychoanalyst, the question of what the neurotic is suffering from therefore essentially leads back to childhood. But this should not be confused with the causal-deterministic notion that the *causes* of a mental illness lie in childhood. When the psychoanalyst turns to the childhood history, he seeks not the causal origination of the neurotic symptoms but, as Freud's introductory quotation demonstrates, their *meaning*.[61]

---

[60] This statement first appears in the *Studies on Hysteria* ('the hysteric suffers mainly from reminiscences', Freud and Breuer, 1895, p. 7) and is used by Freud throughout his works; in 1937, he even makes an equivalent statement concerning delusions (cf. 1937a, p. 268).

[61] 'Sense' is the word used by Strachey in this case to render the German word 'Sinn', which is translated here as 'meaning' (*Translator's note*).

The question 'illness or suffering' therefore seeks to expose the prejudgement that consists in defining psychopathological phenomena essentially as manifestations of illness. It seeks to clarify that the primary question concerning psychopathology is not 'what mental illnesses are' but whether these phenomena are in fact manifestations of disease at all. If this question is answered affirmatively, then we are taking refuge in the *medical-psychiatric discourse* that essentially operates within the twin concepts of *health* and *illness*. If it is answered negatively because a meaning, albeit a hidden one, is imputed to the symptoms, we enter the *psychoanalytic discourse* that is governed by the hermeneutic category of *meaning*.

Daseinsanalytic authors take different viewpoints on the question of 'illness or suffering'. In the 'Historical Part', I indicated that Medard Boss developed a 'daseins-appropriate pathology' that arises from a daseinsanalytic concept of health and is therefore completely indebted to the medical discourse. Ludwig Binswanger, on the other hand, criticises using the concept of illness in psychopathology on the grounds that it implies a biological value judgement (cf. Binswanger, in May et al., 1994, p. 237 *loc. cit.*). For his daseinsanalysis also contains some important hermeneutic elements, although it generally remains governed by the distinction between 'succeeding' and 'failing' or 'successful' and 'unsuccessful' dasein, in which the healthy–ill opposition returns in an inflated form.[62] The daseinsanalysis presented here, however, follows Freud's discovery and so is indebted like psychoanalysis to a hermeneutic discourse.

1.2 The introduction of hermeneutics into psychopathology

Because psychiatric psychopathology subordinates everything attributed to its domain to the concept of illness from the outset, the only epistemological methods it has available are description and causal explanation, but not the hermeneutic method of understanding and interpreting. This can come into play only if a hidden meaning

---

[62] Accordingly, Binswanger entitles a 1956 book about the schizophrenic symptoms of extravagance, eccentricity and affectedness 'Drei Formen missglückten Daseins' (Three forms of unsuccessful dasein) (1992–94, Vol. 1).

is accorded to the symptoms. Now here psychiatric psychopathology can certainly cite appearances: it is obvious to everyone that neurotic and even more so psychotic symptoms make no sense in the situation in which they occur and either constitute exaggerated or understated reactions or show no reference to the situation at all. As such *inappropriate* forms of experience and behaviour, they strike us as disturbing—as not 'normal'. Examples of this are when someone washes his hands umpteen times although once is enough, when someone is frightened to death by a mouse, although these animals are known to be harmless, or when someone blames himself for a small mistake for years as if this were a serious crime. Countless examples could be given. Even if the person affected attributes a meaning to his apparently nonsensical experience or behaviour, this is often a construct that elucidates nothing. Accordingly, the 'ill' diagnosis always steps into the breach in the psychic domain when the limits of understanding have been reached. The enigma of why people, generally with unimpaired intelligence, exhibit such inappropriate forms of experience and behaviour when in fact they could really know better is solved by declaring them to be ill. It should also be noted that the 'ill' diagnosis does not arise from observation itself but constitutes an *interpretation*: we interpret an experience or a behaviour as morbid when it can no longer be understood in terms of its immediate context.[63] What appears inappropriate is interpreted as a sign of a psychic *failure* or a psychic *incapacity*. Someone who exhibits inappropriate experience or behaviour over a long period is supposed to be unable to do otherwise because of a psychic deficiency, such as being incapable of appropriately judging a situation and reacting to it accordingly (distortion of reality), incapable of tackling some work effectively and completing it on time (disturbance of work), incapable of relating to other people appropriately (relational disorder) or incapable of being moderate in alcohol or tobacco consumption (addiction) and so on. As soon as we interpret someone's manifestly incomprehensible experience and behaviour as caused by illness and therefore as something deficient,

---

[63] It is different with physical symptoms because somatic processes cannot be considered meaningful from the outset and are invariably subject to scientific investigation as to whether they are diagnosed as pathological or healthy.

the only recourse is then to examine, describe and classify it. This can only be done by taking healthy (reality-adapted) experience and behaviour as a yardstick and ascertaining how far and how strongly the current symptoms negatively deviate from it. The psychiatric psychopathological description is therefore fundamentally normative. It is amplified by causal explanation, for we also of course want to know how this deficiency came about and exactly what caused it.

Now the psychoanalyst (as well as the daseinsanalyst) also knows that psychic symptoms appear nonsensical, but he disputes the conclusion that this is necessarily a pathologically generated incapacity. Instead he supposes that what manifestly appears nonsensical *can* also have a hidden meaning and that it is therefore important to explore what the symptoms might mean. He therefore introduces the *hermeneutic* method, which has no place in medical psychiatric discourse, into psychopathology. He wants to *understand* the patient's suffering, which is only possible by ceasing to think in the categories of 'healthy' and 'ill'. The fact that psychoanalysts and daseinsanalysts suspend these key medical categories in the aim of understanding does not mean that they are declaring the psychopathological symptoms to be healthy rather than ill, but that they are tackling them by framing the question in a different way. Neither do they dispute the importance and utility of the medical formulation of the problem, since it sheds light on how the mental suffering manifests and what restrictions and blind spots it generates in the conduct of everyday life. Psychoanalysts and daseinsanalysts also change their perspective from time to time in order to assess the manifest obstructive nature of some mental suffering. Nevertheless, it makes a fundamental difference to the therapeutic approach whether we work from the assumption that there is an illness to be treated or a hidden meaning to be discovered and understood (cf. Chapter 1, Part IV on this difference).

1.3 What is 'meaning'?

When Freud refers to the 'meaning' of neurotic symptoms, he is adopting the hermeneutic concept of meaning used in the humanities. Here 'meaning' represents what is comprehensible: what can be understood has meaning—what is meaningful can be understood.

This concept of meaning is not to be confused with the *practical-normative* concept of meaning that is used, for example, when we refer to 'meaningful' rather than 'meaningless' work, enquire into the 'meaning' of life or complain about the 'loss of meaning' in modern life. When Freud attributes a meaning to neurotic symptoms, he merely has in mind their *theoretical comprehensibility*, rather than an especially deep or true meaning hidden in them that—once it has become conscious—might even help to shape someone's future direction in life.

However, the hermeneutic concept of meaning is ambiguous. For Freud's hermeneutic method there are two applicable senses of meaning: 'We have comprised two things as the "sense" of a symptom: its "whence" and its "whither" or "what for" [p. 277]—that is, the impressions and experiences from which it arose and the intentions which it serves' (1917, p. 284). What Freud calls the 'whence' is the *historic meaning* and what he terms the 'whither' and 'what for' is the *intentional meaning as a purpose*. Critically, a symptom does not only have either a historical or an intentional meaning but a combination of the two, and therefore always has a double meaning. This is important to emphasise because mainstream psychoanalysis concentrates one-sidedly on the 'whence' and thus on the childhood history, whereas the daseinsanalytic exposition also considers the 'whither' and 'what for'. It seems in fact that Freud himself one-sidedly emphasises the 'whence' when he defines mental suffering as a 'suffering from reminiscences'. Yet the 'what for' element is incorporated in the phrase '*suffering from*': to suffer from something is not the same as to suffer something. We say, for example, that someone is still suffering from a personal failure, an injustice suffered or a painful loss when we want to convey that he has not got over what he suffered and he cannot reconcile himself with it, but instead rails and revolts against it. His suffering is therefore more than a suffering of something because it also already implies the reaction to what is being suffered, namely a *rebellion* against the fact that this suffering has befallen him. Someone who suffers from something refuses simply to accept what he has suffered and he suffers just as long as he rejects the unreasonable imposition of accepting what has been suffered and secretly demands a revision of the events.

The importance Freud accorded to the 'whither' and 'what for' of mental suffering is indicated by his description of neurosis as a *last technique of living*: 'As a last technique of living, which will at least bring him substitutive satisfactions, he is offered that of a flight into neurotic illness—a flight which he usually accomplishes when he is still young' (1930, p. 84). Understanding mental suffering as a technique represents the strongest alternative to the medical psychiatric conception of illness because it accords the suffering subject a more important, if not the most important, role in the existence and continuation of the mental suffering. This stands in total contradiction to the deterministic medical notion that the subject *suffers* the illness, is at its mercy and is incapacitated by it. If, however, the subject himself actively participates in the mental suffering, his manifest weakness is merely the price he has to pay for being able covertly to pursue his own interests better. For the subject's covert activity in neurotic suffering, Freud coined the concept of 'acting out', which will be presented and daseinsanalytically interpreted in the next chapter.

1.4 What is 'unconscious meaning'?

A hermeneutic procedure encounters certain problems in the domain of psychopathology because the meaning of the symptoms is hidden. The method of understanding developed in the humanities is not adapted to any concealment of this kind. It certainly fully reckons with 'alien' meaning that is difficult to decipher, but not with the hiddenness of meaning characteristic of psychopathological phenomena, which demonstrates *self-alienation* and *self-deception*.[64] For even if it seems easy to talk about an 'unconscious meaning', it is in fact still far from clear how this is to be understood. If it were merely about the 'whence', and if the neurotic symptoms had only a historical meaning, matters would be easier. We could then construe that former childhood wishes that the child repressed because they were dangerous

---

[64] The psychoanalyst Alfred Lorenzer (1970) first explicitly posed the question of how to construct a hermeneutic method of deciphering a meaning that has become unrecognisable through repression and worked out a proposal that he termed 'Tiefenhermeneutik' (depth hermeneutics).

and therefore also banished from memory live on as 'unconscious' wishes and return in the symptoms. Accordingly, the part of childhood history to which the suffering subject no longer had access because of that earlier repression would have lived on in the neurotic symptoms. This is how Freud often explained it and how it was adopted in the general conception of psychoanalysis. However, this theory of the causal impact of repression in symptom formation contradicts Freud's discovery that the meaning of the symptom is ambiguous and also contains a 'whither' and 'what for' that operates as the *unconscious intention* in the symptom. Who can nurture unconscious intentions but the suffering subject who has unconsciously been holding on to this intention since his childhood? That this intention can only be attributed to the patient himself is therefore beyond doubt—but how can an intention be unconsciously pursued? Is it not inherently contradictory even to refer to an 'unconscious intention'?

This reveals how much depends on whether as with Freud the unconscious is reified into something that is present in the mind or it is conceived existentially as the conduct of self-deception. Once it is reified, the notion of an unconscious intention becomes untenable because the subject, who alone can pursue intentions, is situated beyond the unconscious. Freud therefore has to sacrifice his own insight of an intentional meaning in neurotic symptoms and take refuge in the notion of their unconscious determination. The philosopher Jürgen Habermas provided the theoretical justification for this in his interpretation of Freud by explaining that every intention, once repressed and having therefore become unconscious, is transformed into a mere *cause*, for which by analogy with the causality of nature he coined the term 'the causality of fate' (1971, p. 256). This adopts Freud's concept of the repetition compulsion. The neurosis is now no longer maintained because the subject wants to achieve something with it, but only because a repetition *compulsion* is at work here. This returns the neurotic patient to being—as in the medical psychiatric perspective—merely someone who is passively *suffering* at the mercy of some dynamics of his own over which he has long ceased to have any influence. Accordingly, the meaning of the neurotic symptom is a mere relic of childhood—in fact, an 'infantile' meaning that the adult subject in the present, if he only had access to it, would long ago have left behind.

However, if the unconscious is understood existentially, there is no necessity for the unconscious intention to be transformed into a mere cause that operates behind the subject's back. Daseinsanalysis can therefore adhere to an unconscious intention, although it then has to deal with the question of what it means for someone to hide the nurtured intention from himself and what benefits are obtained by his self-deception about the meaning of his own action.

2

Suffering from our own being

Daseinsanalysis considers itself a branch of psychoanalysis. There are grounds for dispute concerning the basis for its claim to the 'label' *psychoanalytic*. Daseinsanalysis certainly regards the recognition of Freud's discovery of an unconscious meaning in mental suffering and the consequent hermeneutic procedure in both psychopathology and psychotherapy as the common denominator of all psychoanalytic schools. This means being guided by both the questions that Freud first formulated: the question as to an unconscious *'what from'* of mental suffering, on the one hand, and an *intention* at work in suffering on the other. The various schools are distinguished by the answers they give to these questions.

2.1 From what does the neurotic individual suffer?

The daseinsanalytic answer is: *the neurotic suffers from his own being.*[65]

This answer accords a special status to mental suffering. It cannot simply be classified with the many other possible forms of suffering, and does not resemble suffering from concrete deprivations, concrete

---

[65] In this chapter, the concept of neurosis is still understood in very broad terms and it represents the hermeneutic rather than the medical view of psychopathological symptomatology: what is neurotic is what certainly manifests as a nonsensical disorder but in fact has a hidden meaning. The distinction between neurosis, borderline states, psychosis and depression follows in Chapters 3–5, Part III, and approaches to a daseinsanalytic psychosomatics are presented in Chapter 1.1.

blows of fate or a concrete personal failure because this 'from what' is situated not on the 'ontical' level of concrete events and actions but on the 'ontological' level of someone's own being. From a daseinsanalytic perspective, mental suffering represents a particular mode of the human being's *relationship to his own being.*

The fact that someone *suffers* from his own being indicates that he is concerned by it to a special degree. Every form of suffering contains an element of openness; it is impossible to suffer from something unless you are also moved by it. To characterise this openness to our own being, I am adopting a phrase used by Medard Boss, who drew a parallel between the schizophrenic's delusional experience and a 'sensitivity to that ordinarily hidden from human perception' (cf. Boss, 1994, p. 234 *loc. cit.*). The word *sensitivity* has the advantage of expressing in positive terms that which makes the suffering person suffer: namely, hearing (and seeing) *more* than the average, including in relation to entirely concrete things in everyday life. Someone who is suffering mentally is orientated towards experiences that the 'healthy' person does not have, or at least not in the same way, because he is not at all concerned in everyday life by ontological matters.

His particular sensitivity makes the mentally suffering person a *reluctant philosopher*. He exists philosophically because he is preoccupied by the basic existential questions of human being; but he does this against his will, driven neither by curiosity nor even wonder at what is hidden behind the concrete matters of everyday life but because an additional philosophical knowledge imposes itself on him by which he is overtaxed. The person who is suffering mentally cannot use his sensitivity as a gift but he *suffers* it, is at its mercy and must therefore apply a particular technique—what Freud called the 'last technique of living'—in order to be able to live with it.

For an illustration of sensitivity, let us turn once more to Binswanger's case example of the girl with the 'heel phobia'.[66] The heel of the five-year-old girl's shoe came loose when she was undoing her skate and got stuck in the skate, which resulted in her first panicking and then fainting. Then until the age of 21 years when

---

[66] The 'heel phobia' was presented in Chapter I of the Historical Part to illustrate Binswanger's concept of the world-project.

she became Binswanger's patient, she suffered from phobic anxieties that arose whenever she noticed that a heel was not firmly attached to a shoe, someone reached for his heel or even just talked about it (her own heels had to be nailed in). From an external viewpoint, this incident on the ice is a mishap that might very well be upsetting at the time but is in fact so harmless that a child normally recovers quickly from his initial fright and either forgets the incident in time or merely remembers it as an amusing story. But the girl clearly had a different experience of this event—namely an ontological experience that intruded into her life as 'anxiety'. Undoubtedly those around her will have coaxed her, explaining that the damage was minor and could easily be rectified. Yet such explanations could have no effect, since they bore no relation to what the girl experienced. She could not be dissuaded from the anxiety because she felt that other people's explanations were superficial and therefore dismissed as mere imaginings something that for her had the status of an incontrovertible and therefore extremely frightening truth. In the conversation we might imagine about the incident on the ice, the girl and those around her therefore talked past each other: the girl lacked the words to express her ontological experience, while the others on their part had no interest whatever in paying any attention to this threatening additional knowledge.

The daseinsanalytic definition of mental suffering intersects with Freud's and is also more radical. Freud defined neurotic suffering as a *suffering from reminiscences*, directing the psychoanalytic psychotherapist to turn his attention to another *temporal dimension* (the past instead of the present); if, however, the neurotic suffers from his own being, then the question 'from what' does not merely exist in another temporal dimension but in another *dimension of being* and it no longer concerns ontical-concrete reality but ontological reality. However, this does not render the psychoanalytic focus on childhood superfluous. The heel phobia example clearly demonstrates that childhood experiences and experiences of being are not to be set against each other but that childhood experiences also need to be accorded an ontological dimension. Whereas for psychoanalysis childhood represents a period of successive developmental phases in which physical and psychic capacities develop and particular conflicts emerge, for daseinsanalysis it represents the period in which the relationship to our own being also develops and becomes differentiated. From a daseinsanalytic viewpoint, childhood emerges as the period of primary and basic experiences of being and therefore as an *eminently philosophical period*. From this perspective, the susceptibility of early childhood to neurotic lapses discovered by Freud consists in the fact that the still relatively unsocialised child of the early years has not yet had any opportunity to acquire the defence mechanisms that he will later generally have available if he participates in common sense (Heidegger's 'the "they"'). Admittedly, daseinsanalysis holds that there is a certain disposition to mental suffering at every stage of life. It is always possible that excessively severe psychic pressures will become the gateway to experiences of being that were previously successfully screened out and generate a neurotic reaction for the first time.

What truth of being the girl experienced in relation to the incident on the ice is a matter of supposition—this could only be confirmed or refuted in analytic conversation with the girl herself. It may initially be supposed that this incident unexpectedly assumed an ontological meaning because the child in no way reckoned on anything of this kind happening at all, since she believed that the heel was part of the shoe and was inextricably connected with it. This is important for once it is known that a heel can theoretically come loose from a shoe because it is only glued on to it, such an incident may certainly cause annoyance and anger but not trigger panic because what has happened is immediately comprehensible. Precisely because the girl has no notion that a heel can come loose from a shoe, it dawns on her emotionally when something inconceivable occurs that anything that appears to be an indissoluble unity can break into separate pieces. This insight is especially uncanny when it is related to our *own being as being-with*—namely to the fact that bonds with other people are also not indissoluble unities but likewise consist only of 'separate pieces stuck together' and therefore can break apart. The question remains as to why the five-year-old girl is sensitive to this particular fact of shared human existence and is so deeply distressed by it. This brings us on to Freud's theory of the Oedipus complex.

2.2 Is the Oedipus complex the nucleus of the neuroses?

The conception of the Oedipus complex as 'the nucleus of the neuroses' is one of Freud's fundamental suppositions (1917, p. 337), to which the daseinsanalyst trained in the Boss school will object that even the claim that all children experience the oedipal conflict is an unreliable generalisation. Yet what is more important here is the insight that the constitutive elements of the Oedipus complex (being in love with the mother, rivalry with the father, castration anxiety or penis envy) express a basic ontological problematic. So let us briefly summarise the experience that in Freud's view heralds the oedipal phase for both the boy and the girl. This concerns the discovery that the mother is a 'whole object'—in other words, a whole person—with her own interests and wishes that she also directs at other people, especially the father, and that the father and the mother share a relationship that excludes the child. This experience is in fact highly explosive in ontological terms, since it conveys to the child the insight that it does not simply belong to the mother and is not an aspect of her world, but is separate from her. The expulsion from the relationship between the father and mother is like a second birth—the birth of the child's self as an *existence* or, in traditional terms, as a *subject*. In fact the bond with the mother is never all-encompassing because from birth onwards the mother is only intermittently available; later, the mother begins to make her own demands on the child and enforce her will on him. However, it can then still remain unquestionable that the child and mother belong together, however imperfect this belonging may be even from the outset. The fundamental belonging proves to be an illusion only in the oedipal phase, which triggers anxiety (not fear!). The oedipal wish arises in response to this threat. In the oedipal wish to win back the mother for himself and exclude the father, the child seeks to deny the ontological fact of his singularity. But why is there anxiety (or in fact, fear) concerning the father? Why is there a fantasy that the father will forbid this wish under the threat of castration? The father actually puts any possible fulfilment of this wish in question not through his prohibition but through his sheer presence, by which he demonstrates to the child the unrealisability of the wish and simultaneously embodies the ontological demand to relinquish the mother and tread the path to becoming a subject.

Binswanger's example of the heel phobia also concerns the threatened belief in an indissoluble unity with the mother:

'Psychoanalysis proved clearly and convincingly that hidden behind the fear of loose or separating heels were birth phantasies ... Of the various disruptions of continuity which psychoanalysis revealed as being frightening to the girl, the one between mother and child was fundamental and most feared' (May et al., 1994, p. 203).

The girl flew into a panic when the heel unexpectedly came loose from her shoe because this destroyed an illusion to which she had previously clung—the illusion of living in indissoluble unity with her mother. The fact that the girl *suffers* from this insight and develops a heel phobia means that her sensitivity makes such a detachment appear unliveable to her. Whether a child resolves the oedipal problematic 'normally' or is made neurotic by it depends on his degree of sensitivity: if he can screen out the ontological meaning of the separation from the mother then, despite being afraid of his new awareness in life that he is a separate self from his mother, lamenting the loss and also feeling some anger at the affront, these negative feelings are compensated by joy and pride in his increased freedom and autonomy. When Freud states that the Oedipus complex is seldom worked through in an ideal way (Freud, 1917), this is reminiscent of Heidegger's statement that actual anxiety is rare and the human being initially and generally seeks to escape it.

2.3 The hidden intention in mental suffering

The question of what the neurotic is suffering *from* must be supplemented by the question of what he is suffering *for*. The supposition that the suffering person is pursuing a hidden intention with his suffering is initially unsettling because it contradicts not only the prevailing medical notion that symptoms are the expression of a pathologically determined incapacity to resist them, but also the personal experience of many patients who feel at the mercy of incomprehensible events. The question as to a hidden purpose to suffering becomes unavoidable, however, once it is conceded that mental suffering is due to a special sensitivity to truths of being that are normally screened out.

'Woe implores: Go!', according to Nietzsche's (1978) expression for the inherent wish in all suffering for a release from it someone who is ill wants to get well: someone who is hungry asks for food; someone who feels lonely wants company and so on. What then does the neurotic want? Does he also want to be well, that is to be freed of his manifest symptoms of suffering? Here we encounter the deepest paradox of mental suffering. For the answer can only be: yes and no. Yes, insofar as he feels constrained by his symptoms and therefore wants to be able to lead a normal life unburdened by them; no, on the other hand, insofar as he has been granted an ontological experience that he finds both incomprehensible and intolerable, against which he is rebelling with his symptoms. He wants to get away from this ontological experience and to be released from the suffering it causes him. Paradoxically, this is precisely why he has to cling to the neurotic suffering because it means overcoming this deeper suffering—the suffering from his own being. In stark terms, the neurotic suffers from his neurosis in order to be released from the suffering from his own being.

2.4 Mental suffering as an acted-out engagement with our own being

Suffering from our own being therefore includes the desire to overcome the reason for this suffering. In what does the 'last technique of living' (Freud) in order to fulfil this desire consist? This can be neither a technique of forgetting nor a technique of interpretation because both have already failed if someone is sensitive enough to be suffering mentally. Freud coined for this technique the term 'acting out', by which he meant a particular, specifically neurotic form of behaviour that is opposed to remembering: the neurotic acts out experiences from his childhood instead of remembering them (cf. Freud, 1914, p. 151ff.). This already explains that acting out is directed at something fundamentally impossible, since past events can only be remembered but never reversed by actions. But this is exactly what is at stake for the neurotic: he is not only anxious to distort his memories in order to have a more tolerable memory of his childhood, but he pursues the unacknowledged intention of acting in a way that can influence something that in reality is only accessible to memory. In the cold light of day, this is an entirely illusory undertaking that is only possible as self-deception. Acting out instead of remembering comprises the illusion of having power of action in a domain where there is nothing left on which to act.

Daseinsanalytically, acting out is related not only to someone's childhood history but also to his own being, which is why it can be termed a 'technique of being' that seeks to change the conditions of his being so he can live with them *without anxiety* even though they are perceived in all their bleak reality. Such a desire for change is hubristic and bound to fail. However, because it arises not from carelessness but from the distress of a special sensitivity, he cannot admit the failure but has to cling to the illusion of a possible success— at the cost of the suffering persisting indefinitely.

Acting out as a Sisyphean task

If we want to convey that a task is meaningless because it can bring no apparent benefit, we refer to a 'Sisyphean task'. This is a reference to the myth of Sisyphus from Homer's *Odyssey* (Book 11), in which Odysseus gives the following account of his encounter with Sisyphus in the underworld:

'Sisyphus too I saw tormented, heaving with both his hands at a massy stone. Straining with hands and feet together, he kept pushing the stone uphill, but just as he should have cleared the top with it, some force would thrust the thing back again; the unregarding boulder would tumble afresh down to the level and the straining man renew the struggle while sweat poured down from his limbs and the dust rose from round his head' (1980, p. 141).

It is tempting to regard Sisyphus as the mythical archetype of the neurotic, but we should also consider that while according to the ancient myth Sisyphus was condemned by the gods to this meaningless activity, we suppose that the neurotic drives his own suffering because he does not even recognise it as a Sisyphean task. Yet this difference becomes less stark if we also consider that the mythical

Sisyphus was condemned because he had twice rebelled against the will of the gods. In both cases there is a certain arrogance, except that the mythical Sisyphus has to suffer for his arrogance towards the gods, whereas the neurotic Sisyphus has to suffer because his special sensitivity has induced him to rebel against the human condition in an arrogant way. This difference aside, the stone-rolling Sisyphus can certainly be interpreted in ontological terms. The enormous boulder that is too heavy for a human being to push then symbolises the burden of being, as it feels to the sensitive person; the willingness to push the block up the mountain by expending enormous effort represents the intensity of the desire to conduct the struggle with his own being at any cost; the never-fading hope of being able to throw the stone over the hilltop this time or the next represents the illusion of possible release from the burden of being, in order then as a Sisyphus liberated from the stone and healed to be able to climb down the mountain and begin a normal—'mentally healthy'—life.

2.5 Confusions

Freud gives a brief example that can be used to illustrate the characteristics of neurotic acting out and how it functions: 'the patient does not remember that he used to be defiant and critical towards his parents' authority; instead, he behaves in that way to the doctor' (1914, p. 150). This concerns a typical transference situation: the patient misreads the analyst by seeing his father in him. The father of that time is thus resurrected for him in the analyst, and he himself feels again as if he were still the young boy from that time who should obey the paternal authority and rebels against it. Purely descriptively, acting out is based on a confusion between past and present. The analysand feels transported back to the past, but in such a way that he takes it to be the present. He therefore inexorably behaves towards the analyst in the way that he did at that time towards his father and indeed from the conviction that the analyst's authoritarian behaviour is providing sufficient grounds for his defiance.

But if acting out is truly an action, then it cannot be said that a confusion between past and present *is occurring* here but rather that this confusion is *intended* and itself constitutes an action that seeks to exert an influence on the past. For this confusion is what gives rise to a new opportunity to compete with his father and bring the battle with him to a more acceptable conclusion. The analysand therefore acts out instead of remembering in order to reverse his defeat at that time. If we consider Freud's example from a daseinsanalytic perspective, it is not only a hurtful past event that is being denied but also irrevocable conditions of being. This already applies to the confusion between past and present that endeavours to suspend the irreversibility of time; it also applies to the rebellion against the father that was part of the oedipal struggle and with which he struggled against the unreasonable demand to renounce the unity with his mother. I have already interpreted the oedipal love-wish as an ontological desire for release from the necessity of existing as a separate self from others.

The fact that neurotic acting out has an ontological intention is also demonstrated by Binswanger's heel phobia example. The girl's acting out (panic-stricken anxiety about loose heels, nailing in her own heels etc.) initially seems only to have the ontical meaning of preventing any possible repetition of the ice-skating incident. However, it conceals the ontological meaning of denying the immutable facticity of a person's selfhood. This (illusory) triumph over immutable conditions of being appears possible through the conversion of the 'anxiety' into a mere 'fear'—here the fear of the (unlikely) possibility that a heel could once again come apart from the shoe, which is now combated with concrete methods. Even this conversion of anxiety into fear does not happen simply, but pursues a covert intention. It enables the girl to pretend that 'all will be well again' when all that her phobic-compulsive precautions can achieve is to prevent a heel ever coming loose from the shoe again.[67]

Neurotic acting out is therefore rooted in basic confusions surrounding both dimensions of time as well as both dimensions of

---

[67] It is of course not obligatory to react to the ice-skating incident with a heel phobia; it constitutes only one possible response. We might also, for example, imagine a hysterical paralysis of the leg as a reaction that made it unnecessary to walk in shoes any more and furthermore that would express more directly (more appellatively) a reliance on staying with the mother, indeed constitute a legitimate claim to do so. Why someone 'chooses' one answer rather than another to an over-taxing experience of being (which does not of course involve a conscious choice) can only ever be answered in part and depends among other things on constitutional temperament, as well as early acquired reactive patterns.

being. Yet how is it even possible for someone equipped with the capacity to perceive and consider the basic difference between past and present on the one hand, and ontical and ontological reality on the other, to deceive himself so that subjectively he can genuinely confuse them? On closer inspection, it becomes clear that the conditions for such a confusion are more conducive than they first appear. First, the past blends seamlessly into the present, and the present is always full of relics of the past for the mentally healthy person as well; similarly, all ontical-concrete events and forms of behaviour have their pre-ontological inclusions. Second, for the person suffering from traumatic childhood experiences the past obtrudes of its own accord and facilitates a confusion between the two dimensions of time; similarly, the over-sensitivity to the ontological renders the normal meaning of an event irrelevant in comparison with its ontological dimension so that only its ontological meaning still counts.

In conclusion, we are faced with the provocative question: is the thesis that the neurotic acts out instead of remembering truly convincing? Is it not contradicted by all the clinical pictures of psychopathological states characterised by inhibitions, blocks, obstructions and incapacities? Can we refer to acting out when someone is unable to leave the house any more from sheer anxiety or when someone is incapable of reaching a decision? This becomes even more doubtful when physiological processes are affected, as for example with sexual impotence or insomnia. However, the answer is a cautious 'yes' that can cite the practice of self-deception. Is it not an important method of self-deception to camouflage our own intentions? And does this not best succeed when someone can pretend to himself that something is happening to him to which he is powerlessly subjected? Seen in this light, merely passive suffering has the advantage over active behaviour of being able to pursue the striving *in an innocent guise*. A man's sexual impotence can therefore have the meaning of avoiding the sexual intercourse that is genuinely making him nauseous, but which he feels he owes to his partner, without having to feel guilty towards her. Insomnia can conceal the intention of staying awake whether because on account of a presumed ideal of achievement someone can allow himself no rest or inactivity, or whether because he is afraid of his own vulnerability in sleep, which is felt to be even more intolerable than sleeplessness. Pretending to himself that everything is only happening to him is important precisely when a special sensitivity to it means that active behaviour makes him feel guilty and therefore has to be avoided.[68]

---

[68] The question as to whether the specifically depressive experience of a loss of *will* also has a covert intention is addressed in Chapter 5, Part III.

3

'Structural disorders'

To talk daseinsanalytically of mental suffering rather than mental illness connects with Freud's discovery of a hidden meaning in *neurotic* symptoms. This raises the question of whether the programme of a daseinsanalytic hermeneutics of mental suffering can be applied to the entire field of psychopathology or only to the limited domain of the classical neuroses. What is the position with what used to be termed 'pre-oedipal' disorders that are now mainly discussed under the heading of 'severe personality disorders'? Can they also be *understood* as forms of mental suffering, or is the hermeneutic method inappropriate here because this suffering results from psychic deficiencies that can be traced back to an excessively early disturbance in the young child's psychic development?

If we turn to consider the more recent psychoanalytic literature on severe personality disorders, the question appears not only justified but already to have been answered in the negative: 'early' disorders are almost unanimously attributed no longer to a conflict but to *a defect in the psychic structure*.[69] Closer examination of why Freud's hermeneutic view of mental suffering is restricted to the oedipal neuroses reveals that this involves an unjustified change to the question being posed:

---

[69] The most important proponent of a psychoanalytic structural theory of early disorders is Otto Kernberg (1975). There is some important counter-argument to Kernberg's replacement of Freud's hermeneutic conflict-defence model with a simple deficiency model in Mentzos 1992, p. 29ff.

instead of asking what people with pre-oedipal disorders are actually suffering from and what hidden intention is hidden in the symptoms, the question becomes what disturbance in their psychic structure lies at the root of these symptoms. The hermeneutic viewpoint is thereby needlessly abandoned in favour of a development-psychological, structural viewpoint. Instead of interpreting the symptoms, it is now a matter of explaining from what they result, namely from the fact that in these cases the norm-appropriate formation of their psychic structure was hindered by an early disorder. The terms 'early disorder' and 'structural disorder' have therefore now become interchangeable. The oedipal neuroses do not fall into this category because here the disorder did not occur until a point in time when the development of the psychic structure was almost already completed.

So far, so good. Only it certainly does not follow from this that early disorders can only be considered from a structural viewpoint. What might have influenced psychoanalysis to change the framing of the question in this way? Presumably it is the fact that in 'early disordered' patients the therapeutic application of the standard psychoanalytic technique usually fails. But this too may be structurally or hermeneutically based: it may either indicate a structurally determined *incapacity* to make use of a psychoanalytic psychotherapy because the requisite ego strength is lacking, or alternatively a *refusal* by these people to make recourse to a therapeutic situation that appears to them too dangerous. Therefore a daseinsanalytic-hermeneutic interpretation of early *qua* structural disorders will next be presented. This will refrain from making distinctions within this spectrum in favour of ascertaining the common features, which is why the concepts borderline disorder and personality disorder will also be used interchangeably.

3.1 Deficient anxiety-tolerance?

Something that is considered characteristic of the symptoms of structural disorders is their *unspecific* nature.[70] Unlike neurotic experience and behaviour, they are generally not restricted to specific domains, selected people and particular situations. The reactions of

---

[70] For the characteristics considered typical of structurally disordered experience and behaviour, I am referring to Kernberg, 1975, pp. 8–47 *loc. cit.*

the borderline personality are therefore much more difficult for people around them to judge than the neurotic's reactions, since it is impossible to predict what may become the object of a threat to them or the cause of an affront. They therefore appear as people who can get into a rage for no apparent reason and commit impulsive actions. Their capacity to perceive their own fault at all and feel it as guilt seems to be only poorly developed, and it is rare to observe any empathic shared experience with others or any genuine involvement with other things and other people. There is a strong temptation in regard to this symptom to conclude that there is a severe defect in the psychic structure that is either acquired early or even innate. Kernberg therefore traces the emergence of borderline symptomatology not only to an early developmental disorder but also to a constitutionally determined 'lack of anxiety tolerance' (1975, p. 22 loc. cit.). This term does not mean that these people are especially prone to intense experiences of anxiety but that their pre-existing somatopsychic constitution prevents them from tolerating an ordinary level of anxiety.

For a daseinsanalytic interpretation of this deficient anxiety tolerance, it is essential to remember Heidegger's distinction between *fear* and *anxiety* (cf. Chapter 4, Part II) and thus to distinguish between tolerance of fear and tolerance of anxiety. Tolerance of anxiety as a being-experience would mean recognising the uncanniness of our own existence in an attunement that incorporates the willingness to take on anxiety and tolerate it. This occurs, as we have explained and justified, only seldom and momentarily. Intolerance of anxiety is therefore not something pathological, whereas intolerance of fear is. What manifests as deficient tolerance of fear is connected from a daseinsanalytic perspective with a (possibly even innate) greater *sensitivity* and *perspicacity* towards the uncanniness of our own being-in-the-world. Concrete dangers always also refer to the fundamental endangered quality of our life, which means that behind every fear that arises lurks the nameless anxiety about our own being that every person initially and generally seeks to escape. The borderline patient therefore cannot tolerate fear because it always indicates to him something more than a mere concrete-ontical threat because of his special sensitivity.

It may rightly be objected that the nameless ontological anxiety is also intense in neurotic anxieties. The difference is that neurotic anxieties are generally restricted to a particular aspect of our existence and accordingly only manifest in a particular domain of everyday life. Thus one person may suffer mainly from hypochondriac anxieties because he is especially sensitive to his physical frailty, while another may live in constant fear of being deceived by his partner because he is acutely sensitive to the fact that his partner as an other remains fundamentally free to enter into other relationships as well. The deficient tolerance of fear in structural disorders is unspecific, however, and can be directed at one thing at one moment and then at another according to the situation. This gives expression to a more comprehensive sensitivity, which, instead of specific conditions of being, concerns the threatened quality of existence itself in a general way.

3.2 The subject's suffering from his weakness

The borderline patient is especially sensitive to the fundamental paradox of human existence, namely to being a subject that has to lead his life but still cannot lead it according to his own will but is subject to conditions that he has neither chosen nor ever accepted. He therefore suffers from the weakness of his subjecthood. The person who suffers from this irresoluble paradox of human subjectivity has two possible means of escape, neither of which in fact attains the goal: either to escape back to before being a subject or to escape beyond it. In the first scenario, this is the attempt to be a mere object that can be entirely determined by the other and others; in the second, it is to acquire the status of a quasi-divine subject that has itself and others freely at its disposal. The borderline personality chooses the second path. He wants to exist as a strong and free subject that obeys only his own will. Therefore everything all too quickly becomes a battle for him; he lives in the expectation of possible obstructions to be combated and he experiences any obstacles put in his way as a severe affront to his self-image. The struggle is always seen in terms of maintaining his self-image as a strong subject. This does not exclude the possibility of the borderline personality occasionally retreating into the role of the passive object and his experience and behaviour temporarily assuming depressive and even masochistic traits. Yet this rarely involves a genuine alternation between the two possibilities of escape because the retreat to object status usually serves the purpose of manipulating others by a skilful presentation of his own weakness and innocence.

The borderline patient's combative attitude seems to indicate an '*excessive development of aggression*' (Kernberg, 1975, p. 27 *loc. cit*). Because this is as unspecific as the deficient anxiety tolerance, Kernberg supposes a constitutional factor here too in the form of an excessively strong aggressive drive. From a daseinsanalytic standpoint, it seems more obvious to relate the constant combativeness to the deficient anxiety tolerance. Someone who is continually confronted with the weakness of his own subjecthood because of an excessive sensitivity also knows that he is constantly defencelessly exposed and thus vulnerable to attack. He reacts to this with an underlying basic mood of *hatred and mistrust*, which can often erupt in impulsive angry outbursts that are apparently unmotivated. Yet not only hatred and mistrust but also the initially mentioned negative symptoms of *deficient guilt feelings, lacking empathy and deficient involvement* become comprehensible in the light of the borderline suffering from the weakness of his own subjecthood. What appears as a mere defect from the structural perspective emerges as a *refusal*. The borderline patient is not willing to admit a mistake because any acknowledgement of guilt means an admission of his own weakness, whereas disregard for moral rules demonstrates strength. The same applies to the deficient capacity for empathy. The borderline refuses to deal empathetically with his fellow human being because he knows this means giving up control over the other person and thus weakening his own position. For the same reason he also avoids a deeper involvement in something or with a fellow human being, since this would mean a betrayal of his independence.

The much bemoaned *exploitative quality* of his relationships with other human beings can also be understood as a reaction to the threat that is posed for the sensitive borderline patient by every other human being. The other may not appear as a subject with his own rights and claims but must be treated as a mere object for satisfying his own needs because this is the only way that his position as a strong subject can be maintained. Also useful here is the borderline patient's proverbial *black-and-white thinking*, which manifests itself mainly in judging everything and everyone as either good or bad, and indeed as good or bad *for him*, namely for his illusory demand to be confirmed as a strong and free subject. Therefore the attribution is continually subject to change: what was still good one day may already be considered bad the next. The abrupt shift from idealisation into radical denigration of another person reflects the fragility of his sense of his own strength and freedom. The borderline personality is reliant on the people around him 'playing along with him'. Anyone who breaks free from his domain of power or is not impressed from the outset by his claim to power thereby demonstrates a self-given authority that triggers anxiety and must therefore be diminished by denigration.

3.3 The meaning of splitting

The most important diagnostic characteristic of structural disorders is considered to be the predominance of *splitting* as a defence mechanism rather than *repression* (Kernberg, 1975, p. 25ff *loc. cit.*). According to psychoanalytic structural theory, splitting involves the development-psychologically earlier and correspondingly more primitive defence mechanism that belongs to a lower structural level of ego development. The child only has repression at his disposal, however, after he enters the oedipal phase, which is why Kernberg considers it to be a 'higher-level' mode of defence. Does this justify the conclusion, however, that the adult borderline patient also makes recourse to splitting as a defence mechanism because he still lacks the capacity to repress instead of only to split? This is clearly not so. If we move from the structural-theoretical to the hermeneutic perspective, there is no longer any question of whether a particular defence mechanism is already available or not, but which defence mechanism is more apposite and is therefore preferred. Working from the premise that the borderline patient is suffering from the irresoluble weakness of his subjecthood and is attempting to overcome it, we must suppose that splitting as a defence mechanism represents a far more appropriate 'technique' than repression for (apparently) attaining this goal. Can this be demonstrated for the phenomenon of splitting?

I will first give a simple example to explain how splitting and repression operate: we are all familiar with the situation in which someone has a sexual or aggressive wish that presses for a satisfaction that is contradicted by his moral ideas. What is to be done? The real resolution of the conflict would consist in renouncing the wish, and yet because no one likes renouncing things, two escape routes from the conflict situation present themselves: repression or splitting. Both eliminate one of the two parties in the conflict from consciousness and enable inner peace to be restored. But this is exactly where the similarity between the two escape attempts ends. For repression concerns wishes, whereas splitting allows both the wish and the prohibitive moral ideas to be banished from consciousness. Repression always works in the service of good conscience, whereas splitting does not. Yet at least as significant and serious is the fact that a wish that was once repressed generally remains repressed for a long time, whereas a split-off wish can return to consciousness at any time. Thus the person who chooses the mechanism of repression persistently identifies with one of the warring parties, namely morality, whereas the choice of the splitting mechanism leaves someone free to identify at one moment with the wish and at the next with the morality. Splitting therefore has the advantage of being able to live both, if not at the same time, then at least one after the other. It makes it possible to live out the unacceptable wish without any moral consideration in order at a later point in time to be a complete 'moralizer' with no knowledge of any inappropriate wishes of his own.

What is termed 'splitting' thus consists in shifting and accordingly non-binding identifications with one or other of the warring parties. This shift in identification results in the experience, judgements and behaviour of splitting personalities lacking any constancy or continuity: these people possess no coherent self-image that persists over time and they present themselves to others without any stable identity.[71] If we assess the defence mechanism of splitting only by

---

[71] The fact that the psychoanalytic concept of the unconscious as an autonomous realm of the psyche is only compatible with the defence mechanism of repression only receives passing mention. The discovery that most psychopathological phenomena are determined not by repression but by splitting actually turns the reified concept of the unconscious on its head. This is because splitting does not produce a stable unconscious but only ever a momentary unconsciousness that can be rescinded at any time with no internal resistance. This presumably constitutes the main reason for abandoning the hermeneutic viewpoint in favour of the structural viewpoint in relation to early disorders. Maintaining the hermeneutic framing of the problem would in fact require a radical revision of the psychoanalytic concept of the unconscious that would lead to its de-reification (cf. here Chapter 6, Part II).

its consequences for a successful conduct of everyday life, then it comes out badly because it leads to much more serious distortions of reality than repression and furthermore causes confusion, rejection and even moral outrage in fellow human beings. Another picture emerges, however, if we relate the result of splitting to the borderline patient's urgent desire to be released from the weakness of his own subjecthood. In this regard, splitting is in fact extremely successful, since it enables the subject to have the constant feeling of being at one with himself. Unlike repression, splitting creates the appearance of a *seamless unity with himself* and thereby conveys a feeling of strength, albeit an illusory one. This is because it banishes all inner conflicts and even seems to overcome the fundamental difference between 'I' and 'me' that defines the human being's relationship to himself. In succinct terms, splitting thus allows an *escape from the relationship to the self altogether*. As Kernberg emphasises, this achieves a victory—albeit completely unstable—over anxiety: 'as long as these contradictory ego states can be kept separate from each other, anxiety is prevented' (1975, p. 26 *loc. cit.*). The strength of the splitting subject therefore consists in no longer being in any relationship with himself at all and thus also being able to avoid doubts and scruples about himself and his actions. The borderline patient therefore always asserts his own wishes as legitimate needs and insists on their satisfaction as if he had a rightful claim to them. If obstacles are nevertheless placed in the way of their satisfaction, he feels unfairly treated, deeply affronted and at the same time morally outraged.

This confirms that splitting is the technique for providing release from the suffering from the weakness of subjecthood. It is a defining characteristic of every defence mechanism, thus also splitting, that it operates 'unconsciously'. If we do not want to make do with this magic psychoanalytic formula, then we must ask how someone can make sudden shifts in identification without noticing it himself. This enigma can only be resolved if we consider the special relationship that the splitting personality has with time.

3.4 The denial of temporality

Repression and splitting have the opposite relationship to time. Because repression persistently shuts out threatening wishes from consciousness, it leads to a more or less constant self-image. This always also incorporates a particular image of the individual's own history, however incomplete and distorted this image may be by the repression of important memories. It also contains an image of the person he would like to be in future. Someone who represses therefore lives with memories and expectations that keep open both temporal dimensions of past and future. Splitting, however, gives rise to a pure present that is severed from the past and the future because every shift in identification denies what had just been established as an undoubted reality. Splitting thus achieves a life in the '*here and now*' and inadvertently turns out to allow an ideal of living that is today highly prized, which promises release from the burdens and restrictions that are always imposed on the present by both the past and the future.

People who live only in the present are relieved of the burden of dealing with their own beginning and their future end as the two poles of temporal existence that are also reminiscent of the weakness of subjecthood: the weakness of not having brought ourselves into life, as well as that of having no control over our own death (see Chapter 2, Part II). At the same time, living purely in the present gives some freedom for an uninhibited satisfaction of needs because neither memories of what went before nor expectations of what is to come impinge in any inhibiting way. Someone who remembers must and wants to be able to integrate what he is doing now as a meaningful part of his life history. Similarly, the orientation towards the future restricts the possibilities in the present because someone who knows that he will have to bear the consequences of whatever he does today recoils from many temptations that people who live only in the present can accede to in a carefree way. The happiness obtained by denying temporality is hollow, though, because purely present-based experiences, however intense they may be at that moment, leave hardly any traces. Borderline personalities therefore suffer from an inner emptiness that cannot be filled by the mere concatenation of activities but only ever provides momentary anaesthesia, which often leads to an addictive quest for experiences.

3.5 Is splitting a contemporary defence mechanism?

Could it be that the defence form of splitting is especially appropriate for our times today? This would shed a new light on the rise in 'structural disorders' and also relativise the hierarchical psychoanalytic view that the predominance of this defence mechanism indicates an early disorder in development-psychological terms that is therefore especially severe. The notion that defence mechanisms are also temporally conditioned does not contradict an ontological interpretation but amplifies it. For although mental suffering occurs in all times and places because it involves the suffering to which the human being is disposed as a human being, the techniques of relief from being that are applied to it are by necessity culturally conditioned. If we compare repression and splitting from this viewpoint, repression fits Freud's time, which required the individual to form a stable and constant ego-identity (in accordance with the strict moral norms). This is different today: confronted with globalisation, the arbitrariness of world views and mass unemployment, what is required of the individual is no longer a stable ego identity but 'flexibility' (Sennett, 2006), which consists in being able to identify with arbitrary demands without succumbing to inner conflicts. This new form of adaptability to ever-changing conditions that have become incalculable can only be achieved by splitting. Furthermore, the capitalism of today that is largely exempt from moral considerations demands not only flexible but 'strong'—i.e. fearless, guiltless and shameless—subjects, who pursue their own interests uninhibitedly; contemporary economic conditions demand and thus foster the mental characteristics that belong to the symptomatology of borderline personalities.

4

The psychotic wish

Medard Boss describes schizophrenic illness as both the most human and the most inhuman of all forms of suffering because it affects the 'basic ontological nature of human existence' (1994, p. 223 *loc. cit.*). He explains his understanding of schizophrenia with the example of a man hallucinating the sun, and he acknowledges his capacity for 'superhuman penetrability' in relation to 'that ordinarily hidden' (p. 234). He describes this special transparency by referring to a 'schizophrenic sensitivity' (p. 234). We have adopted the concept of sensitivity and extended it to apply not only to the schizophrenic but to everyone who is mentally suffering. This makes the question as to the particular characteristics of schizophrenic sensitivity even more urgent.

Sartre gives a description of the madman that can be interpreted as methodological guidance for an existential construction of psychotic suffering. He writes: 'Even a madman in his own way realizes the human condition' (*BN*, p. 396n.). If this is correct, psychotic suffering has a purely ontological meaning that can only be deciphered if we relate its thinking and behaviour to the human condition. It is different with neurotic suffering, although daseinsanalytically this is also to be understood as a suffering from our own being. There the current life circumstances and the childhood history are also indispensable reference-points for daseinsanalytic understanding because neurotic acting out is related to both. In the case of psychotic suffering, however, placing too much emphasis on the current situation and / or the individual past can be misleading because psychotic suffering constitutes a direct and immediate rebellion against the basic ontological situation of human existence.

What this means will be elucidated with the example of two wishes expressed by a young woman. Both wishes are directed at the past, and seek to perpetuate the childhood state, which is why at first sight they appear to be typically neurotic wishes, but in fact they have a purely ontological meaning. They are the wish for an adoptive mother and the wish to return to the parental home.

4.1 The wish for an adoptive mother

When she was 18 years old, Barbara, who was then still living at home with her parents, fell increasingly into a vague mood of anxiety. The external situation was that she was approaching the end of her schooldays. But instead of developing some ideas and wishes concerning a professional training, she increasingly expressed the wish for an adoptive mother. This wish was accompanied by desperate outbursts against her biological mother, whom she denied was her 'actual' mother. What could she have meant by this, when she was casting no doubt on the fact that her real mother had given birth to her? In other words, what was she seeking in an adoptive mother?

What is immediately striking is that the young woman is not highly selective: the first woman she chooses is someone in the neighbourhood and she besieges her front door. Rejecting explanations prove futile and she continues to direct her thoughts and endeavours at this for a considerable period of time. She later directs the same wish at her grandmother who is already living in an old people's home and, following her death, at a great-aunt. Another striking thing is the point in time at which this wish emerges. At the age of 18 years, people become legally responsible. The possibility of an adoption then disappears because in principle only children can be adopted. Yet such logical arguments do not impress Barbara. The only possible reason for this is that this wish follows a different logic. Let us proceed daseinsanalytically and hermeneutically and ask what *being-related desire* is concealed in this unrealistic wish that emerges only as she approaches the threshold of adult life.

We begin to approach the covert meaning of this wish if we consider what it is denying: namely the fact that the period of childhood is over. But what is the reason for this denial? Barbara was a special child from birth. As a newborn child, she appeared neither completely awake nor ever to fall into a deep sleep. Her passive and phlegmatic manner seemed to suggest that she had not fully arrived in the world and also was not really interested in taking the step into the world. Even as a young child, she gave little impression of a desire for anything new. Her playing remained stereotypic and an imaginary world hardly developed, which is why 'autistic traits' were diagnosed at a very early stage. Nevertheless, or precisely for this reason, she later happily went to school; she liked being in a clearly defined context, learnt eagerly with guidance, took pleasure in her achievements and with strong encouragement and understanding teachers she even obtained some good results from time to time. But she never made any genuine contact with her schoolfellows. When she turned 18, the (extended) elementary school period came to an end and the previously obedient child unexpectedly opposed every effort by her parents and the school to help her seek out a professional path and instead insisted on the wish for an adoptive mother.

Against this background, the denial that childhood has come to an end can be understood as a response to her realising that she was different from others of her age. As long as she was a child, she still hardly perceived her different nature and so did not suffer from it either. Now, however, it became increasingly clear to her that she could not keep up with children of her own age, and even that their interests and activities were largely incomprehensible to her. This insight was intolerable and meant that she found leaving childhood behind not only painful but inconceivable. Her wish for an adoptive mother was therefore the wish to be a child again and to remain one and this wish was a response to the extremely frightening and mortifying insight that she was not like everyone else and so 'not normal'. But why did the wish to remain a child assume the form of the wish to be adopted? This question leads on to the difference between the neurotic and the psychotic wish to 'return to childhood'.

The neurotic wish to be a child again or to be able to live as a child should first be distinguished from the widespread longing for lost childhood that is expressed in countless myths, stories and folk songs, as well as in modern novels and films. This longing only assumes the form of a neurotic wish when the impossibility of its fulfilment is denied and instead covert ways of achieving it are sought. Then begins the Sisyphean task that consists in acting ('acting out') in a domain where only memory remains. Yet the wish for an adoptive mother does not belong in this category because, unlike neurotic wishes, it is not 'acted out' but openly expressed. Underlying this wish is obviously the mad notion that another woman's willingness to accept and take her in as a child would suffice to enable her also truly to remain a child. She now wants to find this woman and her interest and participation in the concrete reality of other people is restricted in practical terms to realising this intention. She cannot understand why the women to whom she presents this wish do not accept it, and it also remains a mystery to her why no one else understands this wish either and no one is willing to support her in her intention.

The neurotic wish also seeks something impossible and is mainly directed at childhood. However, if there were degrees of impossibility we would have to say that the psychotic wish seeks something even more impossible than the neurotic wish. Barbara's wish to remain a child is not identical to the neurotic wish to turn the past back into the present.[72] The neurotic wants to get his own past back in order either to be the happy child of that time again or to reverse unhappy experiences of that time. But nevertheless, whatever his motives for bringing the past into the present, this is always about parts of his individual childhood history that he cannot and does not want to relinquish. For Barbara, however—contrary to first appearances—it is neither about remaining the happy child of that time nor being able to have another better mother to compensate for what she believes she has missed with her own. In that case, Barbara would be able like many other young people to seek out a motherly friend or a fatherly friend so that she could still satisfy her infantile needs. Barbara does

---

[72] Neurotic acting out was discussed in detail in Chapter 2, Part III: Suffering from our own being.

not simply want more than that, but something different, namely to create a world for herself in which she *is not subject to the law of time*, and so will also never grow older—thus a world of a timeless present, in which there is no difference either between past and present or between children and adults.

If Barbara's wish for an adoptive mother were neurotic, it would necessarily be ambivalent, and would be competing with the opposite wish to be free and independent and not to be interfered with by anyone. It would also contain some idea of how long it is necessary to have an adoptive mother: for example, as long as she is still afraid of her own future or as long as she does not yet have confidence in being an adult and so on. Barbara's wish is neither ambivalent nor time-limited because it is not about a temporary pause in time but the creation of a world in which the law of time has been abolished and in which also therefore nothing can change. To live her whole life as a child means for Barbara to exist *timelessly* and therefore also without a history. If time stands still, we are relieved of the questions that are part of becoming an adult: who am I? What possibilities are open to me? What do I want? Then there is no difference either between then and now nor any difference between generations. Then we are not measured by any kind of yardstick, and there are no demands that we can fail to meet.

4.2 The wish to return to the parental home

In place of the wish for an adoptive mother, the wish to live with her parents again appeared years later when Barbara was living in a home for mentally handicapped people. This wish was also given absolute priority, preventing her from summoning an interest in any other kind of activity, even care of her own body. She most liked to spend the whole day thinking about the possible fulfilment of her wish. Her conversations with other people also revolved almost exclusively around this wish and were directed only at gaining their understanding and support. When instead she received well-meant explanations as to why it was not sensible still to live with her parents at her age, she lost any interest in continuing the conversation or she expressed the wish again as if she had not even heard the other person's viewpoint.

The wish to return home also dominated the visits to her parents that by agreement took place every alternate weekend. To demonstrate her intention to return permanently, every Friday evening she would pack up all her possessions into a trunk, rucksack and bag in order to leave no evidence in the home that she might be returning on the Sunday evening. Once again, this did not involve any demonstrative 'doing as if'—instead she spared no effort to achieve it properly this time. Once she had arrived at her parents' house, she unpacked all her things to take her dirty washing into the laundry room and put the rest away in the cupboard. Then she would go into the kitchen to help with the cooking—all in the intention of behaving as if she had returned home for ever after a short absence. As soon as her parents pointed out that she was only there as a visitor, she fell into a downcast mood. Even suggestions of things they could do together had no more attraction from this moment. She often responded to these suggestions by saying that they were only an attempt to divert her from her wish.

No doubt ever arose about the legitimacy of her wish and she therefore found it inconceivable that it could fail to be fulfilled. According to her logic, there was no reason why she should not live with her parents. Do children not belong to their parents? Do all children not have a legitimate claim to live with their parents? Why was she being refused something to which all children were entitled, and instead forced to live in a strange place that she did not like? Furthermore, her (child's) bedroom was standing empty and thus only waiting for her to move back in. Her wish to return was uncompromising and left open the possibility neither of any partial fulfilment nor any substitute solution. It would therefore have meant nothing to her if she could come for longer and more frequent visits, as a visit remained a visit and did nothing to alter the situation of having to live in a home, which she found unacceptable. In this context, being welcome only to visit invariably meant an exclusion that was both painful and incomprehensible. Barbara could continue to insist on her wish being fulfilled because she equated two meanings of 'being a child', namely 'still a child by age' and being 'her parents' child throughout her life', and she would pretend not to hear when someone tried to explain to her that although she certainly was and remained her parents' child, she was no longer a child in age terms.

It is obvious that the wish to live at home again has the same purpose as the previous wish for an adoptive mother, namely to live in a world in which there is no difference between being a child and being an adult. At first sight this wish appears—unlike the wish to be adopted at the age of 18 years—not to be 'mad', since it is indeed entirely possible and in certain social or economic circumstances it can even be imperative to live as an adult daughter with parents until they die or move into an old people's home. What is 'mad' is the object of this wish—whereas the analogous neurotic wish would mean prolonging childhood, and further postponing growing up, Barbara's wish is directed at not having to go out into the world at all, but being able to remain inside a protective shell for ever. What is also 'mad' is the idea that the desire to be 'at home' in the ontological sense can be achieved by continuing to live in the parental home. This wish does not stem from concrete memories of that time and does not seek to repeat the individual's childhood but to achieve a prenatal state, and indeed permanently. Whereas the neurotic remains bound to his own childhood because he either suffers from the fact that events took one particular course rather than another better one, or instead suffers from becoming an adult and does not want to relinquish the advantages of being a child, Barbara remains bound to being a child because it was the time in which she lived in a dreamlike, timeless and therefore also oblivious way. She thus wants to return to this period of timelessness and oblivion. Her misfortune is being subject to time at all. Unlike the neurotic, she does not deceive herself in any way about the meaning of her wish. When asked by a carer at the home what was making her suffer so much, she replied: 'They're forcing me to grow older'.

A state of being in which there is no ageing can be achieved only in dreams. The strong similarity between the psychotic's world and the dream world has already been pointed out by Freud (1924, p. 151). Barbara also retreats into an *idios kosmos* (Binswanger in which, as in dreams, the rules that govern the waking world have no validity. The illusory conviction that the being-related sense that she is 'not at home' could be escaped by returning to live in the parental home is reminiscent of the dream from Boss's dream book to which we have twice referred (cf. Historical Part, Chapter 2.4, and Methodological

Part, Part II, Chapter 7.3). Just as the dreamer awakes from the dream to discover that a war is raging outside the house that threatens his life as well, so Barbara is awoken to the unfortunate truth about herself in adolescence. The solution that she wants to enforce in waking life resembles the solution in the dream in almost every detail: just as the dreamer simply shuts the window again and goes to his mother to lie down in her bed, so she wants to return to her parents. She too believes in the omnipotence of wishes: why should what the dreamer manages to achieve in the dream, namely silencing the noise of warfare and regaining peace as soon as he gets back into his mother's bed not also be achievable in waking life?

A person's relationship to his own time is certainly not the only aspect that distinguishes neurosis, borderline states and psychosis. But it illustrates how the refusal to be subject to immutable conditions of being gradually becomes more extreme: the neurotic merely denies the unbridgeable gulf between past and present and obtains the illusion of being able to manipulate his own past and therefore also indirectly his own future; the borderline patient, however, denies the three-dimensionality of time, reduces it to a mere succession of unconnected presents and obtains the illusion of a freedom in the here-and-now that is neither restricted by the past nor carries any obligations for the future. His rejection of the imposition of temporal existence exists on the boundary between neurosis and psychosis, in which this imposition is rejected altogether in favour of an insistence on a life that is beyond time and individual temporality.

5

The special status of depression

The following considerations work from the premise that depression represents a special form of mental suffering. It is more clearly distinct from all the other forms that can be assumed by 'suffering from our own being'. It therefore receives separate discussion here. If the endeavour to demonstrate its special status and interpret it daseinsanalytically succeeds, the unique nature of other forms of mental suffering can also be more clearly understood.

5.1 The incapacitation of the subject: illness or suffering?

Someone who is depressive retains only a weak sense of himself and no longer feels equal to even the most ordinary demands, judges himself entirely negatively and languishes in passivity. The loss of the ability to want or do anything in depression is entirely different in nature from, for instance, a hysterical weakness and fainting, since in the latter the covert intention to convey a specific self-image remains perceptible, whereas the purely depressive prostration does not produce this impression. The depressive cannot present any kind of self-representation; he can only show himself as he is and as he feels.

When it operates in this way, however, the experience of subjective incapacitation that is central to depression does not constitute any kind of 'symptom' because the latter is defined both psychoanalytically and daseinsanalytically by a hidden meaning to an action and a covert purpose. As exemplified in the Sisyphus myth,[73] the depressive can no longer be understood as the Sisyphus who pushes his stone back up the mountain for the umpteenth time and unswervingly pursues the impossible goal of throwing it over the hilltop. The depressive is at best a Sisyphus, not remotely as he is portrayed in the myth, but a Sisyphus who does not continue but instead lies down by the roadside. But there may also be various reasons for abandoning the Sisyphean task in this way. We can imagine a rebellious Sisyphus who refuses to continue carrying out the task that he has recognised as absurd, in which case it would seem more obvious to run away from it rather than stay lying at the roadside. We can also, however, imagine a Sisyphus who merely feels too tired and decides to take a break in order to regain his strength. Neither version applies to the depressive. He lies at the roadside not because he no longer wants to do anything but because he no longer can and, despite his inactivity, he remains as feeble and tired as if he were still pushing the heaviest of stones up the steepest of mountains. His inactivity therefore has no recuperative effect, which is why lingering at the roadside becomes endless and absurd—not a rest, but a reluctant capitulation to his own weakness.

All psychopathological phenomena have so far been subsumed under the concept of suffering rather than illness and also adequately justified this linguistic usage. Understood in this hermeneutic-analytic sense, it is not only the depressive who 'suffers' from something but also the manic person, however happy he may feel. However, if we refer to a specifically depressive suffering, we are looking at a visible subjective unhappiness: the depressive feels, as the word already shows, downcast, beaten down, hopeless, and in a general and constant way that nothing can make him happy or even divert him. He feels at the mercy of this state of suffering, with no prospect of being able to counteract it in any way. At best, he can still lament, in an expression of his despair.

Because the depressive can no longer find anything but fault with himself and he experiences his suffering state as something to which he is passively subjected, it seems obvious to infer that this is

---

[73] See Part II, Chapter 2.4 for a daseinsanalytic account of the Sisyphus myth.

a disease process that cannot be further interpreted. All the more so when the depressive appears to have lost all his previous capacities, and he feels incapacitated by alien events. The depressive's self-experience therefore accords with the psychiatric hypothesis of a process that is senseless and therefore pathological, which happens *to* the individual and deprives him of his capacity to lead his life. Freud opposed this with another hypothesis, namely that 'melancholia', like the 'normal affect of mourning', constitutes *a reaction to the loss of an important object* (1917, p. 243). This recognises melancholia as a mental suffering that is just as meaningful and therefore as explicable with hermeneutic methods as other psychopathological symptoms.

5.2 Loss in depression

Freud works from the observation that mourning and melancholia reveal the same characteristics, namely a deeply painful dejection, a cessation of interest in the outside world and a loss of the capacity to love, as well as an inhibition of all activity (1917, p. 244). Why then is this mourning considered to be a normal state while melancholia is considered a pathological one? Mourning is generally known as the reaction that sets in when someone has suffered a severe loss. Freud concludes from the similarity between their two appearances that the depressive must also have suffered a loss and that his symptoms are to be understood as a reaction to it. Adopting Freud's approach here, we also consider depression from the perspective of a loss that has been suffered. The question is only from what loss the depressive is suffering. Whereas in the case of a mourning reaction both the mourner and those around him know whom or what is being mourned, in the case of depression it is often impossible to detect any loss at all or at most a minor one, which is why the reaction invariably appears disproportionate. If we nonetheless suppose that depression concerns an experience of loss, then this must be an 'unconscious' loss. What is critical now is the level at which this unconscious loss occurs, whether at the ontical level of someone's relationship to concrete 'objects' (close relationships, a job, important goals) or the ontological level of the relationship to his own being. For psychoanalysis, this can only involve a concrete loss, because the ontological dimension has remained neglected in its theory. Hermeneutic daseinsanalysis, however, adds to this that it is not a concrete loss as such, whether conscious or unconscious, that causes depression but the loss of the *meaning of being* on which life has previously been based, in which this ontological loss may or may not be triggered by the loss of something concrete.

What the depressive has lost can be inferred from statements such as 'everything has become meaningless' or 'life in general is futile and worthless'. He has lost what previously—usually in an unconsidered way—gave his life a meaning and made life appear to be something worth getting involved in. But it remains open to question what it was that previously gave his life a meaning and thus a foothold. Has he lost the 'normal' confidence in meaning that is shared by everyone who participates in common sense? Has the depressive thus departed from the common sense that teaches us to leave unsettling questions about the meaning or meaninglessness of life to philosophers or theologians? But this loss is also borne by neurotics. Their suffering consists precisely in their inability to screen out the anxiety-inducing pre-ontological inclusions and therefore having to resort to pathological techniques for combating anxiety, shame and guilt. This is an important point because it implies that the loss of the unquestionably natural belief in meaning that supports normally functioning everyday life certainly can induce depression, but does not have to do so. When does the loss of the naïve equation of being with meaning lead to depression instead of a neurotic practice of coping with life?

Let us return to the mythical figure of Sisyphus, who—from an external viewpoint—is doing something completely futile that he nevertheless has no wish to abandon as long as he can cling to the belief that the impossible undertaking of transporting the stone over the hilltop will still have to succeed for him sometime. This Sisyphus has indeed abandoned the natural common-sense belief in meaning, but he still knows what is he is living for; he has a goal, even if this goal is actually unattainable. This Sisyphus would immediately let the stone roll back down and sit down despairingly at the roadside if he had to admit to himself that the goal was and remained unachievable for fundamental reasons. From then on, he would also lack the strength and impetus for the completely ordinary obligations of everyday life, because now everything would have lost its meaning. In psychiatric terms, he would from this moment have fallen into a state of depression.

If we compare the mythical Sisyphus who continues what he is doing with the image we have created of a Sisyphus lingering exhausted at the roadside, it is clear that the latter knows more than the figure from the ancient Greek myth. He knows *too much*—too much to be able to continue pursuing his life's undertaking because what used to give his life strength and impetus has been exposed as an *illusion*. This sheds light on the special nature of the loss that is bemoaned by the depressive. I will first compare it with the loss of the person in mourning: he has indeed lost an 'object' that is highly significant to him, so that to go on living without it must for a certain period seem empty and worthless. But he has not abandoned the conviction that life itself could have meaning and also still would have meaning without the loss suffered—hence the mourner's intense yearning for the lost object. It is precisely this conviction that the depressive has lost. This distinguishes him not only from the mourner but also from the neurotic.

The depressive provides negative confirmation of Nietzsche's (1977) view that as human beings we are reliant on illusions concerning the fundamental questions of life. It is different with concrete life situations because here it is generally better to acknowledge the truth, for example to know the severity of a physical disease from which we are suffering or what real prospects we have of finding a job and so on. The existentiell (rather than merely intellectual!) confrontation with the immutable basic conditions of our own being, however, is generally too anxiety-inducing and is therefore resisted. There are three available means of defence against this: simply screening out the ontological truth, shrouding it in a transcendental meaning or combating it with pathological techniques. If all three forms of defence fail, for most people depression is all that remains. The depressive not only exists outside the world of common sense and its (illusory) assurance that everything has some kind of positive meaning and reason, but he can also no longer deceive himself like Sisyphus that he can have an influence on the human condition by 'acting out'.

The depressive is *dis*illusioned in the deepest sense. He suffers from the most radical disillusionment that can affect us as human beings because it concerns the ontological desire for a flawless life that is the basis of both so-called mental health and all non-depressive psychopathological modes of living. The depressive knows that this desire is unrealisable. This greater knowledge means that depressive suffering is the most philosophical form of suffering. A person becomes depressive only when he has lost that twofold illusion that generally protects people from a stark confrontation with themselves—with their own being. This is the illusory belief that his own being is fundamentally immersed in meaning, even if this often remains hidden, and the alternative illusion that it is possible by acting out to improve what are recognised to be the flawed basic conditions of life. The statement attributed to Aristotle that precisely 'exceptional people' are afflicted by depression to a special degree cannot be understood in any other way.[74]

5.3 The 'affective' nature of depressive suffering

Depression is classified as one of the 'affective disorders' in psychiatry. This diagnostic classification is based on the observation that this is primarily a change in 'mood' (World Health Organization, 2000, p. 272). A daseinsanalytic interpretation of this general symptomatology is made possible by Heidegger's insight that moods or attunements are never merely accompanying phenomena to perceptions or experiences, but have their own world-disclosing and self-disclosing force.[75] Moods or attunements reveal 'how we are', which means how things stand around us (*BT*, p. 127). This also applies to depressive dejection. In dejection, the depressive discovers how things stand around him and the illusionless truth about his being imposes itself on him. The fact that he is dominated by this mood shows that he *can no longer in any way escape* this truth.

---

[74] 'Why is it that all men who are outstanding in philosophy, poetry or the arts are melancholic, and some to such an extent that they are infected by the diseases arising from black bile, as the story of Heracles among the heroes tells?' Aristotle (1936, *Problems*, Vol 2. Book XXX, p. 155).

[75] Cf. *BT*, §29, p. 126ff., and the explanations in Part I, Chapter 1 and Part II, Chapter 4.

We started from Freud's premise that the depressive is suffering from a loss just like the person in mourning, and have established the difference that the mourner has lost an extremely significant relational object, whereas the depressive has lost the illusion that previously sustained his life. It follows from this that Freud's parallel between mourning and melancholia is slightly inaccurate because it overlooks the difference between the intentional feeling of *mourning something* and the mood of *sadness*. Depressive dejection is obviously neither an (intentional) feeling nor a composite of various different feelings but a mood and it cannot therefore be compared with mourning but only with the mood of *sadness* to which it is also possible to succumb without having anything concrete to mourn but instead feels generally sad on account of 'nothing' and about 'nothing'.

The fact that these are both moods proves that they involve experiences of loss that relate to our own being. To talk about loss at all in this connection now proves to be questionable because after all it is only possible to lose what was once possessed, whereas the human condition is something immutable and predetermined that characterises our life from the very outset. The longed-for flawlessness and wholeness of our own existence is therefore something that the human being has *always already lost* on entering the world. Therefore neither sadness nor depressive dejection involve a real loss but the loss of the corresponding illusion. What is common to both moods is that they emerge when the truth about the finitude of our own being imposes itself and replaces the previous illusions. So what is the exact difference between the two moods?

For this we need to recall Heidegger's indication that even a mood-based insight always presupposes a *standpoint* towards what is recognised through the mood or attunement (cf. *BT*, p. 127). Sadness and depressive dejection are not distinguished by what they disclose but by the kind of position they adopt towards it. Someone who is in a sad mood is not only disillusioned but sadly concurs with the disillusionment. Such an acceptance is not to be conceived as a single act and accordingly the sadness is not to be conceived as a static condition. Mourning a severe loss is known to be a long-term process that comprises various phases, including depressive ones. The person in mourning vacillates about recognising what he would prefer to deny. This is strenuous and absorbs a great deal of energy, which is why Freud referred to the '*work* of mourning' (1917, p. 245, p. 255 *loc. cit.*). Such work would also be necessary when a person has lost an illusion about his own being. But this does not occur in depression. The depressive person does not mourn, but persists in a state of refusal. He refuses to recognise what is imposed on him as an inalterable fact of his existence. It is no coincidence that we refer to not being 'in tune' in depression.[76] The depressive is out of tune insofar as he persistently tunes out what imposes itself just as persistently on him. He rejects both the imposition of existing without legitimation by a higher agency and the imposition of fundamentally failing at every task and being able to incur guilt through his own decisions. These two combined, however, are what make the person a subject, which is why the depressive can also be said to capitulate at the task of being a subject.

5.4 The meaning of depressive symptoms

Incapacitation

If depression is understood as a refusal of the obligation to lead life as a subject, this also sheds light on the meaning of the key symptom of incapacitation. This does not manifest any psychic (or even organic) disease process but a *refusal to take on life under the conditions of subjecthood*. The depressive must therefore feel himself to be someone who no longer has any will for anything, nor any wishes, because even wishing, let alone the intentional preparation for something is a subjective act that presupposes a tacit consent to his own subjecthood. The depressive complaint of loss of will[77] obscures the fact that willing is not permissible because it would impose precisely what the depressive rejects as unreasonable: being a subject that takes on the risky venture of life without any illusions.[78] Precisely the depressive lack of will for anything makes it clear in

---

[76] '*Verstimmung*' means both a bad mood and being out of tune in the musical sense (*Translator's note*).

[77] This is the title of a book by Brigitte Woggon (2000).

[78] Cf. here Sartre: 'Actually it is not enough to will; it is necessary to will to will' (*BN*, p. 467).

negative terms that the will represents the strength that presupposes an affirmative relationship with oneself. This also explains why the depressive does not perceive his own activities as such and if his attention is drawn to this, also does not want to admit it, since he would then be abandoning the depressive standpoint that life under flawed conditions is neither liveable nor worth living.

Loss of appetite and 'morning blues'

These can be interpreted as a basic expression of the refusal to live under unreasonable conditions. How can someone be hungry when he has no appetite for life itself? How can he feel fit in the morning, when he is tired of life? Emmanuel Levinas has construed the phenomenon of fatigue as follows: 'to be weary is to be weary of being' (1978, p. 35). This contains the familiar expression that someone is 'tired of' doing something or other, which conveys that for whatever reason he is no longer prepared to engage with it any longer. This construction certainly does not apply to every form of fatigue but to fatigue as a depressive symptom. The depressive has grown tired of 'being' and is weary of life. His tiredness is an expression of the refusal of his own existence in the sense of 'I no longer can be, like or want myself any more under such obviously flawed conditions'.

Self-hatred

The rejection of oneself as a person who cannot escape from anxiety, guilt and shame manifests itself in self-hatred. Freud established the distinction between mourning and melancholia in terms of the self-criticism and self-abasement that are rarely apparent in the mourner but in the depressive can extend to 'a delusional expectation of punishment' (1917, p. 244). His interpretation that his hatred in reality applies to the lost object is only correct if this object is located on the ontological level. The depressive hates the human condition to which he knows he is subjected; he is ashamed of being a mere human being, even feels guilty for being incapable of creating flawless conditions like a god.

Altered experience of time

The relationship to our own time is indeed specifically altered in every form of mental suffering but it is only in depression that this change is perceived and *experienced as painful*, which is why it is considered a typically depressive symptom.[79] The depressive experiences himself as cut off from intersubjective time (cf. Fuchs, 2002). It passes him by and continues only for others, whereas his own time stands still. Has he 'fallen out' of shared time (Fuchs) or has he taken himself out of it? If we understand the depressive as the Sisyphean figure who capitulates at the impossible task and sits down despairingly on the roadside, then his relationship to time as well as his temporal experience acquires another meaning. The depressive rejects time because taking over his own life and subordinating himself to the law of time are one and the same thing. He would prefer to be a 'living anachronism' (Fuchs), who neither accepts that what was has been and is therefore irreversible, nor opens himself up to an uncertain future.

The end of depression

This is usually experienced as a 'surfacing'; the comprehensive feeling of dejection, meaninglessness and personal worthlessness subsides as if spontaneously, without any knowledge of how this is happening to one. This experience already reveals that this must essentially involve a *return to the old, familiar pattern of living* that is naïvely equated with mental health. Being cured of depression generally means someone has gone back to being the person he used to be for himself and for other people. Reproducing this state is the stated intention of medication-based treatment. Such treatment is the therapy of choice for many depressives, not only because they hope that it will effectively relieve the severe symptoms from which they are suffering

---

[79] The special nature of the depressive experience of time has been examined and described in detail primarily in phenomenological psychiatry, albeit from the viewpoint of the presence of a mere disorder. Another work to consider here is Ludwig Binswanger's *Melancholie und Manie* (melancholia and mania), published in 1960 (1992–1994. Vol. 2, pp. 351–428), which belongs to the last stage of his work that was philosophically indebted mainly to Edmund Husserl's theory of transcendental consciousness, which led him to attribute the mental illnesses of melancholia and mania to a 'failure in the construction of inner temporal consciousness'.

but also because they are only partly addressed as subjects by such a treatment. They only have to agree to take the medication; everything else happens automatically, and is neither their concern nor their responsibility. But because medication can only free someone from the acute symptoms of depressive suffering but not the previous illusion, the danger of relapse is great, so that in fact it is only possible to refer to depression-free intervals of a shorter or longer duration. Ideally, however, there is also another way out of depression, namely the egress into a *mourning process* in which the illusions are recognised as such and are left behind. Only then can depressive suffering strictly become an experience from which something has been learnt so that someone therefore returns to life more experienced.

5.5 Is depression a typically modern form of suffering?

If depression is understood as a suffering from subjecthood, the question arises as to whether western modernity as the *age of the subject* is more prone to depression than other ages and cultures. Certainly the pre-modern religious meanings on offer are still available, amplified by innerworldly-utopian world views, but none of these retains any force of authoritative validity. This means that the task of 'reassuring being' is today left largely to the individual. He has to select what seems good and right to him from the various meanings on offer. Such a choice rarely proves to be so convincing that it can effectively protect him from overtaxing experiences of being. This fact alone makes the modern human being more susceptible to depression.

Depression from out of the blue

It is due to the special situation of the modern subject that depressions often seem to come from out of the blue because before the outbreak of depression the depressive has led not only a psychopathologically inconspicuous life but often even a socially successful one. If our daseinsanalytic view of the link between depression and disillusionment is correct, the previous manifestly healthy state must also already have borne pathogenic traits; it is only that these did not impinge as a noticeable disorder. Succinctly expressed: normality itself must have had a pathological quality insofar as it not only served the concrete mastery of life but at the same time the acted-out and thus illusory triumph over immutable conditions of being. We can point to two typically modern lifestyles that can both be used for the purpose of alleviating being and are then especially prone to depressive outbreaks. Although they are opposite, these two lifestyles are interdependent: one has the characteristics of the free, self-employed entrepreneur, the other those of the dependent employee.

The entrepreneur lifestyle

Someone who chooses the entrepreneurial lifestyle fully embraces the modern task of asserting himself and fulfilling himself as a subject. He likes making decisions and seeks opportunities to play an active part in events and achieve things. Obstacles are just there to be overcome. But here also lies the very crux of the matter because insurmountable obstacles can unexpectedly get in the way, which belie the promise that he who dares also wins. As long as he is successful, the entrepreneurial type can cherish the illusion that he is free to shape the world according to his own will. Since he combines this with being a strong rather than merely a weak subject,[80] he can only love himself as long as he remains successful. Even minor setbacks can trigger intolerable shame or deeply injure his narcissism. Succumbing to depression here means refusing to live as a weak subject. The depressive who has lost the illusion of his own invulnerability and power therefore does not blame himself alone but also the world, finds fault not with himself, but with the others who have mistreated him.

The employee lifestyle

Someone who chooses this lifestyle relies above all on fulfilling duties in which he is orientated by other people's expectations (superiors, spouse, his own children and so on). By working hard, and showing perseverance and reliability, he is generally valued. The desire to place himself at the service of others and their projects and put his

---

[80] Cf. Part II. Chapter 3.2.

own needs last seems pre-modern. Unlike the entrepreneur type, the employee type does not want to change the world but to fit into a pre-existing world and fulfil the expectations that are thereby placed on him so that he cannot be criticised or blamed. For him, limitations have the opposite meaning and are experienced as supportive rather than restrictive. He also takes a different view of his fellow human beings, who instead of being rivals are parental figures by whom he is guided and by whom he would like to be recognised and loved. Therefore it is crucial for his self-worth that he can perform the tasks required and that these are also valued. For the employee type too, therefore, nothing must go wrong. It goes wrong, for example, when someone loses his job, grown-up children have left home or the boss who was a father figure retires; and certainly also when his own powers are no longer adequate, whether because he overtaxes himself from fear of incurring guilt or because the working world exploits such people's excessive readiness for tasks. Exhaustion invariably leads to an exhausted depression ('burn-out') when it has also brought the failure of someone's own project of being, which promised blamelessness.[81]

Whereas the entrepreneurial lifestyle mainly battles against the insurmountable *weakness* of subjecthood, the employee lifestyle rebels against the non-delegable *guiltiness* of existence. The modern subject carries the constant burden of having to earn his right to a place in the world (cf. Part II, Chapter 5.2). His fear of existing in a merely arbitrary way and without any grounds for justification can only be assuaged by the successful life itself; the entrepreneurial type feels legitimised as long as his activity is not obstructed, the employee type as long as he is needed and can feel useful.

---

[81] Hubertus Tellenbach (1980) has coined the concept of the *typus melancholicus* for this lifestyle and demonstrated in some brilliant phenomenological analyses of its characteristic behaviour patterns how they inevitably lead to depressive breakdown.

Daseinsanalysis
Daseinsanalysis
Daseinsanalysis
Daseinsanalysis
Daseinsanalysis
Daseinsanalysis

IV

Therapeutic conclusions

Daseinsanalysis
Daseinsanalysis
Daseinsanalysis
Daseinsanalysis
Daseinsanalysis
Daseinsanalysis

Introduction

As a psychotherapeutic movement, daseinsanalysis is unique in the central importance it accords to philosophy.[82] For it is only in daseinsanalysis that philosophy is used not only to lay the foundations for a particular concept of the human being or to explain the state of a particular theoretical corpus, but also serves directly as a guide for discovering and understanding the hidden meaning even of everyday experiences that the patients have in relation to themselves and the world. The strict boundary that otherwise pertains between philosophy and psychology is therefore removed in daseinsanalysis.

The fourth and final part of this book is devoted to the therapeutic conclusions that emerge from a philosophical definition of mental suffering. All the chapters are therefore subordinate to the guiding question as to the role that falls to philosophy in daseinsanalytic practice. The starting-point is the question of whether daseinsanalysis can in fact be understood as a therapy that is centred on shared philosophical contemplation; whether the basic philosophical themes and experiences from which the patient has previously suffered because of his special sensitivity, without being able to reflect on them as such, should form the content of the therapeutic conversations.

---

[82] This already applied to the daseinsanalyses of Ludwig Binswanger and Medard Boss, although they did not understand mental suffering as a suffering from our own being.

However, the first chapter makes clear that, despite its philosophical interpretation of mental suffering, daseinsanalysis cannot become a philosophical therapy in the narrower sense but remains, as Binswanger appositely stated, 'psychoanalysis informed by daseinsanalytic perspectives' (1955, Vol. 2, p. 293). The following chapters will explain why daseinsanalysis must remain indebted to the psychoanalytic procedure precisely because of its philosophical interpretation of mental suffering.

In the past two decades, a development has occurred in psychoanalysis itself that is celebrated by its proponents as a true paradigm shift and termed an 'intersubjective turn' that moves away from the focus on the patient's inner mental world to the relational events between patient and analyst, which are reinterpreted using key terms such as intersubjectivity, mutuality and relationality. Looking back from this shift in psychoanalysis to the critique of psychoanalysis put forward by Binswanger (1992–94, Vol. 1, pp. 159–189)[83] and Boss (1982 [1957]; 1994 [1971]) many decades earlier, it becomes obvious that both can be considered important intellectual precursors of this shift. Both already contain a radical critique of Freud's Cartesian and naturalistic approach, as well as his one-sided interpretation of the therapeutic relationship merely as a transference relationship. For both, the essence of the therapeutic relationship consists in enabling the patient to have new, positive relational experiences and Binswanger sees the therapist and patient as being 'on the same level' and describes the therapeutic relationship as an 'encounter' between two 'partners in Dasein' (1992–1994, Vol. 3, p. 261).[84]

In the light of its own history, what standpoint should daseinsanalysis adopt towards intersubjective psychoanalysis? Is it not the order of the day to be integrated into what is now a broad movement within psychoanalysis? This seems all the more self-evident because there is also a group within intersubjective psychoanalysis that argues for an interweaving of philosophical and psychoanalytic dimensions and draws philosophically on Heidegger's daseinsanalytics

---

[83] cf. Historical part, 1.4.

[84] Cf. The proximity of the daseinsanalyses of Binswanger and Boss to relational psychoanalysis has been rightly indicated by Daniel Burston and Roger Frie (2006, p. 180, 190).

in *Being and Time*, as well as Gadamer's philosophical hermeneutics (cf. Stolorow et al., 2002).

Yet how close daseinsanalysis and contemporary intersubjective psychoanalysis actually are does not depend on how far the latter has departed from Freud's theory of the drives and thereby approached phenomenological standpoints. The criterion is in fact whether its proposal to replace Freud's conversation technique with a dialogical form of conversation is still compatible with Freud's discovery of a hidden meaning in mental suffering. And the proximity between daseinsanalysis and Robert Stolorow's group, with a Heideggerian and Gadamerian orientation, depends on exactly what therapeutic conclusions are drawn from Heidegger's analysis of dasein and Gadamer's hermeneutics.

To anticipate how daseinsanalysis might be positioned in this intrapsychoanalytic dispute: it can only concur with the intersubjective critique of traditional psychoanalytic practice insofar as this relates to the 'standard technique' that has developed in the name of an orthodoxy in Freud's line of succession. It disagrees with the critique, however, when it is also applied to Freud's proposed form of analytic conversation based on the three fundamental rules of free association, abstinence and listening with free-floating attention.

The insight that our philosophical understanding of mental suffering does not in fact deviate from Freud's analytic understanding of therapy nor from his technical instructions but points back towards them is developed in the chapters that follow. The focus there is on Freud's three fundamental rules and the demonstration of why it is only by observing these rules that a hermeneutic access is gained to the hidden meaning in mental suffering and on why these rules create the unique therapeutic situation that also allows room for the ontological (philosophical) experiences that underlie mental suffering according to the daseinsanalytic conception. The suggestion that these three fundamental rules should be abandoned in favour of a Gadamerian conversational dialogics is discussed and rejected because this would mean abandoning any understanding of the unconscious philosophical meaning in mental suffering.

My case for the indispensability of Freud's rules does however require interpreting them more deeply in an existential and ontological way without changing their meaning. If that succeeds, the objection raised by proponents of intersubjective psychoanalysis that these rules are indebted to Freud's so-called one-person psychology and have therefore been superseded becomes invalid. This applies above all to the rule of abstinence, which is interpreted as a special (ontological) *relational offer* to the patient because it enables the patient to experience *through* the abstinent analyst—and specifically not *with* him—what primary experiences of relatedness form the basis of all actual relationships, whether these are close or distant, whether they are satisfying or painful.

What is new here is the reintroduction of *interpretation* into daseinsanalysis (Chapter 5). Interpretation could play no explicit role in Boss's daseinsanalytic psychotherapy because it was equated with subjectively arbitrary reinterpretation that does violence to phenomena instead of treating them with reverence. Yet this obscures the real reason for any 'for' or 'against' in this connection: as long as mental suffering is conceived in the medical-psychiatric sense as 'being ill' (Boss), there is nothing to interpret, whereas interpreting is unavoidable if a hidden meaning that is worth understanding is imputed to mental suffering. Daseinsanalysis can only take over from psychoanalysis the *principle of interpretation* rather than the actual practice of interpretation, which makes it necessary to work out the characteristics of a daseinsanalytic interpretation.

Finally, I take a step back and ask what form a specifically daseinsanalytic therapy offering would take. This question arises because even if it is understood as a 'psychoanalysis from daseinsanalytic perspectives' daseinsanalysis cannot simply take over what is offered by psychoanalytic therapy. It cannot do this because it makes a difference whether mental suffering is understood psychoanalytically as a 'suffering from reminiscences' or daseinsanalytically as a 'suffering from our own being'. Daseinsanalysis is therefore the only psychotherapeutic movement that must ask itself what kind of therapy can be offered if the patient is understood as a 'reluctant philosopher' who suffers because of his special sensitivity to the ontological negativity of human being that is not 'curable' by any human measures.

1

Is daseinsanalysis a philosophical therapy?

Freud evidently recognised that the psychotherapeutic procedure depends on the underlying conception of mental suffering that is held. The concept of psychopathology comes first; from it follows the therapeutic practice.

In Part 3, a specifically daseinsanalytic view of mental suffering was elaborated. While this is based on Freud's discovery that apparently meaningless symptoms have a hidden (unconscious) meaning, here meaning is philosophically rather than psychologically determined. The difference must be reflected in the therapeutic procedure in such a way that philosophy also has an important role to play in a daseinsanalytic therapy. This raises the question of *how* philosophy is to be integrated into the therapy. Is the daseinsanalytic conversation to have a philosophical content? Can and should daseinsanalysis be understood as a philosophical therapy that is connected with the ancient notion of philosophy as therapeutics that is also being revived today in philosophical circles?[85]

---

[85] The ancient idea of philosophy as therapeutics has been revived in German-speaking countries mainly by Wilhelm Schmid (2004), who refers to a 'philosophical praxis' that can be applied in therapy, consultation, mediation and adult education; cf. Staude (2010).

1.1 What form a daseinsanalytic philosophical conversation might take

The daseinsanalytic understanding of the mentally suffering person as a 'reluctant philosopher' seems to argue in favour of using the philosophical conversation therapeutically. And does the term 'sensitivity' not contain a reference to a special openness to what is 'normally' a philosophical matter? So it seems obvious to conclude that the therapeutic assistance must be philosophical in nature. Only in a philosophical conversation, or at least so it initially appears, can the philosophical issues from which the patient is suffering according to the daseinsanalytic view be thematised and addressed therapeutically.

This possibility can be considered by replacing Freud's 'analytic' listening with the 'philosophical' conversation. This would pursue the same goal as the analytic conversation, namely to transform the patient's 'acting out' into 'remembering'. A philosophical conversation would also entail acquiring self-knowledge—not so much knowledge about oneself as a particular person with an entire individual biography (as in psychoanalysis) as about oneself as a person subject to the basic conditions of human being who suffers from them because of his sensitivity. The memory to be gained in a philosophical conversation would therefore mainly be philosophical in nature; it would consist in transforming the individual's previously acted-out struggle with ontological misery into a verbal engagement with the human condition.

As soon as we try to imagine a philosophical conversation conducted for therapeutic purposes, it immediately becomes obvious how this differs from other forms of philosophical conversation and how it would have to be differentiated from a philosophical conversation conducted for purely educational purposes. The latter can be conducted without direct reference to the individual concerned, whereas the therapeutic conversation would have to be orientated towards what the patient is suffering from: the object would therefore always be an individual one despite being concerned with a universal problematic that is part of the human condition. Accordingly, the philosophical conversation with each patient would also be a different one and unrepeatable. And like the psychoanalytic conversation it would relate to the entirely personal concerns inherent in a person's own suffering. The daseinsanalyst would therefore have a different task from a philosophy teacher who is teaching pupils. He would be allowed to bring nothing to the patient's attention that he—being sensitive—does not himself already fundamentally know. Only his unconscious philosophical knowledge that is manifested in his symptoms should be jointly understood and thus brought to the level of conscious reflection.

What form might this take in a specific case? Let us consider Binswanger's example of the girl with the heel phobia that is already sufficiently familiar.[86] If our ontological interpretation is correct that when the girl's heel becomes detached from her shoe and remains stuck in the skate in the harmless incident on the ice, she is having a traumatic experience of being, the hidden meaning of the phobia that develops from this would have to constitute the main theme of the philosophical therapeutic conversation. As a first step, the daseinsanalytic therapist could explain to the girl that her panic-stricken anxiety about the incident on the ice is not based on any subjective misapprehension of reality but on an above-average degree of sensitivity. This reference to her special sensitivity could itself have a therapeutic effect. For patients always suffer not only from their symptoms but also from being considered by those around them as people who misapprehend reality, who are imagining something and therefore are suffering from delusions. If the phobic girl then were to gain the insight together with the daseinsanalytic therapist that her 'abnormal' phobia has a universally valid philosophical basis, it would be possible for her to see herself in a different way: no longer as someone afflicted with a flaw but as a person who because of a special sensitivity also has to bear a special burden that the average person can remove by escaping into forgetting.

This would lay the foundation for reviewing the actual theme: the fundamental fact of each person's irreversible separateness from all others, the most vivid example of which is birth as the physical separation from the mother. A daseinsanalytic conversation about the question of why experiences of separation belong to human

---

[86] Cf. the explanations in the Historical Part 1.2 and the Methodological Part III, Chapter 2.1.

life would differentiate between separations in the plural and the separation in the singular that makes every person an 'individual' (Kierkegaard). The discussion would move on to the fact that all actual separation experiences have a philosophical basis and that it makes a big difference whether because of a special sensitivity someone is involuntarily confronted with it or can turn a blind eye to it. The girl could at this point be introduced to the distinction between fear and anxiety in existential philosophy because that would help her to understand the meaning of her anxiety attacks on the ice as well as the ensuing phobia instead of condemning them as a mental disturbance. The daseinsanalytic therapist could even refer to Kierkegaard as the philosopher who discovered anxiety as a philosophical basic emotion that makes the human being experience his irremediable singularity and therefore also his freedom. This would enable the girl to understand why the incident on the ice, although harmless in itself, became a traumatic experience for her, to which the initial panic and its ensuing phobia constitute entirely appropriate reactions.

This recognition may have a further positive therapeutic effect. For the extent of subjective suffering always also depends on the shame-inducing knowledge of being perceived by other people as mentally ill, as well as on the concomitant guilt about being unable to fulfil expectations of 'normality'. It is likely that a philosophical interpretation of mental suffering can alter that substantially. For can these feelings of shame and guilt not be overcome if someone can see his own pathological symptom as the expression of an ontological truth? And can someone who has learnt to see his own irrational fear in the light of the anxiety that lies waiting in all human beings not cultivate greater tolerance towards the feeling of fear, removing the need for compulsive rituals that provide protection from it?

So far the prospects for a special characteristic of daseinsanalysis that relies on philosophy rather than psychology seem to be fairly good. For it is a convincing suggestion that such a conversation might give the patient the unique opportunity to gain the insight that his suffering has a philosophical meaning that has so far been hidden from him, enabling him to engage verbally, together with the philosopher-therapist, with the traumatic experiences of being.

Two doubts

Some doubts now emerge though. The first concerns the patient's motivation: can it be assumed that people who have undergone traumatic experiences of being because of their special sensitivity are necessarily therefore interested in having a philosophical conversation about them and also have the capability? This seems questionable because the philosophical knowledge that has a powerful impact in mental suffering derives not from philosophical contemplation but from an involuntary sensitivity. To infer from this a definite interest in philosophical considerations is at best premature. It would therefore be at most a highly exclusive clientele for whom daseinsanalysis in the form of philosophical conversations would form a special therapeutic offering.

Yet even if it were to emerge that all patients can be motivated towards a philosophical contemplation about the hidden meaning of their mental suffering, the other assumption would remain questionable—namely that the philosophical orientation of the conversation is the therapeutically appropriate and therefore also curative means of exploring the unconscious meaning of their suffering. Let us consider the *form* of such a conversation and the resulting *allocation of roles*. Despite the orientation to individual suffering, this kind of conversation belongs by its form to the type of explanatory or informative conversations that are centred around the transmission of knowledge or insight. The relationship between therapist and patient would thus closely resemble the relationship between *tutor and student*. It makes no difference if the therapist explains to the patient that he considers him an equal partner in conversation without whose contributions it would be impossible to gain the insights that are being sought.

However, as *Freud* already had to recognise, informative conversations remain therapeutically ineffective: 'There was a time when we thought this was a very simple matter: all that was necessary was for us to discover this unconscious material and communicate it to the patient. But we know already that this was a short-sighted error [p. 281]. *Our* knowledge about the unconscious material is not equivalent to *his* knowledge; if we communicate our knowledge to him, he does not receive it *instead of* his unconscious material but *beside* it; and that makes very little change in it' (Freud, 1916–17, p. 436). It is important to realise that the transmitted knowledge remains ineffective not because the patient does not take it up but because even if he makes it his own knowledge, it remains separate from the 'unconscious knowledge' at work in his symptoms.

This recourse to Freud is in turn open to the objection that the patient may not in fact have been presented with any accurate interpretations of his suffering in which he had been able to recognise himself, and that the patient may have agreed with him from sheer obedience. No conclusions can therefore be drawn from Freud's experience about the therapeutic ineffectiveness of philosophical conversations that deal with what the patient is really suffering from.

1.2 Why a philosophical conversation cannot have a healing effect

It may be surprising that Freud's insight concerning the therapeutic ineffectiveness of guidance is even more apposite in relation to the hidden ontological meaning of mental suffering. When philosophical conversations are conducted with a therapeutic purpose, the fundamental difference between *emotional experiences of being* and an *understanding of being* is in fact obscured. According to Heidegger, however, it is necessary to differentiate rigorously between them because whereas understanding always concerns the *meaning* of our own being, it is in moods that our own being is disclosed in its 'bare' and therefore senseless *facticity* that cannot be comprehended in words at all.[87] As soon as the therapist speaks in philosophical terms about the patient's experiences of being, he covers or enfolds them with words that give them some kind of meaning. Whatever form this attribution of meaning takes—whether completely basic or highly elaborate and whether plausible to the patient or not—it is in any case separated by a gulf from the mood-based experiences of our own being that form the basis of mental suffering and that by definition are not *experiences of meaning*.

---

[87] Cf. Methodological Part I, Chapter 2 on 'Existence as attuned understanding of our own being'.

The supposition that philosophical conversation could bring about a change in the patient's relationship to his own being can only be maintained by ignoring the gulf between a verbally constituted *understanding* of being and the non-verbal emotional *experience* of being. If mental suffering were due for instance to an extravagant or illusory interpretation of our own being, a philosophical conversation would presumably have a chance. But this is not how matters stand. It has therefore constantly been necessary to separate *mood-based experiences* of the bare *'that I am and have to be'* from hermeneutic experiences of the *what and how and why of our own being*. The former can have a traumatic effect precisely because they cannot be transposed into words.

This was illustrated by the example of the girl on the ice who was unexpectedly seized by anxiety as a completely mysterious experience and thrown off-course. This experience of anxiety is certainly philosophical in nature and is nevertheless separated by a gulf from philosophical thinking about anxiety. Approaching the traumatic experience on the ice through philosophical explanations of the nature of anxiety cannot therefore succeed. Either the two forms of 'knowledge' continue to coexist and the conversations remain, as already demonstrated by Freud, therapeutically ineffective or they have a negative effect, because the suffering patient feels misunderstood by the therapist's 'clever-clever' talk and therefore also abandoned by it.

With reference to the fundamental difference between understanding and mood-based disclosure of our own being, the idea that the philosophical quality of mental suffering therapeutically requires a philosophical conversation proves erroneous. Yet this does not invalidate the idea that philosophy plays a special role in daseinsanalytic psychotherapy. All that has become clear is that it would be short-sighted to believe that philosophical questions could form the *content* of therapeutically effective conversations. The next consideration will be the *form* of conversation: is there a form of therapeutic conversation that could be termed *philosophical?*

2

Daseinsanalytic therapy as 'psychoanalysis from daseinsanalytic perspectives'

The insight gained in the previous chapter that a daseinsanalytic therapeutic conversation with a patient cannot and may not have the quality of a philosophical conversation raises the question of what therapeutic role is left to philosophy. To proceed further here, a distinction must be made between the *content* and the *form* of conversation. This makes it clear that the negative assessment concerns only the kind of philosophical conversation in which two people explicitly discuss philosophical subjects. Such a form of conversation is inappropriate because it cannot access the philosophical dimension in which we are situating mental suffering. In fact, a philosophical conversation inevitably remains in the dimension of *verbal meaning*, whereas the mentally suffering person is enmeshed in philosophical experiences of his own human being that are emotional in nature and revolve around the 'anxiety' discovered by Kierkegaard.

This brings us to the question of whether there is a form of conversation in which the philosophical content of mental suffering can *be experienced*. This form of conversation must be able to open up an experiential space that can also accommodate ontological experiences that are intrinsically devoid of meaning. The question of whether this conversational form must be invented or whether it already exists is rhetorical because I am seeking to explain in this chapter why the psychoanalytic form of conversation inaugurated by Freud fulfils the necessary conditions.

It is far from obvious that daseinsanalysis should adopt the psychoanalytic form of conversation since in the last two decades this has been severely criticised within psychoanalysis in the name of a further post-classical development. Yet this criticism may be validly applied to the 'standard technique' that has been established in Freud's succession, but not to the form of conversation itself, which is based on three completely unique rules. It is therefore absolutely essential to distinguish between these to avoid prematurely dismissing the 'analytic' form of conversation in favour of a 'dialogical' form and throwing out the baby with the bath-water.

For the daseinsanalysis I am putting forward, there are two reasons for maintaining the psychoanalytic form of conversation: one being psychoanalytic and the other specifically daseinsanalytic. The psychoanalytic reason consists in Freud's discovery—also indispensable to daseinsanalysis—that mental suffering has an unconscious meaning. This discovery can in fact no longer be made therapeutically productive in a dialogical form of conversation, which is why in Chapter 5 I will defend Freud's form of conversation, including its associated principle of interpretation, against its critics within psychoanalysis as well. The daseinsanalytic reason, as already mentioned, is that only this form of conversation can accommodate the patient's philosophical experiences without misunderstanding them as ontical experiences from the outset.

Because daseinsanalytic practice adopts the psychoanalytic form of conversation, it can be defined with Binswanger's expression as 'psychoanalysis from daseinsanalytic perspectives'. In this chapter, the special nature of this form of conversation is elaborated. The emphasis here lies on what Ricoeur called the 'anti-technical' nature of psychoanalysis. Psychoanalysis is anti-technical because its conversational form is based on 'rules' that turn out on closer inspection to be 'anti-rules'. But anti-rules have a completely different function from technical rules, which is why a conversation that is subordinate to them can accommodate experiences that remain excluded from the outset in the usual kind of rule-bound professional conversation—including philosophical experiences. Chapters 3 to 5 will then deal with the 'daseinsanalytic perspectives' that arise from the ontological as opposed to the purely historico-genetic view of mental suffering and also still shed further light on Freud's rules.

2.1 What makes the psychoanalytic conversation a 'procedure *sui generis*'?

It is the three rules of *free association, listening with free-floating attention* and *abstinence* that make the psychoanalytic treatment what Freud called a 'procedure *sui generis*' (Freud, 1926b, p. 189). At first sight, these rules only have the function of allocating roles in the conversation. The rule of free association defines the patient's role; the rule of listening with free-floating attention defines the analyst's role. The rule of abstinence applies to both insofar as it defines the context of the therapeutic encounter, even if it means something different to each party and the analyst has sole responsibility for its observance.

A clear allocation of roles is a feature of every professionally conducted conversation. How is it then that Freud's three rules create a form of conversation that not only runs counter to the usual notion of professionalism but is entirely lacking in any model? This can only be due to the fact that these rules assign both to the patient and to the therapist a role that is entirely atypical. If we focus on the role assigned to the patient by the rule of free association, the conversation between close friends seems to substitute for a professional conversation, since the rule requires the patient to say everything that spontaneously occurs to him and to exclude nothing, even if he would prefer for various reasons not to say it (Freud, 1913b, p. 134). Yet conversation between friends is based, if it is as unconditionally open as the rule of free association requires it to be, on *reciprocity*. In a conversation between friends, both are in principle ready to talk openly about themselves and trust each other on a reciprocal basis. However, the rule of free association that Freud also characterises as the actual 'fundamental rule' of psychoanalysis applies only to the patient and therefore creates no reciprocity but a definite *asymmetry*. This is reinforced by the fact that the fundamental rule of free association corresponds on the analyst's side to the rule of listening with free-floating attention.

It is no wonder that this form of conversation, which can fulfil neither the criteria of a professional conversation nor those of a friendly dialogue, is felt to be a challenge. While it lacks the clear structure and intent of a professional conversation, it also lacks the necessary reciprocity for a personal conversation. What is interesting now is whether these apparent deficiencies do not conceal a positive element. I will not pursue this question comprehensively here but only in relation to the crucial question of how far the psychoanalytic form of conversation provides the space that is being sought here for ontological experiences.

The general protective function of rules

Recognising the special nature of Freud's rules requires comparing them with the rules that normally govern a professional conversation. Rules of this kind state how a conversation is to be expertly conducted. By knowing and having practised them, it becomes possible to apply a *conversational technique* that methodologically determines the course of the conversation.

Which conversational technique is applied depends on the specific objective that is being pursued with the conversation. An exploratory conversation in the context of an application in the job market is therefore differentiated from a conversation giving guidance on problems in the workplace or marital difficulties. What these conversations have in common, however, is that they are determined by technical rules that also structure the course they take. This has an extremely important advantage that is usually overlooked—it eliminates the dangers to which anyone who gets involved in a free, unregulated conversation is exposed.

In an unstructured conversation, no one can know in advance what the other person will say. Such a conversation can therefore not only take an unexpected turn at any time but an unwanted direction. It is no accident that many couples guard against talking personally about themselves and their relationship unless a third person is present who is regulating the conversation. Rules for conducting a conversation help each person to safeguard against the conversational partner's uncontrolled reactions. Rules therefore have a protective function. The more the course of a conversation is governed by rules, the more secure both can feel in the position assigned to them by the rules because each knows what is expected of him and what he can expect of the other or reject as unacceptable.

In the case of a psychotherapeutic conversation, the need for protection is especially great both for the patient and for the therapist. The patient is extremely exposed since he reports not only highly personal and intimate things but also experiences that have traumatised him, events that are extremely painful for him or his own perverse even criminal actions about which he feels ashamed or guilty. The medical obligation of confidentiality certainly serves to protect the patient in the outside world but it does not safeguard against the therapist abusing the knowledge with which he has been entrusted to make the patient dependent on him. Conversely, the patient's open talking also makes heavy demands on the psychotherapist: it is not he but the patient who determines what anxiety-inducing or abhorrent stories he must listen to, which may involve denigrating him either as a therapist or as a person.

Scientification as pseudo-protection

The current trend towards a strict regulation of psychotherapy in the name of scientificity must also be seen as a reaction to the perception of the specific dangers inherent in the therapeutic conversation. But why is the aspiration to be scientific so suitable for immunising against the anxieties that a psychotherapy generates both in the patient and in the therapist? I have demonstrated in detail elsewhere (2002, pp. 19–85) that the scientification of psychotherapy is synonymous with its *depersonalisation*, the first step of which consists in interpreting mental suffering as a mental *illness* on the model of somatic medicine. This makes it possible to transform an intimate conversation into a conversation that is related to the illness and therefore factual with an expert who assumes responsibility for its progress. Depersonalisation, expertise and guidance (control) are therefore inextricable and together constitute the therapeutic conversation conducted according to (pseudo-)scientific standards. In it the therapist regains a strong position and thus a feeling of security that usually has a reassuring effect on the patient as well. So it is not surprising that the regulation of psychotherapeutic procedure in the name of professionalism and scientificity is advancing inexorably.

In 1967 in his book *From Anxiety to Method in the Behavioral sciences,* George Devereux interpreted the methodological regulation of procedure in the behavioural sciences as a protection from the anxieties that can be triggered among scientists by data in this field of research. In comparison to a researcher, however, a therapist is much more strongly and also more directly confronted with 'sensory' data that affect him immediately. It is therefore immediately obvious that the scientification and professionalisation of psychotherapy also serve as a defence against anxiety.

2.2 Freud's fundamental rules and anxiety

The psychoanalytic rules as anti-rules

Paul Ricoeur's description of Freud's rules as anti-rules (1974) is no overstatement.[88] In fact, they neither determine the course of the conversation nor surrender the conduct of the conversation to either of the two participants. This means that they do not carry out any protective function—either protection from oneself or from the conversational partner. Instead they instruct the patient and analyst to adopt an openly unprotected position and stay in it. The three rules therefore require closer examination.

Listening with free-floating attention

The rule that applies to the analyst concerns listening. First I will move away from how he is to listen in order to emphasise that his role as an analyst primarily consists in listening as such. Now any conversation depends on listening because where there is only talking without listening, no conversation takes place. The psychiatrist who investigates the patient using a questionnaire must also listen to how the patient answers. But as long as he takes the investigator's role, all that he hears will be answers to the questions posed. The analyst, however, is challenged much more rigorously as a listener because he must listen to what the patient says without being asked and therefore

---

[88] Here Ricoeur describes the psychoanalytic technique as an 'anti-technique' or a 'non-technique' because rather than 'manipulate forces and energies directly', it seeks 'access to true discourse' and thus 'remains within the dimension of veracity and not that of mastery' (pp. 187–189).

spontaneously. If the analyst has the listener's role, he must therefore abandon the conduct of the conversation.

From the perspective of a professionally conducted conversation, this role attribution seems counterproductive because it precludes planning, setting objectives and an efficient realisation of the purpose of the conversation. In fact, the rule requires the analyst to abandon the power that is gained from directing a conversation. As a listener, however, the analyst is in a passive and to that extent unprotected position. The defencelessness is intensified by the instruction as to *how* the analyst has to listen. According to Freud, in listening the analyst should be 'not directing [his] notice to anything in particular', but treat everything that he gets to hear with the same 'evenly-suspended attention' (1912, p. 111ff). This is therefore another anti-rule that merely requires deliberately excluding nothing from attention. However, listening without selective criteria means remaining unconditionally open to everything that the patient says and therefore unprotected from it. But this is possible only for someone who is willing to suspend his previous knowledge and, instead of yielding to the wish to have understood already, to tolerate not yet being able to know and to keep going back to not knowing.

It would be a serious misunderstanding to equate this listening role with the role of an uninvolved observer. Whereas value-free observing requires an active distancing from what is to be observed and therefore itself constitutes a protective attitude, listening with free-floating attention is a receptive attitude that entails assimilating whatever is received to be heard. Here the analyst surrenders control not only over the course of the conversation but also over what the things he hears may trigger in him.

Free associating

This rule applies to the patient and instructs him first to say *everything* that comes straight to mind even if he would prefer not to mention it for certain reasons and, second, to say it exactly *as* it directly occurs to him (Freud, 1913b, p. 134). At first sight, what is impressive about this rule is that it gives the patient a licence to talk freely that he is never otherwise so unrestrictedly granted. Does this not accord with a hidden wish that we all cherish—namely, to be finally allowed to rattle on to our hearts' content regardless of any other considerations? Yet as Freud himself had to discover, communicating this rule to the patient does not in fact achieve any free flow or stream of thoughts and fantasies but instead a faltering that may include the statement that nothing is occurring to him.[89] Obviously following the rule is not a pleasure but an imposition, and for several reasons. First this is also an anti-rule that provides neither stability nor orientation. Second, it requires the speaker not to communicate what he has always wanted to unburden but everything that occurs to him, and therefore also what it is extremely unpleasant to say, whether from consideration for the analyst or because of how he would like to be perceived by the analyst. The patient therefore struggles against following this rule because the requirement to be unreservedly honest with himself makes him anxious. Third, the rule requires something that also, if the resistance to it is abandoned, proves to be impossible. For after all thoughts do not emerge in such a way that they can be told in a sequence but often arise almost simultaneously and are mixed up so that it is possible to do little but select which of the thoughts will be given preference and how long will be spent on it. However, instead of this choice remaining unconscious as in ordinary speech, the reasons for the selection now obtrude unavoidably and confront the analysand with all the previous unadmitted secret wishes and apprehensions that normally guide his speech. Fourth, this rule requires the patient not only to be as honest as possible with himself but to be so in the analyst's presence and thus to expose himself defencelessly before a person who is mostly unknown to him.

It becomes abundantly clear from these explanations that the 'fundamental rule of free association' and the 'rule of listening with free-floating attention' correspond to each other. The analyst's listening does not involve surrendering control of the conversation to the patient who now exercises it. Instead the two rules that belong together create a situation in which there is neither a leader nor a follower but in which both parties, albeit in different ways, are

---

[89] Cf. Freud's statement: 'The first thing we achieve by setting up this fundamental technical rule is that it becomes the target for the attacks of the resistance' (1916–17, p. 287).

undirected and so encounter each other unprotected. Certainly the
patient has the more active part to the extent that it is he who speaks
spontaneously. But this activity does not give him control over the
situation and the analyst but forces him to reveal himself by talking
to another person, without being able to know what this person is
listening out for and what he may be thinking about it.

The classical analytic setting in which the patient lies on the
couch and the analyst sits behind him may alienate many people today
and with reason as long as it is regarded as staging a power imbalance
between analyst and analysand. Yet even if the power aspect may in
fact enter in and must therefore always be considered critically, the
setting has a different meaning. Instead, this setting should enable both
patient and analyst each to follow his own rule. Lying on the couch
requires the patient to talk more autonomously because it prevents
him from doing what we all do involuntarily when we sit opposite
another person, namely adjust our own talking to the other's facial
expressions, gestures and gaze. Sitting behind the couch allows the
analyst to devote himself to listening more freely than when he is
feeling constantly watched by the patient.

Abstinence

When Freud explains that the psychoanalytic 'treatment' must 'be
carried out in abstinence' (1915b, p. 165), he makes it clear that not
only the patient but also the analyst has to behave abstinently. For
the analysand this means refraining from 'acting out' his wishes in
the sessions and merely speaking as freely as possible about them.
What it means for the analyst to be abstinent is the subject of intense
controversies in psychoanalysis. The orthodox standard technique took
literally Freud's instruction that the analyst has to remain 'opaque ... like
a mirror' (1912, p. 118) to the patient and inferred that the analyst has to
remain as impersonal as possible, even unapproachable, disclose nothing
about himself as an individual person, show no emotions, answer no
questions from the analysand, not even ask questions himself but limit
himself entirely to listening and interpreting what he is hearing.

This construed the rule of abstinence in positive terms,
instead of taking it as an anti-rule, and misunderstood its meaning.

The rule of abstinence assumes its true meaning only in the context of Freud's hermeneutic (instead of medical-psychiatric) view of mental suffering.[90] For if in suffering a hidden *wish* is always also at work that is pressing for satisfaction, it is part of the normal course of an analysis that the patient should direct this wish at the analyst and expect him to fulfil this wish. The analyst must remain 'abstinent' towards this wish, which means he should indeed answer it but never in the intention of fulfilling it by his own behaviour but only in order to discover and understand its hidden meaning with the patient. However, correctly understood, the analyst's attitude of abstinence contains something more: he may in fact in no event suggest to the patient that he would be essentially capable or even internally willing to fulfil his (neurotic and thus intrinsically unfulfillable) wish; he may not therefore act as this were a wish that is in principle fulfillable or even meaningful that he must refuse only on professional grounds.

It is critical for the rule of abstinence that this also entails an anti-rule, which is why what it requires of the analyst cannot be encapsulated in a code of conduct. Actually this rule only urges the analyst never to exchange his role as an analyst for the role of a (pseudo-)healer or even (pseudo-)saviour. For as soon as the analyst imagines himself to be capable in reality of fulfilling the wish that the patient directs at him, he is already succumbing to the temptation of seeing himself as a potential saviour instead of an analyst. Therefore no analyst can answer the question of what it means to be abstinent in any specific case except by reflecting on himself as honestly as possible. This mainly entails admitting his own narcissistic wish to surrender the analyst's self-denying role instead of acting this wish out unconsciously towards the patient. If the rule of abstinence is understood in this way, it may even be doubted whether this is actually an independent third rule at all or whether it is not already contained in the rule of listening with free-floating attention. For as long as the analyst sees his most important task as this special kind of listening and accepts this, he also behaves abstinently.

The reference to the rule of listening already shows that the patient tempts the analyst to diverge from his analytic attitude not

---

[90] The difference between a hermeneutic and a psychiatric approach to psychopathological phenomena is tackled in Part III, Chapter 1, 'Mental illness or mental suffering?'.

only with sexual wishes. At least as often, if not more often, it is about the *analytic form of conversation* that the patient would like to suspend in wishing the analyst to allow him to take over control in the conversation or to consent to the kind of symmetrical and reciprocally open conversation that is usual between friends. In the context of the 'intersubjective turn' in psychoanalysis, the wish above all for more reciprocity in the conversation and with it more personal openness from the analyst is understood as a legitimate wish and the rule of abstinence that causes the asymmetry in the conversation is accordingly criticised.

The patient's wish for greater reciprocity and symmetry in the analytic relationship appears justified because it seems to accord with the new empirical insight into the fundamentally intersubjective structure of human dasein. The rule of abstinence, however, is then interpreted as an expression and at the same time as a therapeutic implementation of the obsolete 'one-person psychology' to which orthodox psychoanalysis has too long been indebted. Accordingly, the analyst's attitude of abstinence is imputed with preventing the emergence of a beneficial therapeutic relationship. From this perspective, the word 'abstinent' assumes negative overtones of 'artificial' and 'inauthentic', even 'hard-hearted' and 'inhuman', which in turn leads to 'abstinence' and 'authenticity' having to emerge as mutually incompatible attitudes.[91]

Nevertheless, daseinsanalysis does not want to abandon the rule of abstinence, although it insists on differentiating between abstinence as an anti-rule or negative principle and its reinterpretation as a positive requirement to observe neutrality and opacity as strictly as possible. This difference was already indicated by the German psychoanalyst Johannes Cremerius (1984). If the rule of abstinence is understood as a requirement for the analyst to be aware of and reflect on the constant temptation to escape from the analytic attitude, it cannot be pitted against an authentic or personally adapted relationship with the patient, because then it does not instruct the analyst how to behave in every specific instance or what to avoid in each particular situation.

---

[91] I go into these arguments in more detail in Chapters 4 and 5.

I think it is therefore impossible to overemphasise that the orthodox psychoanalytic standard technique that has rightly come under fire since the intersubjective turn in psychoanalysis was based on a *reinterpretation of the three anti-rules as positive rules*, which specifically directed how an analysis had to proceed by the rules of the profession. This also conferred on the psychoanalytic form of conversation—contrary to its original meaning—the function of warding off anxiety. This function was reinforced when the analytic setting was comprehensively understood as a scientifically based arrangement that created conditions comparable to a research laboratory. The patient thereby unexpectedly assumed the role of a 'research object' and his free associating became merely a tool for approaching 'unconscious material'. Accordingly, the analyst's role changed from being an open listener to an active observer who examined and classified the material according to metapsychological theories.

This pseudo-scientific interpretation of the analytic situation as a laboratory situation has been readily connected to this day with the magical notion of a direct communication between the patient's unconscious and the analyst's unconscious. For this too Freud himself provided the impetus by describing the analyst's unconscious as a 'receptive organ' that can attune directly to the patient's 'transmitting' unconscious (1912, p. 115).

Back to Freud's (anti-)rules

It is now clear that daseinsanalysis differentiates between Freud's three anti-technical rules and the orthodox standard technique. It is orientated by the former because they create the conversational situation in which anxiety is no longer warded off by the application of a method. I have until now referred interchangeably to 'anxiety' without considering the existential philosophical distinction between (ontical) *fear* of specific dangers and (ontological) *anxiety* about the basic conditions of human being. There I followed Devereux, whose demonstration that method in the behavioural sciences serves to ward off anxiety also refers to anxiety in a broad sense. But this does not mean that this distinction with reference to Freud's anti-rules is now considered superfluous—quite the opposite. Observing positive rules not only gives protection from the fear of literally making a mistake and being held responsible for it; it also deflects the ontological anxiety that would reveal that following positive rules can only ever produce a semblance of safety.

Freud's rules of analytic conversation serve to deflect neither fear nor anxiety. This is not intended to suggest, however, that Freud's rules have the function in the daseinsanalytic view of intentionally triggering fear and/or anxiety in the patient or the analyst. Their negative nature merely opens up the conversational space in which fear and anxiety emerge and can be experienced and addressed as such.

3

Listening with a philosophical ear

I explained in the last chapter why daseinsanalysis maintains the psychoanalytic form of conversation. Now this is based on the rule of *free association* intended for the patient and the rule of *listening with free-floating attention* that applies to the analyst, which are both in fact anti-rules. As already shown in the last chapter, the two rules are inextricable and both incorporate the third rule of abstinence. This chapter is devoted to the rule of listening—more precisely to a daseinsanalytic interpretation of what Freud termed 'free-floating attention'. The question now is therefore what it means for the daseinsanalyst to listen with free-floating attention.

To Freud, the analyst should listen without any intention and not try to make a note of anything explicitly because then he would already be making a selection according to his own expectations and inclinations. Freud could have great confidence in this intentionless listening because, as already mentioned, he believed that in this way the analyst's unconscious rather than his ego was listening and that it established a direct access to the patient's unconscious. Based on the daseinsanalytic concept of existence, this mystifying notion of the unconscious as an independently functioning organ of perception in the human psyche cannot be maintained.[92] Nevertheless, Freud's insight that the hidden meaning of mental suffering can only be

---

[92] Cf. my existential interpretation of the unconscious orientated to Sartre in Part II, Chapter 6.

deciphered when the analyst listens without intention also applies to the daseinsanalyst. Only in that way will he in fact be open to the ontological experiences to which the patient is exposed by his special sensitivity. In the daseinsanalytic view, listening with free-floating attention is therefore the necessary correlate to the patient's special sensitivity.

Freud's student Theodor Reik devoted a book to listening with free-floating attention in 1948 and described it—borrowing an expression of Nietzsche's—as 'hearing with the third ear': 'One of the peculiarities of this third ear is that it works two ways' (Reik, 1948, p. 146). Someone who listens in two channels simultaneously hears two messages. This dual hearing needs to be learnt however. It requires more than taking a passively receptive attitude: 'the psychoanalyst … has to sharpen his sensitiveness to [this almost imperceptible, imponderable language *of the unconscious*], to increase his readiness to receive it' (p. 147).

When Reik refers to the 'language of the unconscious' to which the Freudian psychoanalyst must listen with the third ear, what he means is the language of the patient's unconscious past. The patient who according to Freud 'suffers from reminiscences' always speaks, without noticing it, in two channels: in one he speaks about his conscious memories and current events; in the other about his repressed childhood experiences. Therefore the psychoanalyst only listens appropriately when he is open to both temporal dimensions. According to the daseinsanalytic view of mental suffering as a suffering from our own being, the patient also speaks in a third channel: in his speech not only past and present experiences but also ontical and ontological experiences are intermingled. The daseinsanalyst should therefore actually listen in three channels, and hearing in the channel that sends philosophical messages distinguishes him from the psychoanalyst.

This gives Freud's discussion of free-floating attention a daseinsanalytic meaning. It now means *also* listening with a *philosophical ear*. This listening also needs to be learnt because it entails cultivating a special 'sensitiveness' (Reik) to the hidden ontological meaning of the patient's narrations. I will explain what it means also to listen with a philosophical ear with two examples.

3.1 A comparison between psychoanalytic and daseinsanalytic listening

Two examples

The *first example* is drawn from a text by the psychoanalyst *Wilfred Bion*, which is fascinating precisely because Bion does not know the distinction between listening to the ontical-concrete and the ontological, but introduces another distinction that closely resembles the daseinsanalytic one. In the 1973 *Brazilian Lectures*, Bion refers to the example of a stocking phobia mentioned by Freud in the essay on 'The unconscious', which consists in a young man becoming unable to put on stockings because he must 'pull apart the stitches in the knitting, i.e. the holes' (1990, p. 21), which makes him intolerably anxious. With reference to this example, Bion now encounters the distinction between a *macroscopic* and a *microscopic* vision that leads him to diverge strongly from Freud's perspective (1915c, p. 200). Instead of following Freud's sexual interpretation of this phobia, or even mentioning it, Bion is evidently fascinated by the fact that this man cannot disregard the fact when putting on his stocking that the fabric consists merely of small holes and that he becomes unable to continue putting stockings on because of his microscopic vision. For Freud though the infantile-sexual meaning of this symptom is beyond question and he only mentions this example because the young man suffering from this symptom—contrary to what would be expected of a neurotic—is supposed to have shown no resistance to revealing the hidden sexual meaning of his inhibition or phobia to the therapist.

For Bion, however, it is irrelevant whether this young man also connects a sexual phantasy with the stocking-holes. Instead he identifies a special observational gift in this man. This patient in fact perceives something while putting on the stocking that is correct and yet is overlooked by most people: that the material of every stocking consists on closer inspection of 'a lot of holes knitted together' (1990, p. 21). Bion therefore attests this patient's special capacity for microscopic instead of only macroscopic vision, which gives rise to his phobic fear of stockings.

Here the analyst must appropriate the 'microscopic vision' not in order to know more than the patient but to avoid falling short of what the patient is capable of perceiving.

It is not difficult for the daseinsanalyst to recognise the 'ontical' in the vision that Bion describes as macroscopic and the 'ontological' in the microscopic vision. Normal everyday life functions relatively free of mental disorders because macroscopic vision predominates there. Macroscopically (ontically) seen, the stocking is nothing other than a stocking worn to cover the legs, and is thus an ordinary item of clothing that in Freud's day belonged in a man's wardrobe. It is only because that young man has a capacity for microscopic vision that he is confronted when putting stockings on with a truth that must make him anxious and therefore makes it impossible for him to continue with this action. Listening with free-floating attention as an analyst in this case means following the patient's especially lucid perception and recognising and acknowledging its truth content.

With the requirement that the analyst must cultivate the same microscopic vision and hearing that belongs to the patient, Bion goes beyond Freud. For Freud's sexual interpretation remains within the dimension of macroscopic vision. This means that he considers the small holes in the stocking that are making the patient anxious as intrinsically meaningless and therefore can only accord a hidden meaning to the anxiety that arises when putting on the stocking by identifying it with infantile castration anxiety. To Freud the patient is therefore not clearer-sighted; rather than seeing more than the normally-sighted person, he succumbs because of his unconscious transfer of an early childhood anxiety on to the stocking to an illusion that makes it impossible for him to continue seeing the actual stocking that he is to put on as a harmless stocking and use it accordingly.

If we identify Bion's microscopic vision as 'ontological', then we also go beyond Bion. For Bion's discovery that the patient sees more than the normally-sighted person cannot itself explain why the perception of the small holes in the stocking must trigger panic-stricken anxiety in him. His phobic reaction only becomes comprehensible when the experience the patient is having because of his microscopic vision is recognised as an *ontological experience*. This means that the patient not only perceives the ontical-concrete lacunary nature of stocking fabric but that with it he is having the ontological experience of a lacunary quality that is general and fundamental because it concerns the being of all things. The stocking's hole-ridden fabric becomes so deeply threatening for the patient because the truth dawns on him through this ontical perception that on closer inspection the supposed compactness and constancy of all things and so the entire world turn out to be an illusion.[93] Only someone who is ontologically sensitive can have the experience with such a harmless item of daily use as a stocking of essentially living in a 'lacunary' world into which the anxiety that was already defined by Kierkegaard as 'the nothing of anxiety' can intrude at any time (1980, p. 62).[94]

Listening to the philosophical truth. Listening with a philosophical ear only makes sense if it is assumed that the patient is also reporting a philosophical experience when he misconstrues this as an ontical-concrete experience and thus in the above example believes that he is afraid of the stocking when he is actually anxious about the lacunary nature of the world. This means that rather than lacking any presuppositions, the daseinsanalyst's listening is rooted in existential-philosophical considerations of the human being's relation to his own being. This assumes however only that what a patient is experiencing involves an ontological experience, which is why it remains the daseinsanalyst's task always to listen anew to *which* experience of being might be in play here. Existential philosophy therefore provides no prior knowledge that restores to the daseinsanalyst the security he abandons by observing Freud's anti-rule of listening with free-floating attention.

Listening philosophically is not intended as a substitute for psychoanalytic listening. What Freud discerned from the stocking phobic's experience may also be correct. The daseinsanalyst should therefore always also remain open to an ontical (in this case infantile-sexual) meaning. For him though—unlike the psychoanalyst—childhood castration anxiety also has another double meaning, namely ontical and ontological. He will thus listen with 'free-floating

[93] In Thomas Bernhard's literary text *Gehen* (walking) (1971), Karrer likewise insists when visiting a shop that sells trousers that all the trousers on sale there have 'thin patches' and breaks down with regard to this fact of which all those present with 'normal vision' try to dissuade him.

[94] On the 'lacunary world' see also Kolakowski, 1967, pp. 118-121.

attention' to what anxiety may be hidden in the fear of castration: whether the anxiety about the fundamentally indissoluble otherness and mysteriousness of the opposite sex, or the anxiety about the collapse of fundamentally fragile male sexual identity, or even the anxiety about a possible loss of self altogether as a result of sexual fusion with a woman. Freud's warning not to stop listening too early on the assumption of having already understood also applies to listening to the ontological dimension in the fear of castration.

Listening while dwelling on the phenomenon. Daseinsanalysis has always been committed to the phenomenological method, although Binswanger and Boss connected it with completely different views of 'phenomenology'. It is impressive that listening with a philosophical ear also leads to dwelling on the manifest phenomenon—not because there is nothing to be sought behind it, as Boss in particular believed, but because what is sought, namely the hidden ontological meaning, lies hidden *in* the manifest ontical phenomenon and nowhere else. Or to put it another way: unlike the psychoanalyst, the daseinsanalyst can dwell on the given phenomenon because he imputes a special ontological sensitivity to the patient, whereas in the psychoanalytic view the patient is merely 'transferring' a historical experience on to the manifest phenomenon, which therefore only constitutes a more or less incidental 'substitute' or at best a sexual 'symbol'. For the daseinsanalyst, the stocking is therefore no mere substitute for something else because he assumes that the patient because of his microscopic clear-sightedness about the stocking is having a true and also deeply uncanny experience of being. In listening he can therefore dwell on what is important to the patient himself instead of having to devalue it as a mere 'substitute formation'.

The different evaluation of the manifest phenomenon cannot fail to influence the relationship between patient and analyst. The forms this takes differs if the patient is assumed to be blinded by the 'return of the repressed' to the phenomenon from which he is manifestly suffering rather than being attributed with seeing and listening more deeply into manifest reality than the normal average human being.

The *second example* concerns a symptom that relates to the therapeutic setting, more specifically the beginning of the session.[95]

---

[95] This is an example from my own clinical practice.

A female patient consistently turns up to the session as arranged but almost equally regularly arrives late. To her, this is always to do with some incident that has ruined her good resolve to be punctual. She usually arrives about a quarter of an hour late, having run breathlessly up the stairs, complaining or ranting about the annoying incident as she apologises for being late: she just couldn't find the piece of clothing she wanted to wear, or the car keys weren't in the usual place or the garage driveway was blocked by an unknown car, or she was held up by a neighbour or a sudden traffic jam added to the journey time and so on.

Listening with free-floating attention forbids drawing any premature conclusion as to a hidden resistance to the therapy. It requires initially tolerating not yet being able to know what this symptom may mean and therefore just continuing to listen. This is also advisable in this case because the analyst does not have the impression that the patient is making up stories from a need to conceal a completely different purpose to her late arrival. It actually sounds credible every time that yet again some obstacle has thwarted her good intention to be punctual on this occasion. All that is remarkable here is that she draws no conclusions from her previous experiences and does not allow more time. She always calculates this so that she could, in favourable circumstances, be there exactly on time at the beginning of the session. What this prevents at all costs is arriving too early and having to wait for the beginning of the session. What does the daseinsanalyst listen to when she also listens to her 'philosophically' in this connection?

It may be helpful first to envisage what the analyst would listen to psychoanalytically. It is necessary to distinguish today between traditionally Freudian and post-Freudian-intersubjective listening. If the analyst listened in a *Freudian* way, then she might discern here an unconscious realisation of infantile wishes to rebel against parental authority—perhaps also something else, but even if she left open for a long time what the late arrival actually meant, the 'free-floating attention' would still be orientated towards both the temporal dimensions of the manifest present on the one hand and the patient's repressed early childhood past on the other. She would therefore work from the premise that the symptom of the delayed beginning of the session had a 'transference meaning' that would be revealed by patiently listening to 'both channels' (Reik).

If on the other hand the analyst listened in a *post-Freudian intersubjective* way then she would work from the premise that the late arrival has something to do with the real relationship between her as an individual person and the patient. She would therefore listen for whether the patient with this symptom might be indicating a lingering conflict in the relationship between them that she only dares to express in this indirect way. In listening, the analyst would therefore remain open to the possibility that the patient is indirectly trying to draw her attention to something that she is reluctant to admit to herself. It might indicate, for example, that the patient does not feel welcome with her and that this is much more than a matter of a 'transference' of the infantile feeling of not having been loved enough by the mother; instead, she might be sensitively perceiving something that relates to the person of the analyst or her relationship with the patient—for instance, that the analyst is secretly disappointed or even aggrieved by the slow progress of the analysis, or that the analyst has become accustomed to punishing the patient for her late arrival with a cool manner of greeting, or that this analyst would find it difficult to tolerate an overt criticism from her patient and she therefore only dares to express her criticism in the form of a supposedly involuntary late arrival.[96]

These two forms of psychoanalytic listening should not be opposed because neither makes the other superfluous: the analyst who listens in a classically Freudian way should also consider the possibility that an aspect of her own behaviour may be partly responsible for the symptom and, conversely, the analyst listening in a post-Freudian intersubjective way should remain open to what the symptom could mean in the transference.

What is added or what changes when the daseinsanalyst (also) listens with a *philosophical ear*? She is then listening to a truth that belongs neither only in the patient's childhood nor in the present-day interaction between her and the patient, but in the patient's philosophical relationship with the basic conditions of human being. She is able to do this because she works from the premise that mental

---

[96] Stolorow et. al. provide a similar example (2002, p. 104); cf. the following Chapter 4.

suffering is always (also) a suffering from our own being. She will therefore listen for whether the beginning of the analytic session has a hidden ontological meaning for this patient.

To discover something more specific about this, it is also necessary to listen patiently. I emphasise that because those familiar with Medard Boss's daseinsanalysis may suppose that the analyst's philosophical reflection concerning the 'essence of beginning' can itself provide the crucial insight. But the phenomenology of being that characterises Medard Boss's daseinsanalysis can provide no information concerning to what *this* patient is especially sensitive and *what* ontological meaning not every beginning has for her but very specifically *the beginning of the analytic session*. For this patient certainly does not arrive late everywhere and to every appointment. Could it be that this patient finds it especially difficult to arrive on time to the analytic session because with it a session always begins in which she can neither take the passive role of the listener nor, when talking, follow any rules that give her security, but has to begin by talking herself? Could it be that for this woman the fact that an analytic session begins so that *she herself makes the beginning* is charged with an ontological meaning that causes anxiety?

Now not only is there the ever-new beginning of the individual analytic sessions, but the analysis or psychotherapy itself once began. And this patient has also begun the psychotherapy in the expectation of a change. Some years have passed since this beginning, without any appreciable change having occurred. This patient has long hoped that it would be enough to begin an analysis and to attend the arranged sessions regularly for something to change *as if of its own accord* because this has corresponded with her general attitude of *passively waiting* for an event that would change her life. This hope has since disappeared. It may therefore be that the beginning of each individual session is anxiety-provoking because every time she is inexorably reminded that change will only be possible if she dares to give up the chronic waiting and to begin *herself*.

Even the mere thought of beginning herself in the sense of beginning a life of one's own terrifies this patient. The *ontical* dangers consist in leaving the familiar protective space and in that connection leaving behind the ageing mother who clings desperately to her.

The implicit *ontological* threat here consists in finally taking over one's own life—in the sense of a delayed psychic birth—as something that is *one's own in a way that cannot be delegated*. She recoils from this because—unlike the 'healthy' average—she is especially sensitive to the immanent ontological burden in our own beginning.

It is often said that 'every beginning is difficult'. This may not always be ontically and literally correct, but it certainly is ontologically. The daseinsanalyst must know about the ontologically burdensome nature of beginning in order to be open and sensitive to this patient's suffering. Only then can she listen to the guilt feelings that immediately arise in this patient at the mere idea of beginning herself and taking control of her own life.[97] She can then understand the notorious lateness as an 'acted-out' refusal of the imposition of becoming guilty with our own beginning in a two-fold sense. For in the ontological (pre-moral) sense actually every beginning of our own—even our own beginning of an analytic session—incurs guilt because we must authorise ourselves to it. The patient repeatedly talks about her conscience pangs that immediately arise when she merely begins to try to free herself from the parental home. She also talks about the certainty that she is lacking something fundamental in order to be able to take her life into her own hands. If we try to find out what it is she is lacking, what occurs to her is that she lacks the sense of being entitled to it, instead of which she is pervaded by the feeling that a beginning of her own would be an act of hubris for which she would be punished.

Yet our own beginning is burdensome in yet another respect. Many of the patient's statements indicate that she also recoils from her own beginning because she knows that it inevitably entails making a choice. We can begin in one way or another but however we begin we have decided in favour of one possibility and thereby surrendered other possibilities. This is also experienced by this patient as an imposition that is hugely threatening: having to choose *how* she herself wants to live life without being able to know whether or not she will later regret the choice.

The beginning of the analytic session symbolises for this patient the beginning that one must make oneself and that alone allows a

---

[97] On two-fold ontological guilt, see Methodological Part II, Chapter 5 in this book.

life of one's own. In so frequently arriving late, she is acting out the wish not to have to begin herself at all or at least to be able to delay her own beginning a bit longer. For when she arrives late, the session has already begun without her, which despite her outward agitation at the annoying obstacles obviously has a calming effect.

So if the analyst listens philosophically, she discovers in the late arrival the fear of the two-fold ontological guilt connected with every beginning: that we can only begin when we authorise ourselves to it and that we are responsible ourselves for how we begin. This provides an understanding of this symptom that cannot be gained by a listening that is only psychoanalytic. Yet this does not mean that it can replace the latter. Listening to the hidden philosophical meaning does not remove the need either to listen to the historical and genetic connections or to listen to the current relational dynamics between analyst and patient. In the example described, it was immensely important to hear that even as a small child this woman's own beginning had been challenged by an elder and extremely jealous sister. Later in her childhood, the mother incessantly emphasised a special 'spiritual kinship' that existed exclusively between the two of them and so she managed to bind the patient especially close to her in this way. Claiming a life of her own was therefore presumably also burdened with *moral* guilt for this woman from early childhood onwards. Likewise, it is essential to reflect on the analyst's own role here that inevitably makes her the mother's adversary, since she expects the patient to dare to make her own beginning and so to break away from the mother. The symptom of the late arrival can therefore also be understood in Freud's sense as a compromise formation: while she certainly attends the analytic sessions because they represent for her the vitally important opportunity for her own beginning, she arrives conspicuously late as a form of indirect display of loyalty towards her mother that alleviates her own guilt feelings.

3.2 Fear and anxiety in listening

We have so far presented three kinds of listening with 'free-floating attention': classical psychoanalytic, post-classical intersubjective and daseinsanalytic-ontological. None protects the analyst from either fear or anxiety because when listening he is always exposed to what the patient is saying, without being able to know in advance what he is going to hear or what this will trigger in him.

When the analyst listens in a Freudian way and focuses on the patient's inner world as a particular individual person X with this individual history, a protective distance from what is being heard seems to ensue almost automatically. Yet here too the analyst may inadvertently discover similarities or even connections with his own individual history and so run the risk of being overwhelmed by his own traumatic childhood experiences or even stumbling because of the patient's descriptions on traumatic childhood experiences of his own that he had previously successfully denied.

When the analyst listens in a post-Freudian intersubjective way, he abandons this distance. He can no longer protect himself with the explanation that as an abstinent analyst he is only the projective screen for the patient's infantile wishes and fears; unlike the classical Freudian, he consciously exposes himself to the danger of being perceived by the patient with his individual weaknesses.

If the daseinsanalyst listens with a philosophical ear, yet another distance disappears that remains as long as listening excludes the ontological dimension of what the patient is saying. Now the analyst hears from a patient about something that applies equally to him, namely being subjected to the uncanny basic conditions of human being.[98] In this way, the daseinsanalyst consciously moves, unlike the psychoanalyst, into the danger zone of 'anxiety' and not through a possible emotional contagion or emotional transference but because of the possibility of being seized by his own inner anxiety as he listens.

To summarise, all three variations of listening with free-floating attention expose the analyst to *experiences* that concern *himself*, simply because he sees the patient not as a mentally *ill* person but a person who is *suffering from himself*. Freud had therefore required the psychoanalyst

---

[98] Binswanger acknowledged this fact in a striking way in his 1956 lecture 'Der Mensch in der Psychiatrie' (the human being in psychiatry): 'What for me ... it depends on is bringing home to you at the very beginning of our explanations that we understand nothing about madness as long as we behave towards the mad person as an uninvolved subject or, which amounts to the same thing, set the mad person before us merely as an *object* or in short imagine him as a thing, but that we only understand the madness from the ground of our common human fate, from the ground of the human condition, or what comes down to the same thing, when we see the mad person also as our fellow human being' (1992–94, Vol. 4, p. 58).

'to make himself capable, by a deep-going analysis of his own, of the unprejudiced reception of the analytic material' (1926b, p. 219). The analyst can only listen 'with free-floating attention' when he neither has to 'fear' nor 'be anxious about' what the patient is reporting. Fear always hinders listening when what he is hearing touches on his own unelaborated childhood experiences or on individual weaknesses that he is denying in himself. However, when the daseinsanalyst listens with a philosophical ear everything that the patient reports touches on his own anxiety. Therefore in his training analysis, the daseinsanalyst must not only have come to terms with himself as an individual person but also have learnt to tolerate the existential basic experiences of anxiety, guilt and shame in himself.

But even if what the daseinsanalyst hears may trigger anxiety in him in principle and he should be open to this possibility, the listening certainly does not occur in an atmosphere of anxiety. Listening with a philosophical ear is supported by another atmosphere that I characterise here as 'sympathy'. This atmosphere of sympathy is not though—as I will go on to explain—the condition for being able to listen philosophically, and it therefore does not have to be acquired from somewhere in order to support the listening; instead this sympathy follows from listening philosophically.

3.3 Empathy and sympathy in listening

To understand what I mean by 'sympathy', it must be compared with 'empathy'. Psychoanalytic listening is connected with the capacity for empathy that according to Freud 'plays the largest part in our understanding of what is inherently foreign to our ego in other people' (1921, p. 108). Described as 'empathy' is the capacity to relate to what *another* person is feeling. The psychoanalyst can only listen empathetically to the patient if he is both able and willing to enter as far as possible into the subjective world of his thoughts and feelings.

The daseinsanalyst must also have this capacity and willingness for empathy because it is necessary for being open to a patient's individual otherness. This indicates an important criterion for empathy: it presupposes acknowledging this very fact of the patient's individual otherness. The philosopher Max Scheler created the important distinction between empathising with the other (*Einfühlung*) and feeling at one with the other (*Einsfühlung*) (1973, p. 29). These two are fundamentally different. Where the analyst feels 'at one' with the patient, he denies any difference between them because he *identifies* with the patient or, conversely, he expects the patient to identify with him as his analyst and to think and feel as he does.

If for example a female patient is mourning a specific loss, the analyst can only empathise with this mourning if he also knows that it is *her* mourning and not his and that a loss has befallen her and not him. This does not exclude the analyst being able to approach the patient's mourning so closely while listening empathetically that he might also shed tears.

Scheler seeks to differentiate empathy not only from 'feeling at one' but also from 'emotional contagion' (1973, p. 25ff.). The analyst may for example find the patient's tears infectious and begin to cry without his mourning having to have anything to do with the patient's mourning. He then uses the patient's mourning only as an opportunity to devote himself to a feeling of mourning of his own, but has thereby moved a long way from the patient's mourning.

The analyst requires empathy *because* his patient is another person, and empathy can only be effective if the analyst is *ready to acknowledge* the patient's individual otherness as something fundamentally positive and is furthermore also *interested* in his individual otherness.

Sympathy also has to be distinguished from empathy. Unlike empathy it is a feeling and, as stated, it is the feeling that sets in when the daseinsanalyst listens with a philosophical ear. I am well aware how misleading it is to use the concept of sympathy for this because in current everyday language we talk about 'being in sympathy with someone' when we find a person's individual character especially pleasant and therefore also attractive, so that we feel drawn to him and want to be around him. The sympathy discussed here has little or nothing to do with this personal sympathy or liking between two individuals. The sympathy to which I refer here only arises when I listen as a daseinsanalyst to the ontological meaning of what a patient tells me. The sympathy that I feel therefore does not apply to him as this individual person but to him as a 'reluctant philosopher'. It would be glossing over the realities to pretend that every patient throughout the entire period of an analysis is also personally sympathetic. Instead what happens is that with some patients it is entirely possible to imagine being friendly on a personal basis, while others would be avoided in the private sphere. I disagree with the view that in the latter case the necessary preconditions for a successful psychoanalytic psychotherapy are not met and I think it may even be dangerous because feelings of sympathy based on personal liking can easily switch to the opposite, namely into antipathy, for instance when the patient begins to react negatively to everything the analyst says or does.

Why does sympathy for the patient arise in the daseinsanalyst when he listens to him philosophically? Because then he is listening out in the person's suffering from his ontical–individual fate for the ontological fate of being human that is also his own fate. He is then listening to what connects them *both*, although every person has to bear this fate himself. Could listening to the shared ontological fate not also generate antipathy? Certainly, if the daseinsanalyst is still afraid of the anxiety and therefore has to resist the recognition of this common feature. A fundamental tolerance of anxiety has already been identified as the condition of philosophical listening. The analyst can only listen philosophically when he knows he is ontologically-existentially *connected* with the patient and *affirms* this connectedness. This affirmed knowledge is emotionally expressed as sympathy.

It is extremely important for the therapeutic relationship that the daseinsanalyst can feel this special form of sympathy for the patient independently of how difficult the interaction between the two may be at times. For this sympathy establishes a bond between the two of them that holds even if negative feelings prevail between them and the analyst has difficulty listening empathically.

Why ontological sympathy rather than ontological empathy? It may seem more appropriate to attribute ontological (rather than ordinary ontical) empathy to philosophical listening. Yet what could ontological empathy mean? According to the explanations so far, it would inevitably prescribe that his patient's ontological experiences also concern his individual suffering, which is intrinsically alien to him as the analyst but with which he could and should empathise. This would generate an illusion that would serve the analyst's self-protection and create a distance that is not there at all in reality. Sympathy is more than mere empathy; it is, as the word suggests, suffering *with* the person rather than merely understanding the feeling. Being able to empathise with the patient without feeling *with* him is important for listening to the patient's individual situation. Feeling only empathy for the patient as a 'reluctant philosopher' would amount though to a denial that they are subject to the same conditions of being and remain connected beyond all individual differences.

This particular kind of sympathy therefore arises spontaneously when the daseinsanalyst listens (also) philosophically to this patient and it is at the same time connected with this listening and so to the analytic situation. This sympathy is thus not to be confused with a general philanthropic feeling that would extend to all human beings on any basis. If in listening sympathy ceases to arise and negative feelings prevail instead, this shows the analyst that he has ceased to listen philosophically and thus to be abstinent in the strict sense but has for whatever reason embarked on a battle with the patient. To that extent, the absence of this feeling of sympathy is an important and in fact a highly specific and therefore extremely helpful warning sign that tells the analyst exactly what he has to do, namely to return to philosophical listening.

This chapter was devoted to listening. It has now become clear that the analyst's listening not only defines his role in the analytic conversation but also determines how he relates to the patient and how he enters into the relationship with the patient. It is now therefore important to consider the uniqueness of the analytic relationship from the daseinsanalytic–philosophical perspective.

4

The analytic relationship and philosophical experience

I t is not really changing the subject in this chapter to move from the analytic form of conversation to the *relationship* between (daseins-)analyst and patient. It is now common knowledge that the (successful) relationship between therapist and patient is the central operating factor in every psychotherapy. But when does a relationship between therapist and patient succeed, or to put the question another way: what constitutes a 'good' therapeutic relationship? If we want to get beyond merely cliché notions, the answer can only be given according to a particular school of thought because it depends on both philosophical-anthropological and psychopathological theories. Therefore I will not discuss the therapeutic relationship in general here, but only the *analytic* form of relationship that begins when the therapeutic conversation adheres to Freud's three (anti-) rules.

4.1 The attitude of abstinence as a relational offer

It may be plausible that the analyst's attitude of abstinence opens up a special experiential space in which the patient's hidden ontological experiences can become manifest; it is difficult to see though how this very attitude should contain a relational offer to the patient. The opposite—namely the refusal of a relationship—even seems to apply. There can only really be a relational offer if the person who offers a relationship is prepared to become personally involved in this relationship. This initially justified objection only makes clear however that through the attitude of abstinence a relationship is offered that differs from the customary or 'normal' relationships in some key respects—more precisely: that it creates the possibility of a relationship between analyst and patient that opens up a unique therapeutic opportunity psychoanalytically *and* daseinsanalytically.

For the psychoanalyst, the attitude of abstinence contains the offer to the patient to use him as a figure of projection for his childhood fantasies and thus to enter into a '*transference relationship*' with him. This follows from the psychoanalytic understanding of mental suffering: when the patient suffers from 'reminiscences', he needs exactly this a-personal relational offer in order to re-experience with the analyst his repressed, painful relational experiences and then as a second step to understand them with the analyst and also to be able to process them. The offer of an abstinent relationship here means freeing the patient's present relationships from pathogenic childhood relational patterns and thereby liberating him for new, freer forms of relationship.

From a daseinsanalytic viewpoint, the abstinent analyst makes (yet) another relational offer. This is based on the insight from existential philosophy that every human being, including the analyst, is always present in a two-fold way: ontically as this individual person X *and* ontologically as an other in his pure otherness. The presence as a pure other generally remains hidden because the ontical presence as each individual person is in the foreground. Accordingly, the analyst's willingness to hold himself back as an individual person also has an ontological meaning. It now contains the offer to the patient to experience through him as an abstinent analyst what it means to relate to another person not as *this individual* but as *an other in principle*.

From an outside perspective, this is an artificial relational offer that can only be justified by the ontological understanding of mental suffering as a suffering from our own being. For then the patient needs exactly this offer, to have relatively 'purely' the ontological experience of the irresoluble otherness of the other, to which he is especially sensitive, and to be made aware of the latent anxieties that are contaminating his everyday relations with his fellow human beings. Here the analyst takes on the task of representing the other as other for the patient, so that the patient learns in the protected framework of the analysis to distinguish between the ontological experience of the other's irresoluble otherness and the many kinds of ontical experiences (of personal closeness or distance, intimacy or strangeness, attraction or repulsion and so on). It is important to learn this because from the daseinsanalytic view relationships generally fail when ontological experiences of the other's otherness intrude and are then struggled with in the actual partner. Here too the a-personal relational offer has a liberating function: many patients will only gain the psychological knowledge of human nature required to perceive the individual uniqueness of other human beings intuitively in everyday life and to observe what kind of relationship is possible with whom once they have experienced the irresoluble otherness of every other person with the analyst and have learnt to accept it.

Conclusion: The attitude of abstinence is a relational offer that is based on the recognition that every personal relationship has both a historical and an ontological dimension. The analyst's attitude of abstinence is supposed to provide the patient with the possibility of becoming involved in both these dimensions in order to gain a freer relationship with both. Having recognised that only the attitude of abstinence provides this opportunity, the criticism that it manifests the analyst's refusal of a relationship can be confidently rejected because this criticism then proves to be the result of an excessively narrow view of relationships, which underestimates the defining power of both the dimension of repressed childhood relational experiences and unrecognised predominating ontological relational experiences.

The criticism of the abstinent attitude is only justified where this deteriorates into a mask-like anonymity on the analyst's part in the aim of establishing a false authority over the patient.

4.2 Dialogue and reciprocity instead of abstinence?

The attitude of abstinence has so far been justified as a relational concept without going into the radical criticism of the rule of abstinence made by representatives of intersubjective psychoanalysis. This should now be remedied because their objections are directed not only at its incorrect application in practice but at the attitude of abstinence as such and therefore refer in particular to more recent empirical infant research.[99]

The decisive theoretical argument against the rule of abstinence is that it belongs to the now superseded '*one-person psychology*'. This designates a psychology that posits the human being as a fundamentally solipsistic individual. Freud is criticised for having taken on this one-person psychology unhesitatingly and further cemented it by his theory of the drives. For if the human being is conceived as constituted essentially by the drives, his relationship with his fellow human being (Freud's *Nebenmensch*) can only ever have the function of serving his own drive satisfaction. What corresponds to this is that Freud assumed a primary narcissistic state of the infant, in which the latter seeks to satisfy his needs by hallucinatory means. The turning outward—generally to the mother—is according to Freud a secondary occurrence that results from the 'bitter life experience' of being unable to remove the tensions of these needs by hallucinatory means (cf. Freud, 1900, p. 565).

The results of infant research convinced many orthodox psychoanalysts of what Balint, Winnicott and Laplanche had each previously described in their own ways: that the infant is in fact a *relational being* from the outset and that his devotion to the mother also therefore originates from a genuine *wish to be together with her* and is far from being aimed only at using her as a 'need-satisfying object'.

As mentioned in the introduction to Part 4, the daseinsanalysis of both Binswanger and Boss can be considered as precursors of the intersubjective turn in psychoanalysis because both authors—influenced by Martin Buber (Binswanger) and Heidegger (Boss)—much earlier rejected the monadological view of the human being and the one-sided concentration on the individual's 'inner world' connected with it. Accordingly both have also conceived the therapeutic relationship as an 'encounter' or as a 'being together' in which patients could have *new* relational experiences instead of

---

[99] For German-speaking regions, Altmeyer's and Thomä's (2006) reader of texts by writers on this subject from the American region gives a good overview; concerning earlier 'new developments in psychoanalysis' in the European region see Part II Chapter 3 'The other', in this book.

only repeating old pathological relational patterns.[100] Through the so-called 'intersubjective turn', psychoanalysis is catching up on an internal debate about the human being as a relational being that was conducted much earlier in daseinsanalysis.

The proponents of intersubjective psychoanalysis consider the psychoanalytic form of conversation as needing revision because it is based on an obsolete view of the human being. It should assume a *dialogical* nature to account for the new insight into the human being as a relational being. A genuine dialogue is based on *reciprocity* and produces a *symmetry* between the partners in dialogue from the outset. Reciprocity demands in turn that both patient *and* analyst reveal themselves. The concept of 'authenticity', which is known to play an important role in Carl Rogers' client-centred psychotherapy, is now also becoming important psychoanalytically with the requirement for it to be possible for the patient to experience the analyst as a genuine counterpart. How far self-disclosure in the name of authenticity fundamentally may or should go and how much the analyst may or should disclose, and when and with whom, is still controversial though within the intersubjective movement of psychoanalysis.[101]

Critical concerns

The requirement for a dialogical form of conversation has a highly seductive power for various reasons. Yet it seems to me neither theoretically sufficiently well-founded nor practically sustainable. Anchoring the analyst's abstinent attitude in Freud's monadological concept of the human being is in my view misleading. It follows in Freud rather more from his discovery that there is also a hidden meaning in the patient's symptoms of mental suffering. This raises the unsettling question of whether the surrender of abstinence in favour of

---

[100] Boss did not see any contradiction here with Freud's technical instructions, as his criticism mainly applied to the orthodox standard technique and to Freud's metapsychology. He even saw the attitude of abstinence as the realisation of Heidegger's 'leaping-ahead' care instead of 'leaping-in' care, which was to enable the patient to find his way freely himself instead of merely imitating the analyst; cf. Boss, 1982 [1957], pp. 75-87.

[101] Cf. Aron (1996, pp. 221-253) discusses several variations of the psychoanalyst's possible self-revelation towards the patient, including Renik's thesis of an 'ethic of self-disclosure'; cf. also Stolorow et al., 2002, pp. 82-88.

a dialogical form of conversation does not also dispense with Freud's revolutionary discovery, which would mean readopting the traditional psychiatric view of mental suffering as mere 'disturbance'.[102]

Once the attitude of abstinence, as stated at the beginning of the chapter, is understood as a specifically analytic relational offer, it no longer contradicts the anthropological insight that the human being is from the outset a relational and not only a drive-dominated being—quite the opposite. The dispute about maintaining or abandoning the attitude of abstinence therefore no longer concerns the question as to whether psychoanalysis can finally bring itself to make an anthropological recognition of the human being as a relational being or not, but the question of *how* relationship is to be psychoanalytically understood. If in fact Freud's thesis that mental suffering is a 'suffering from reminiscences' is understood *hermeneutically rather than causally and genetically*, it contains a highly complex relational theory. Then it is not simply a matter of a one-sided unconscious dependence of current relationships on early childhood relational experiences, but the recognition that individual human beings are never only related to each reciprocally and thus never only hold a conversation with each other, but that every individual at the same time unconsciously addresses early caregivers of that time, from whom he still (unconsciously) expects something, whether this expectation is negative in the sense of a danger that is supposedly still threatening or positive in the sense of a wish yet to be fulfilled.

This is the meaning of the so-called 'transference' on to current relationships (certainly not only on to the abstinent analyst), which results in the present-day relationships always serving also to overcome old relational anxieties and wishes still pressing for fulfilment. It is obvious that this is a highly sophisticated theory of the connection between relational experiences at that time and in the present. However, to specify and also resolve this connection in a therapy requires the analyst's attitude of abstinence as a relational offer that brings this 'relational confusion' to account.

Some critical doubts concerning a replacement of the psychoanalytic form of conversation by reciprocal dialogue must also be registered by daseinsanalysis. For if one accepts the existential

---

[102] I will return to this in Chapter 5.1.

philosophical recognition that relational experiences have an ontological dimension, then here too the actual interacting partners still mean something else and the concrete relationships are still concerned with more than the reciprocal reference in the here and now. Now it is not (only) the actual caregivers of early childhood who are secretly also in play here but also in the daseinsanalytic view the other in his pure, ontological otherness. For daseinsanalysis, therefore, the patient's current relational problems are not only burdened with hidden apprehensions and wishes that stem from his own past but they are also determined by the (existential) anxiety that enters into actual relational experiences because of his special sensitivity and produces an ontical–ontological 'relational confusion' as well as a temporal one. This can also only become manifest when the analyst adopts an abstinent attitude.

In the light of these explanations, it becomes clear what is lost when the analytic-therapeutic conversation is transformed into a symmetrical dialogue. This kind of dialogue offers in the ideal case the possibility that patient and analyst can talk openly about the reciprocal experiences they are now having with each other personally in the current context, which is undoubtedly an advantage. However, the more the analyst enters into play as this individual person in such a dialogue, the smaller the possibility that remains for the patient of consciously experiencing in relation to the analyst the infantile relational anxieties that are still virulent to this day and above all also relational wishes that have nothing to do with the analyst as this individual person and understanding them as such; also obstructed is the possibility of having the ontological experience of his inalienable otherness in relation to the analyst and thereby learning that many of his current relational problems have nothing to do either with the actual caregivers or with his own actual inadequacies but with his special sensitivity to the worrying fact that every fellow human being is and remains an other. I will next go on to describe in more detail the ontological experience that the patient can have in relation to the analyst through his attitude of abstinence.

4.3 Experiencing *through* the abstinent analyst what it means to be *for* the other

If daseinsanalysis is essentially orientated by the Freudian attitude of abstinence, it is not because it formulates the human being as a primarily isolated individual relating only to himself but because it regards the relations with fellow human beings as *ontically-ontologically ambiguous*.[103] Of course the *ontical dimension* is generally in the foreground: *with whom* I have a relationship, *who* this actual other is, *what* I actually expect of him and he of me, *how* we actually deal *with each other*. But this does not alter the fact that every ontical relationship also has an ontological dimension: *that* this actual other with whom I have a relationship is after all and fundamentally an other who by his otherness always eludes my knowledge, power and control.

This ontological dimension also pertains to the patient's relational experience with the analyst. In it the patient always simultaneously has the philosophical experience *that* the analyst is an other. It is important to note that this philosophical experience would simply remain unnoticed unless the analyst heeded the rule of abstinence (in the sense of an anti-rule).

To summarise: the daseinsanalytic understanding of abstinence is grounded in both anthropology and psychopathology. It is based on the existential-philosophical recognition that every relationship is ontically–ontologically ambiguous; the attitude of abstinence gains its therapeutic function though from the daseinsanalytic view that the actual relational problems are related to the patient's special sensitivity to the other's inalienable otherness. To recognise the resulting confusion between ontical and ontological relational experiences and then to resolve it requires the 'abstinent' analyst.

Sartre's discovery of the difference between 'being with others' and 'being for others'

In *Being and Nothingness* Sartre chooses to designate the relationship to the other not, as would be expected, with the well-adopted expression '*with*-others', but with the unusual expression 'for-others' (cf. *BN*, p.

---

[103] This distinction has already been made in Part II, Chapter 3, The other.

243ff.). On closer inspection, he thereby provides a phenomenological differentiation between ontical and ontological relatedness to the other that subverts the intersubjective approach. With the expression 'for-others' (*pour autrui*) Sartre refers to the existential (ontological) relationship to the other that lies at the basis of the existentiell (ontical) relationship of 'with others'. He thereby indicates that the ontical and ontological relation to the other are differently structured because ontological relatedness does not as generally supposed have the structure of 'with' or 'inter' but 'for'. I think this is a discovery that cannot be overestimated because it makes clear that the entire intersubjectivity debate applies only to the ontical dimension of the relationship to the actual other as an individual person X rather than to the ontological dimension of the relationship to the other as such.[104]

An *inter*action or, synonymously, a *being-together* is always an ontical interaction between actual people because it implies some kind of reciprocal participation, as it is only realisable between actual others. Therefore all actual relationships outwardly have the form of *inter*action *with* others, while they always also realise the ever one-sided being-*for*-the-other.

Sartre thus draws attention to a structural difference in every relationship that is obscured in a purely intersubjective view. This therefore needs to be amplified by the recognition that at the basis of every concrete being-together-*with* lies the ontological primal experience of *for*-the-other that cannot be removed by any other interactions, however successful and exhilarating.

What does 'being-for-others' mean? The question immediately arises of whether 'for' is actively or passively meant: as active and concerned attention to the other or passive subordination to the other? In Sartre, 'for' is clearly passively meant because the other is independent of me and I am in his gaze, whether I want to be or not. The other has priority insofar as his presence is not constituted by me but represents a primal fact that befalls me passively. For this very reason I am not originally 'with' him but 'for' him, namely for him

---

[104] Heidegger did not consider this difference, although his analysis of the 'mineness' of dasein provided the preconditions for it. Therefore 'being together with others in a shared world' also assumes an ontological status in his work without further justification, 'being-with' is stated to be an existential and the being of the other is defined as a '*Mitda-sein*'—cf. BT §26.

as the other to whose gaze I am primarily passively subordinated.[105] In 'for-the-other', Sartre has therefore captured the asymmetry in the ontological relationship to the other as other, which always remains and cannot be removed by any symmetry in ontical-concrete relationships with other people.

Is it not a reasonable objection that the asymmetry is reciprocal insofar as the other to whose gaze I am subordinated is himself subordinated to my gaze? Certainly, only the fact that everyone is 'for' the other does not itself establish any reciprocity in the sense of 'for-each-other', which would relativise the destiny of every individual human being, himself 'to be thrown into the freedom of the other'. There is indeed a 'being-for-each-other', yet this like the 'against-each-other' that corresponds to it is an ontical form of being-*with*-each-other that is based on the ontological 'being-*for*-others'.

For daseinsanalysis it is only the attitude of abstinence that opens up the possibility for the patient to have the ontological experience *through* the analyst that always remains concealed in the interaction *with* him as an actual person and is nevertheless at work—namely the experience of being *for* the other. The entire analytic setting can be understood as staging that a-social primal situation in which the human being always unconsciously finds himself in all actual relations with his fellow human beings. This staging is therapeutically necessary because the patient suffering from relational problems is in the daseinsanalytic view especially sensitive precisely to the primal situation that lies at the basis of all these social interconnections. The analyst's attitude of abstinence thus proves to be the therapeutic relational offer that takes account of his suffering from this.

Who am I 'for' the other?

The question of who I am 'for' the other is somewhat ambiguous. It is directed at the ontological *self-experience* that corresponds to the ontological experience of being *for* the other. This experience is also

---

[105] Sartre's ontological definition of for-others therefore contrasts with Levinas's theory of the Other (1978), in which for-others means active devotion to the other in the sense of a positive (ethical) consideration for him.

in fact obscured if a foundational intersubjectivity is assumed. For then I am only ever the individual person X whose individuality is developed and also changed in interaction with actual others and I also only experience myself in this way. As however I can experience the other in two ways: as this individual person *and* as the other qua other, I can experience myself in two ways: as an individual person (with my unique history, my present situation and my specific future-related wishes and apprehensions) *and* as 'this singular individual' (Kierkegaard), who 'is and has to be' himself in a way that cannot be delegated (Heidegger).

The concept of the *individual* was introduced into philosophy by Kierkegaard on account of the consideration that 'the individual begins constantly anew'.[106] By this he pointed out the singularity that has less to do with the fact that every human being is different from all other individuals because of his individual distinctiveness but with the fact that everyone begins 'anew', that means must take over and lead his own life in a way that cannot be delegated. The non-transferability of this task to anyone else makes every human being ontologically this singular individual regardless of how closely interconnected he is with other people ontically. Following Kierkegaard here, Heidegger therefore characterised human dasein as 'always *mine*' (cf. *BT*, p. 39).

The experience of the inalterable 'mineness' of one's own existence thus corresponds to the other's inalterable otherness. This is another experience that the patient can have only if the analyst behaves abstinently. It is supremely important to be able to have it because many people hope to obtain from a relationship that is as close as possible or as dependent as possible the deliverance from their (ontological) singularity. To experience in relation to the abstinent analyst that there can be no deliverance from the 'mineness' of a person's own existence is what first opens the way in such cases to successful relationships with others in which each person can also remain himself through reciprocal respect.

---

[106] Cf. Kierkegaard: 'At every moment, the individual is both himself and the race ... As the history of the race moves on, the individual begins constantly anew', 1980, pp. 28-29.

Experiences of anxiety, shame and guilt 'through' the abstinent analyst

By focusing here on both the ontological experiences that the patient can have *through* the abstinent analyst, I do not seek in any way to deny that he can also have many important ontical experiences *with* the analyst. My concern here is merely with making clear and acknowledging what remains unconsidered outside a psychoanalysis guided by existential philosophy, which is characterised here as 'daseinsanalysis'. The next question is therefore what distinguishes ontological experiences '*through*' the abstinent analyst from the manifold ontical relationship experiences that he still also has *with* him. Three points of difference are especially important:

1. They are experiences of the pure *that* rather than the concrete *what*, *how* or *why*: the pure fact is discovered *that* one is exposed as an analysand before the analyst and *that* this exposure before him is unavoidable; one simultaneously experiences one's own powerlessness with regard to this fact, for however one strives to influence the analyst, to make the best possible impression, for instance by keeping some things quiet or glossing over them or by flattering him, none of that does anything to alter the fact of being exposed before the analyst as an analysand. This includes the experience of not being able to know what is going on in the analyst's 'head' and therefore not knowing what kind of image he is creating of one, while knowing with certainty that he has the power to perceive one from his own perspective, which it is impossible as an analysand to adopt; in precisely this again lies the experience that one cannot escape the fact of being 'for' the analyst as the other.

2. The experience of being *for* the other is originally purely emotional in nature because as demonstrated in Part I, Chapter 1.3, only moods can open up the dimension of the conditions of being in their pure facticity. This constitutes a major difference from actual

relational experiences *with* the analyst as this individual
person, where it is the actual perceptions or fantasies
that evoke corresponding emotions: the patient may
for example receive the impression that the analyst is
not remotely interested in him personally and react to
this with feelings of disappointment or rage, or he may
believe he can discern that what he is relating is being
deplored by the analyst and become afraid of his moral
condemnation and so on.

3. The ontological experience of being *for* the analyst as
the other *is* as such the experience of existential anxiety,
shame and guilt, although these mostly appear in the
guise of (ontical) fear of the analyst's judgement or the
(also ontical-conventional or moral) shame and guilt
about one's supposed inadequacy as an analysand. To be
distinguished from this are the feelings evoked in the
patient by the actual, real or only imagined experiences
with the analyst as a real person or as a transference figure,
such as being in love, admiration or gratitude on the one
hand, and dislike, envy and contempt on the other.

Examples of statements that (also) indicate an ontological experience

In the following comments made by patients, thus or often similarly
expressed, the daseinsanalyst who listens with a philosophical ear can
also discern experiences of being that are stirred in the patient by the
analyst's attitude of abstinence:

- I don't know if I'm talking too much or too little and
  whether that's really what you want to hear from me;
  this makes me really uncertain and sometimes almost
  despairing.

- I want to show myself as I am here, try to say everything
  that comes into my head, but I'm always afraid it seems
  ungenuine, that after all I'm only deceiving you and myself.

- I simply don't know how to relate anything today; this has been depressing me all morning and I can't stop thinking you'll be bored and think, oh here she is now back already with the same old stuff.

- I feel ashamed about just coming here and expecting you to listen to me, while you're perhaps tired or had something much more important to do.

- I can't stand not being able to get into your head and know for certain whether you like me or not and what you think of me.

- I always have to look at the clock so that I know myself when I have to stop talking because whenever I'm surprised by the end of the session, I have the unpleasant feeling that I'm being thrown out because I've become a burden to you.

4.4 For a coexistence of alternative views of analytic relationship

If the classical psychoanalyst receives the patient's statements presented above with a historical ear, he will discern in them early infantile relationship experiences that are transferred on to him because of his abstinent attitude and relived with him. If though he listens with 'intersubjective sensibility' as an advocate of intersubjective psychoanalysis (Stolorow), he will take such comments as an indication of a problem in the personal relationship between him and the patient and will want to find out in the conversation with the patient what he himself has contributed to it through his own behaviour. If the daseinsanalyst listens (not only, but also) with a philosophical ear, though, he will discern the ontological meaning of these experiences that impose themselves on the patient because of his 'ontological sensibility'.

Any perspective is in danger of being absolutised. This also applies to the daseinsanalytic perspective on the philosophical experience of being-for-others, which the patient has *through* the abstinent analyst. This too requires amplification by the psychoanalytic perspective, which has existed in two variations since the 'intersubjective turn'.

Why the analytic relationship also has a historical transference dimension

The daseinsanalyst should not listen only with a philosophical ear or he will miss the *historical* dimension in the patient's relationship to him. He must know that mental suffering is always also a 'suffering from reminiscences' and that the patient unconsciously transfers the 'eternal childhood wishes' (Freud) involved in the memories on to him. The above-listed comments by patients as to how they experience the analytic setting therefore express not only ontological but also historical experiences.

It is also important for the daseinsanalyst to know that the ontological and historical-genetic perspective can only be abstractly separated, for on the one hand the patient's sensitivity often goes back to actual early infantile experiences, on the other childhood itself is a supremely philosophical time because the child only slowly acquires the collective defence mechanisms that protect the 'healthy' adult from the incursion of ontological experiences.[107] The daseinsanalyst can therefore safely assume that such and similar comments by patients to their analyst contain their ontological (philosophical) experience of being an individual *for* the other but *at the same time* also repeat actual historical experiences that they have had with important caregivers in early childhood.

Why the analytic relationship also has an interactional dimension

What the patient perceives *through* the analyst even when the latter remains abstinent is never only his inalterable otherness. It is therefore always possible and often also probable that what the patient perceives in relation to the analyst also actually applies to the latter, regardless of whether the analyst recognises himself in it or not. On the model of intersubjective psychoanalysis, the daseinsanalyst should therefore take seriously what the patient perceives in relation to him as also a potentially true view of him as an individual person or what is

---

[107] In *Das Subjekt in der Kur*, Chapter 16, I have discussed the 'philosophical dimension of childhood' in more detail; cf. A. Holzhey-Kunz, 2002, p. 225-239.

actually happening between them. This requires him to be prepared for a *personal truthfulness* that safeguards him from using the attitude of abstinence as a 'cordon sanitaire' (Stolorow et al., 2002, p. 91) to protect himself from unpleasant arguments with patients.

An example. Stolorow et al. present three examples in all of which the patient says something about the analyst that the latter spontaneously considers completely inaccurate. Therefore these examples also raise the question of where, or more precisely with whom, 'reality and truth' lie in such cases. In the first example, to which we are limiting ourselves here, a female patient relates how she was extremely upset that she had been described by the analyst as a borderline case.[108] Not only can the analyst not remember making such a statement, it also seems to her entirely alien because psychiatric diagnoses play no role in her thinking. She therefore feels the spontaneous impulse to tell the patient that she can only have imagined that—to which she does not accede though.

There is undoubtedly a strong temptation with this very example to consider either a 'transference' on to the analyst or an ontological experience 'through' the analyst. However Stolorow et al. point out that the analyst's not being able to remember such a statement does not itself disprove the truth of what the patient is saying. For every analyst must know that he has a tendency to repress statements of his own that he suspects he would have done better not to make. The analyst in this example knows this, which is why she remains open to the potential truth of the patient's criticism and enters an open dialogue with the patient. Thanks to this willingness, the analyst realised that she had recently without noticing it herself taken an increasingly overbearing and know-all attitude, as if she wanted to say to the patient: 'I'm so clever and I can tell you what the trouble is'. Now it becomes clear that the patient's criticism applies to this attitude and it is therefore secondary whether the term 'borderline' was really used by the analyst or not.[109]

---

[108] Verbatim: 'I've been so upset, I can't get it out of my mind that you called me a borderline. I can't stop thinking that that is what I really am that that is how you really see me' (2002, p. 103).

[109] verbatim: '... that something had gone very wrong between them, and the analyst's instant denial—verbally expressed or not—signaled her unawareness of what had happened' (2002, p. 118).

This example shows what is new in comparison to the psychoanalytic standard technique: it consists in the analyst's willingness to learn something about herself from the patient instead of passing the criticism back to the patient by interpreting it and setting herself above her (2002, p. 118f.). Yet this benefit does not justify now stopping at that. For it does not make either a transference interpretation or an ontological interpretation of this patient's criticism untrue or therapeutically superfluous.

I therefore argue for a 'peaceful coexistence' of the three perspectives on the analytic relationship, as each alone can only bring a part of the truth into view. So the patient's subjective impression that the analyst is overbearing and know-all towards her could also have originated from her special *sensitivity*—the sensitivity to what it means to be defencelessly exposed before the analyst. And the *anxiety* that this causes could have been transformed unnoticed into ontical *fear* of being negatively judged by the analyst. Taking the daseinsanalytic perspective, it even becomes probable that the patient with her complaint of having been diagnosed by the analyst as a borderline has also given expression to an ontological experience. The term 'borderline' would then relate not only to her own family history (diagnostic concepts played an important role in conversations of her family of origin), but could symbolise for the patient the ontological reality of the indissoluble border that separates every human being from the other as other. And taking the classically psychoanalytic perspective, it is obvious to suppose that the analyst's overbearing attitude has become the cause for the patient to relive infantile relationship experiences with early authority figures.

In conclusion, this again makes clear how complex the analytic relationship is and how rich is its potential, so that both psychoanalyst and daseinsanalyst should take care not to squander this potential by a fixation on only one of the three perspectives.

5

The reacquisition of interpreting for daseinsanalytic practice

reud chose the verb 'deuten' (interpret) to refer to the analyst's hermeneutic activity: 'Interpreting means finding a hidden sense in something' (1916-17, p. 86). Interpreting is therefore not synonymous with 'understanding' or 'construing' but is used only when the meaning is *hidden*. That is the case with psychopathological phenomena that manifest themselves as deficient divergences from the healthy norm. Here what is obvious is incomprehensible. It becomes comprehensible only when it becomes interpretable, so that its hidden meaning can be discovered and construed.

Unlike Medard Boss's daseinsanalysis, the daseinsanalysis put forward here can no longer dispense with interpreting because it too imputes a hidden meaning to mental suffering. This links it with psychoanalysis, although it does not simply adopt its specific interpretative practice. The daseinsanalytic interpretation differs from a psychoanalytic one in being based on an ontologically deepened understanding of mental suffering as a 'suffering from one's own being' and it therefore seeks a hidden 'ontological' meaning in the symptom. Whether this involves only a difference in the content of the interpretation or whether the form of the interpretation also changes with the content-related orientation to the philosophical dimension in mental suffering is an important question in the second part of this chapter.

5.1 The rehabilitation of interpreting

Although the postulate of a daseinsanalytic interpretation follows from the understanding of mental suffering presented in Part III, the introduction of interpreting into daseinsanalysis still requires justification. Daseinsanalysis has always been indebted to the phenomenological method, which raises the question of whether interpreting is in fact compatible with the phenomenological approach. *Ludwig Binswanger* did not make any statement on this, presumably partly because his daseinsanalysis was primarily intended to be a new (phenomenological) research movement in psychiatry, while interpretation has its place and function in therapy. Nevertheless it can be shown that his theory of the individual world-project allows an interpretation of the manifestly meaningless symptoms, as already shown by the 'heel phobia' example in several places in this book (last in Chapter 4.1). For Binswanger interpreting did not therefore seem to be an intrinsically un-phenomenological act, and my intended introduction of interpretation here into the therapeutic practice of daseinsanalysis can at least implicitly refer to him. It is entirely different with *Medard Boss*, who understood his movement of daseinsanalysis also as a therapeutic movement in itself. He rejected any interpreting in the name of phenomenology. Interpreting a phenomenon meant for him fundamentally imposing an alien meaning on it and thereby violating it. In his view there could therefore be no right or wrong interpretations; instead, every interpretation is a misinterpretation because it seeks a hidden meaning behind manifest phenomena. And he would have considered the notion of a 'daseinsanalytic interpretation' to be a contradiction in terms.

The question of whether Boss could justify his radical condemnation of all interpreting with reference to Heidegger cannot be definitely answered. The answer is yes based on the 'Zollikon Seminars'—the records of their joint seminars between 1959 and 1969 as well as the simultaneously conducted dialogues (cf. Historical Part 2 in this book)—but no with reference to § 7 on 'The phenomenological method of the investigation' in his early major work *Being and Time* in 1927. For whereas in the late phase of his thinking Heidegger again equated phenomenological seeing with 'a full view into the unfolding essence' (*Wesensschau*) (Heidegger, 2001a, p. 166) and recommended the psychiatrists taking part in the Zollikon seminars to practise 'a simple looking at the essence' (*Wesensblick*) (2001a, p. 263), he firmly put forward the view in *Being and Time* that phenomenology must become hermeneutics when it turns to the phenomena of human existence, and indeed a hermeneutics of the hidden, because the ontological meaning of human phenomena is not merely random but actually necessarily concealed (cf. *BT*, p. 31ff.).[110]

The daseinsanalytic interpretation of mental suffering put forward here is based on the phenomenological hermeneutics of the hidden that Heidegger not only justifies theoretically in *Being and Time* but also demonstrates throughout the book. It is nevertheless necessary to devote a whole chapter to daseinsanalytic interpretation. There are two important reasons for this: first, in *Being and Time* Heidegger is concerned with a purely ontological interpretation of the human relationship with one's own being, whereas a daseinsanalytic interpretation always relates to the suffering of a unique individual from his own being. Therefore the question of the specificity of a daseinsanalytic interpretation can only be partly answered based on Heidegger. It also requires a comparison with the psychoanalytic interpretation because daseinsanalysis adopts 'interpreting as a principle' from classical psychoanalysis.[111] Second, interpreting is receiving criticism today also within psychoanalysis and especially by advocates of intersubjective psychoanalysis, as already discussed in detail in the two preceding chapters. Interpreting appears here as the expression of a power position arrogated by the analyst that is itself based on the previous monadological concept of psychoanalysis rather than the intersubjective one. Interpretation as the analyst's solitary act should be replaced by *conversation*, in which analyst and patient agree *together* on what can be considered 'real' or 'true'.[112]

---

[110] In *Leiden am Dasein* (2001) I have discussed in detail the relationship between phenomenology and hermeneutics; cf. loc. cit., pp. 36-49 and pp. 181-184.

[111] Hans-Volker Werthmann (1997, p. 318) draw a helpful distinction between 'interpreting as an isolated verbal act' and 'interpreting as a principle' because it is 'interpreting as a principle' that has to be rehabilitated daseinsanalytically. Like psychoanalysis, daseinsanalysis subordinate itself to 'interpreting as a principle', which does not imply that interpreting should become the principal activity of the psychoanalyst or the daseinsanalyst.

[112] Because dispensing with interpreting in favour of dialogue *with* the patient follows from the intersubjective view of the analytic relationship, the example of the borderline diagnosis given at the end of Chapter 4 could also be cited here.

On closer inspection, there is no declaration of war on interpreting here, as in Boss, but on the analyst's interpretative sovereignty. Therefore interpreting is not to be replaced by 'a simple looking at the essence' either, which is after all exercised just as one-sidedly by the analyst as interpreting, but by dialogue. This raises another question, which can be formulated as: can intersubjective understanding achieve the same as interpreting? Or: can an intersubjective understanding between patient and analyst not be just as successful as and perhaps even more successful than discovering the hidden meaning in mental suffering?

This question must be pursued here because *Stolorow's* group led by *Donna Orange* has made recourse to *Hans-Georg Gadamer's* hermeneutics in this connection. She puts forward the hypothesis that Gadamer's hermeneutics can serve as a hermeneutic foundation for intersubjective psychoanalysis because this involves a *hermeneutics of conversation*.[113] Now Gadamer's hermeneutics is based on Heidegger's analysis of existential understanding in *Being and Time* as well as on his later understanding of language. Gadamer is therefore considered to belong to the inner circle of Heidegger's students. This is reason enough to examine this proposal here. The two above questions should therefore be considered in relation to Gadamer's hermeneutics, so that it is now a question as to whether Gadameris actually offering a dialogical hermeneutics that supersedes the analyst's interpreting.

To understand by reaching an understanding through conversation

The title *Truth and Method* already gives some indication of the purpose of Gadamer's hermeneutics: it seeks to reveal the illusory nature of the hope that goes back to *Wilhelm Dilthey* that 'understanding' can be developed into a 'scientific method' that has an equivalent status to 'scientific explanation' and to show that even professional interpreting is always temporally conditioned because the interpreter exists inside a tradition from which he cannot diverge even if he reflects on it critically.

---

[113] Hans-Georg Gadamer: *Truth and Method* (henceforth TM); Stolorow et al, 2002, loc. cit.; Orange, 2010.

With the false ideal of a methodologically established and
therefore 'objective' understanding as method, Gadamer contrasts
understanding as reaching an understanding with the text. He
refers to the interpreter having to enter into dialogue with a text
or generally with the tradition. To demonstrate how this has to take
place, Gadamer uses the model of the 'living' conversation between
two people. It is these passages in particular that are enthusiastically
taken up in the intersubjective psychoanalysis of Stolorow and Orange
because they rely on the dialogical nature of understanding. In these
Gadamer discounts the possibility of an unprejudiced understanding
on the model 'I can understand you as you are'. That is not possible
merely because all understanding is conditioned by prejudices that are
inevitably projected on to the other. Understanding the other requires
entering into dialogue with him and reaching an understanding
about him together. In such a conversation neither party can claim
the prerogative but each must listen to the other and also allow
himself to be challenged by the other (cf. *TM*, p. 383). To illustrate the
common nature of understanding, Gadamer referred to a 'real fusing
of horizons' of the respective conversational partners (*TM*, p. 307).
This 'fusion' allows an expansion of the horizon of understanding of
participants in a successful conversation, so that neither remains the
same after the conversation as before it.

All this appears to confirm the intersubjective criticism not only
of the practice of interpretation but generally of the conversational
form of orthodox psychoanalysis. Confirmed above all is that the
analyst cannot and may not claim for his own insight-perspective
any precedence over that of the patient because it too is necessarily
laden with prejudice; an understanding of the patient's problems only
becomes possible by reaching an understanding with him in which
the analyst also reveals himself personally instead of hiding behind
the mask of abstinence; and the analytic process is a shared process of
understanding from which not only the patient but also the analyst
emerges changed.

Yet this astounding agreement should not yet allow us to
conclude that it is legitimate to invoke Gadamer's hermeneutics
against the psychoanalytic hermeneutics that is based on Freud's three
anti-rules as well as the concept of interpretation. This is determined

not by these individual points of agreement but by the entire concept of Gadamer's hermeneutics. And this is characterised by being a textual hermeneutics.

Understanding as dialogue with the text

It is questionable first whether Gadamer would have concurred with the proposal to replace the psychoanalytic model of conversation with the model of the 'hermeneutic conversation'. For him in fact both the therapeutic and the educational conversation need their own rules in order to fulfil their specific functions.[114] More important, however, is the factual question of whether his dialogically conceived understanding can in fact be invoked against psychoanalytic interpreting. Gadamer demonstrates that interpreting is not a method that can be taught and learnt and that it also cannot claim any objective validity; yet it does not necessarily follow that interpreting can be replaced by a dialogical process of understanding in Gadamer's sense.

My preliminary objection to this is that Gadamer's hermeneutics cannot be introduced into psychoanalysis because it constitutes a textual hermeneutics, while psychoanalysis deals not with texts but with subjects who are suffering in themselves. On closer examination, Gadamer does not actually present a hermeneutics of conversation, as Donna Orange in particular repeatedly emphasises, but merely adduces 'the model of conversation between two persons' (*TM*, p. 386) so as to be able to conceive textual understanding as a dialogical rather than a monadological process. According to Gadamer, the interpreter should refer to the text to be understood *as if* it were a 'thou', a living partner in conversation. Gadamer himself knows very well that the text only has the characteristics of a 'thou' to a very limited extent: 'It is true that a text dos not speak to us in the same way as does a Thou. We who are attempting to understand must ourselves make it speak' (*TM*, p. 385). The fact that a text does not speak to us spontaneously but we interpreters have to make it speak undoubtedly creates new problems for his interpretation, but at the same time it removes all

---

[114] Cf. Gadamer's observations on the role that hermeneutics has to play in the context of a psychoanalysis in: 'Rhetoric, hermeneutics, and ideology-critique' (1997) and 'Hermeneutics and psychiatry' (1996).

the problems that make personal conversation between two people
difficult, to say nothing of the problems that begin when it concerns
the hidden meaning of their suffering in therapeutic conversations
with people who are suffering mentally.

It could be pointed out in favour of the project to introduce
Gadamer's hermeneutics into psychoanalysis that textual understanding
is ambiguous and can also entail seeking to discover the author's intended
meaning. If in referring to the dialogue with the text Gadamer had
in view above all the dialogue with its author, the difference from the
therapeutic conversation would actually be rather smaller, even though
the author of a historical text can only ever be a fictional conversational
partner. But Gadamer clearly argues against this variation of textual
understanding: his hermeneutics seeks specifically not to reconstruct
the author's intended meaning but to capture the meaning of the text
itself because 'the sense of a text reaches far beyond what its author
originally intended' (*TM*, p. 380). Gadamer is therefore concerned
with a pure textual hermeneutics and it is highly questionable whether
a hermeneutics specifically aimed not at the 'subjective, intended
meaning' but the meaning expressed in the text itself is a suitable
methodological basis for the psychoanalytic conversation.

Because Gadamer is concerned only with dialogue with texts, his
reflections on the conversation between I and thou are comparatively
sparse because he is concerned only with what can also be applied
to conversation with texts. So he assumes for example from the
outset that the conversational partners reach an understanding on
a particular matter (cf. *TM*, p. 375; p. 386). Conversations between
friends in which intimate personal things are confided are not allowed
for at all precisely because they are not a suitable 'model' for a dialogue
with texts. But these would be far closer to an analytic conversation
than conversations in which it is a matter of being 'conducted by
the subject matter' (*ibid*) so that the better argument (!) can prevail.

So on closer inspection Gadamer's analysis of conversation only
contains two considerations that have any relevance to the analytic-
therapeutic conversation: first, that the play of question and answer
between conversational partners follows a logic of its own to which both
must surrender without seeking to manipulate it in their own interests;
second, the consideration that a successful conversation generally takes

a course that cannot be anticipated by either of the two conversational partners, so that 'the partners conversing are far less the leaders of it than the led' (*TM*, p. 401) and therefore also 'something emerges that is contained in neither of the partners by himself' (*TM*, p. 438).

Gadamer emphasises that one merit of his textual hermeneutics is its universal applicability. Not only historical events but also economic and social relations, as well as intellectual developments, can and must be read as texts because their meaning cannot be ascribed to the intentions of actors (of politicians, military commanders, financial magnates, philosophers or artists) but has become autonomous. Yet this merit of a universal scope also constitutes the weakness of this hermeneutics. In relation to people, subjective-intentional, i.e. consciously or unconsciously intended meaning is reduced to mere textual meaning. It is only because Stolorow's group neglects this difference between subjectively intended meaning and pure textual meaning that it can argue for the introduction of Gadamer's hermeneutics into psychoanalysis. For only then does it appear unproblematic to conceive of everything that is to be understood in a psychoanalytic therapy as 'text': 'For the text" [in Gadamer we may substitute the patient's history, the patient's suffering, a misunderstanding between patient and analyst, or the heating or cooling system in the analyst's office' (Stolorow et al., 2002, p. 114).

This is a perplexing sentence because anyone who is convinced that the 'patient's suffering' poses the same problems of understanding as 'the heating system in the office' has departed from Freud's conception of a hidden meaning in mental suffering. It cannot be overemphasised that for Freud a subjectively intended meaning is concealed in the symptoms of suffering and that interpreting seeks to discover this meaning.[115] As soon as it is assumed that everything that the patient refers to in the conversation, whether it is his own suffering or the heating in the consulting room, can be understood as a text in Gadamer's sense, interpreting becomes superfluous because here the suffering is understood only as a 'blind spot' but no longer as a suffering from one's own being.

---

[115] Cf. Freud: 'In most of our researches we can replace "sense" by "intention" or "purpose"'. (1916–17, p. 40).

It is no coincidence that the title of Donna Orange's book published in 2010, *Thinking for Clinicians. Philosophical Resources for Contemporary Psychoanalysis and the Humanistic Psychotherapies*, refers to psychoanalysis and humanistic psychotherapy in the same breath. As soon as a psychoanalyst reads mental suffering like a 'text' and thereby negates the key part of Freud's discovery, he approaches humanistic psychology and its positive, if not naïvely optimistic image of the human being. It is precisely this positive image of the human being that knows neither irresoluble inner conflicts nor 'anxiety' in Kierkegaard's and Heidegger's sense that is also found by Donna Orange in Gadamer's hermeneutics, which she therefore describes as a 'hermeneutics of trust' and pits against Freud's hermeneutics, which the French philosopher *Paul Ricoeur* had termed a 'hermeneutics of suspicion' (1970). Although it is strictly meaningless to describe textual hermeneutics as a hermeneutics of trust because the question of whether something can be trusted is faced only with people rather than texts, Orange nevertheless indicates here a characteristic of Gadamer's hermeneutics that distinguishes it not only from Freud's hermeneutics but also from those of his teacher Heidegger.

From Gadamer back to Heidegger

The arguments presented so far against the proposal of orientating psychoanalytic practice towards Gadamer's hermeneutics also apply to daseinsanalytic practice, and in spite of their common philosophical roots in Heidegger's daseinsanalytics of *Being and Time*. In fact on closer examination of where Gadamer does and does not concur with Heidegger, there turns out to be yet another objection to an orientation to this hermeneutics.

This second objection concerns Gadamer's entire one-sided reception of Heidegger's existential-hermeneutical approach. Gadamer in fact refers only to sections 31 and 32 of *Being and Time* concerning 'understanding' and 'interpretation' and excludes section 30 on 'attunement'. He makes no mention of Heidegger's discovery that 'attunement' has an equal status to 'understanding' and represents its own source of knowledge independently of understanding (cf. *BT*, p. 126). This has huge implications for hermeneutics and for the image of the human being intrinsic to this hermeneutics. For it makes the human being's *relationship* with the world and himself identical with his *understanding* of the world and himself. All that remains in Gadamer of Heidegger's restriction of understanding by moods is a general emphasis on historical contingency and the finitude of all human understanding; what remains unnoticed though is Heidegger's discovery that the human being's own being is disclosed originally not in understanding but in *moods* and unconcealed only in the mood of anxiety.

Although Gadamer's hermeneutics is greatly indebted to Heidegger, it is nevertheless separated by a gulf from his approach. For whereas Heidegger's hermeneutics assumes 'anxiety' as the basic experience in which our own being is disclosed to existence *in its pure facticity*, Gadamer's hermeneutics makes no reference to emotional experiences of being. Now it might be objected in favour of Gadamer that this does not have to constitute a deficiency for textual hermeneutics because texts are not people and therefore have no relationship to their own being. This argument is invalid though because this concerns the interpreter. Nowhere does Gadamer reflect on the interpreter's attunement to the text, nowhere does he ask what kind of emotional experiences the interpreter undergoes when he opens himself to an unknown text. There is no consideration of the role that existential moods of anxiety, guilt and shame, including the resistance to them, can assume in the interpreter's dialogue with the text.

In conclusion, there are two good reasons why daseinsanalysis should not be orientated by Gadamer's hermeneutics: first, because it is a textual hermeneutics that can give no guidance as to how unconsciously intended meaning is to be discovered and interpreted in psychoanalytic practice and, second, because it concerns a hermeneutics that absolutises understanding instead of relating it to emotional experiences that are inaccessible to understanding, namely experiences of the meaning-less '*that it* [dasein] is and has to be' (cf. *BT*, p. 127).

5.2 Characteristics of daseinsanalytic interpretation

Proceeding from the recognition that intepreting is as indispensable to daseinsanalysis as to psychoanalysis, an enquiry should now be made into what characterises daseinsanalytic interpretation. This suggests a comparison should be made with psychoanalytic interpretation. For although there have been various approaches to psychoanalytic interpretation that have to some extent moved far away from Freud, what still remains as their common factor is that they only address the disparity between conscious and unconscious or present and past (childhood) experiences. The difference between ontical and ontological experiences is still neglected. But this specific difference is at the centre of daseinsanalytic interpretations because these assume that emotional *experiences of being* are at work in mental suffering that need to be discovered by interpreting.

Interpreting as indicating hidden experiences of being

The reference to experiences of being not only determines the content of daseinsanalytic interpretations but also characterises their form. There are four identifiable points that also differentiate these from a psychoanalytic interpretation. They are first listed here and then elucidated by Freud's 'stocking phobia' example, already adduced several times:

> 1. The daseinsanalytic interpretation operates in a different interpretative horizon from the psychoanalytic one; 2. It discovers a different truth; 3. It remains necessarily incomplete; 4. It is phenomenological in nature.

On 1. A different horizon of interpretation

Because daseinsanalysis defines mental suffering not as a 'suffering from reminiscences', but as a 'suffering from our own being', it has a different horizon of interpretation. Whereas the psychoanalytic interpretation remains within the horizon of life-historical experiences, the daseinsanalytic interpretation also operates in the horizon of ontological experiences. With the example of the stocking phobia: Freud interprets the phobic fear of the holes in the stocking as a *fear with a displaced content*, which in reality refers to the female sexual opening; daseinsanalysis though interprets the same fear as concealed *anxiety*, in which the phobic is confronted with the lacunary nature of his own being. For psychoanalysis this is also a *temporally displaced fear*, since this actually belongs to a past time, namely the early infantile oedipal phase of the now adult man. With its re-emergence as a stocking phobia, a piece of the past replaces the present without this being recognised. It is therefore essential for the psychoanalytic interpretation that it operates in a temporal horizon that encompasses both present and the (repressed) early infantile past. It is also critical that this temporal horizon is simultaneously a *horizon of meaning* because the revived early infantile experiences exist in ontical contexts of meaning.

The horizon in which a daseinsanalytic interpretation operates is neither a temporal one nor a horizon of meaning, although even a daseinsanalytic interpretation refers to ontically meaningful experiences from childhood or from the present. This is because a daseinsanalytic interpretation relates all these ontically meaningful experiences to ontological experiences of 'that I am and have to be'. The horizon in which the daseinsanalytic interpretation operates is therefore not simply broader than the psychoanalytic one; it is no longer a horizon of meaning but transcends this so that senseless ontological experiences can also be accommodated. Literally this means that inadequate emotional reactions such as the present stocking phobia are not interpreted by going back to specific childhood experiences but by going back to 'anxiety' or to what the patient experiences in anxiety, namely the lacunary nature of human existing as a senseless fact. It is important for a daseinsanalytic interpretation that anxiety as an original experience of being forms the last reference point that can no longer be integrated into any context of meaning. Threatening childhood experiences can certainly *trigger* anxiety but never *produce* it. The fact that on the occasion of a specific threat *anxiety* (instead of only fear) is experienced always has its basis in a special *sensitivity* to the immutable and also uncanny facts of the human condition.

On 2. A different truth

Psychoanalytic interpretation proceeds from the recognition that
a *truth* is concealed in neurotic symptoms. But this is a *historical*
truth that is no longer valid under the conditions of adulthood. The
example of the stocking phobia makes this clear: what could still
appear to the small boy as a real danger, namely the discovery of
sexual difference and the woman's lack of a penis, no longer represents
any real threat to the adult man. From a daseinsanalytic viewpoint
though, the truth enacted in the symptom is timeless, which is why
the phobic fear of putting on stockings is inappropriate because it is
actually a harmless matter and yet it contains a *timelessly valid* truth
that always makes the human being anxious.

Psychoanalytic and daseinsanalytic interpretations therefore
have different points of emphasis: in a psychoanalytic interpretation,
fear certainly has a true historical core because it was justified and
therefore also appropriate as an infantile fear but is now baseless
and lives on as an unreal fear as long as the patient confuses past
and present. It is therefore an important task of the psychoanalytic
interpretation to draw the patient's attention to the disparity between
historical–infantile and adult truth. This also contains the positive
message for the patient that the fear that holds him so captive is not
only conquerable but dissolves spontaneously when he recognises
that it actually belongs to early childhood (Freud, 1938, p. 185). A
daseinsanalytic interpretation works differently: it indicates to the
patient that the manifestly meaningless fear of putting on stockings
arises from his realising anew a truth from the stockings every day,
which is and remains anxiety-inducing. In fact it also draws the
patient's attention to a confusion, namely to the confusion between
ontological and ontical experience and it interprets the phobic fear
as ontically misinterpreted existential anxiety. This interpretation also
contains a positive message, since it promises that the unreal fear
will dissolve if the patient is able and willing to distinguish between
the ontical specific threat and the ontological one. This message is,
however, simultaneously a negative one because it also reveals the
wish to be freed from the anxiety as an illusion. A daseinsanalytic
interpretation therefore contains the implicit challenge to the patient

to confront what he is sensitive to—in the case of the stocking phobia the lacunary nature of the world and self—and to recognise the *truth*, although it induces anxiety.

On 3. Its inconcludability

Because the daseinsanalytic interpretation refers to experiences of being, it remains incomplete in comparison with a psychoanalytic interpretation in a specific way. For experiences of being can only be *indicated*, without any 'meaning' yet being discernible in these experiences. Returning to the stocking phobia example: a psychoanalytic interpretation is concluded and complete because it understands the fear of the stocking as a repetition of the boy's childhood fear of the maternal vagina, which is forbidden under the threat of castration. A psychoanalytic interpretation is always simultaneously an interpretation of *meaning* because it manages to integrate the manifestly nonsensical fear into a meaningful context (that of childhood sexuality and its accompanying temptations and dangers), in which it becomes comprehensible as a *meaningful reaction*. That is something a daseinsanalytic interpretation cannot achieve because it does not relate the current fear of the stocking to another, again specific, fear albeit in the past but to the person's anxiety about his own being and about the wish to escape its lacunary nature. But this experience of anxiety unlike childhood apprehensions can no longer be located in a meaningful context and therefore a daseinsanalytic interpretation must limit itself to indicating what may certainly be experienced emotionally but eludes every interpretation in its pure facticity.

The specifically daseinsanalytic interpretation is therefore indicative in nature because what it discovers would be obscured again by a meaning-based interpretation. Certainly there are numerous ontological *meaning-based* interpretations of human existing and its constitutive conditions. But such interpretations are always based on philosophical or religious convictions as to a foundational and therefore unquestionable meaningfulness of human existing. Daseinsanalysis is as far removed from this as psychoanalysis. Freud had already discovered the 'analytic' understanding that discovers and interprets 'motives', distinguished it from 'synthetic' understanding and emphasised that the psychoanalyst has to be content with the former (Freud, 1919, p. 158ff). The reason why even existential-philosophical theories are not on the agenda of a daseinsanalytic psychotherapy has already been explained in Chapter 4.1.

On 4. Its phenomenological nature

Heidegger's existential hermeneutics does not spring only from phenomenology but remains indebted to the phenomenological formulation that interpretations must be designable to the directly given phenomena. That also applies to the daseinsanalytic interpretation of symptoms of mental suffering. Whereas the psychoanalytic interpretation generally moves far away from the patient's communicated experiences, the daseinsanalytic interpretation always remains related to them. This fidelity to phenomena in the daseinsanalytic interpretation results, however, not from a dutiful compliance with the phenomenological formulation but follows from the recognition that the patient is especially sensitive to the ontological truth that is hidden *in* the concrete phenomena. What follows from this for the ontological interpretation is the instruction to seek the hidden meaning *in* the directly manifest phenomena themselves—in the case of the stocking phobia in the fear of the small holes in the stocking fabric—because the patient has a direct experience of the unfathomability of human being in these specific phenomena. For the psychoanalytic interpretation, though, the stocking becomes a purely arbitrary substitution for an entirely different, much more meaningful object, namely the maternal vagina.

The fact that the step from conscious panic-stricken fear of the small holes in the stocking fabric to unconscious anxiety about the 'lacunary' nature of his own human being requires fewer intellectual acrobatics of a patient than the step from conscious fear to the repressed infantile fear of the woman's 'hole' is certainly not the reason why the daseinsanalytic interpretation adheres more closely to phenomena but rather a positive effect. For interpretations that refer to what the patient is directly suffering from are in less danger of seeming authoritarian and merely being obediently swallowed by the patient.

Interpreting as opening up the ontical–ontological difference

It would be a misunderstanding to conceive the above explanations of the daseinsanalytic interpretation using Freud's stocking phobia example as a specific instruction as to *how and what* should be daseinsanalytically interpreted. There is no model of a typically daseinsanalytic interpretation because the form of an interpretation depends on the current therapeutic situation: on the particular patient, on the current course of the analysis, on the present transference and countertransference relationship and not least on the analyst as a person.

It seems important now to differentiate between two kinds of interpretation in terms of content, for which the stocking phobia can again serve as an example: one consists as already mentioned in *indicating the anxiety-inducing truth of being* to which the patient is defencelessly exposed by his sensitivity, here the immutably lacunary nature of human existing; the other consists in *interpreting the acting-out in his struggle with anxiety*. The quintessence of this interpretation lies in pointing out that the patient's belief that the anxiety about the lacunary nature of his own being can be overcome by taking measures against the fear of the small holes in the stocking fabric is an illusion.

Both interpretations draw attention to the ontical–ontological difference that is always denied in mental suffering. Therefore I would like to conclude by considering this important if not determining factor in every daseinsanalytic interpretation. It is evident that the psychoanalytic and daseinsanalytic interpretation converge here insofar as the psychoanalytic interpretation always also aims at opening up a difference, namely the *difference between then and now* as two temporal dimensions that in the patient are (still) inextricably confused. Similarly a daseinsanalytic interpretation always seeks to open up the *difference between ontical-concrete and ontological experiences* that are confused by the patient.

I will next be considering only interpretations that explicitly refer to the patient's active negation of the ontical–ontological difference and discover its hidden meaning. As this negation of the difference manifests itself in three ways, three variants of interpretations ensue that build on each other: 1) the discovery of the patient's tendency to absolutise ontical events erroneously; 2) the discovery of his tendency to connect the absolutised ontical occurrences with illusory expectations; 3) the interpretation of a hidden intention in denying the ontical–ontological difference.

- On 1) As a first step, the analyst can point out to the patient that it is strange that despite his intelligence he constantly generalises and absolutises isolated incidents. To give a few examples: 'I find it surprising that for you the fact of having done *something* wrong becomes evidence that you *always do everything* wrong' or: 'it seems to follow for you from the fact that your father did not take your childhood wishes seriously then that *you yourself* may also not allow yourself any wishes of your own now'; or: 'whereas others feel guilty when they have done *something unjust*, with you guilt feelings arise when you merely *undertake activity yourself*' and so on.

- On 2) As a second step, the analyst can indicate to the patient the illusory expectations that are connected with the absolutised concrete events: 'No wonder you feel an ordinary misfortune is as bad as a crime if you want to go through life totally free of guilt'; or: 'How can you do anything other than postpone this decision if you require an absolute guarantee that you will never regret it'; or: 'of course you have always to be the best if you may only claim a place in this world by the highest achievements'; or: 'it's understandable that you may not forget the slight inflicted on you and must demand satisfaction for it if you hold an aspiration to be able to order the other person how to behave towards you'.

- On 3) The references to the exaggeration of specific incidents and the illusory expectations associated with them already contain what can be thematised explicitly as a third step, namely the patient's hidden interest in mistaking ontological experiences for ontical ones *in order* not to have to abandon illusory expectations concerning his own being. As this is a hypothesis, it is best formulated as a question: 'Do you believe perhaps that you can buy yourself a right to live if you do everything right by everyone?'; or: 'Do you hope then to be able to eliminate the uncertainty factor from your life by trying to keep everything under control?' or: 'Does it seem to you possible to remain free of any possible guilt by flawless behaviour?'

The third step in particular confronts the patient with a necessary renunciation—namely renouncing the illusory wish to intervene in conditions of being by acting out and to be able to remove their negativity. Recognising the ontological difference therefore always involves a painful dis-illusionment. What motivates the patient to accept this disillusionment, what makes him willing to differentiate between the ontical and ontological dimensions, to distinguish between (fundamentally conquerable) fear and anxiety and to take on the immutable truth about his own being? These questions lead on to the concluding chapter, which will discuss whether the patient is able and also willing to take on the negative truth about his own being.

6

How much truth can the sensitive patient tolerate?

n the five preceding chapters, therapeutic conclusions were drawn from the daseinsanalytic view of mental suffering as a suffering from our own being. Binswanger's formulation that daseinsanalytic therapy is a 'psychoanalysis from daseinsanalytic perspectives' has been unfolded step by step. Psychoanalysis is concerned with truth: Freud has aptly described analysis as 'educating himself to the truth about himself' (1916–17, p. 433). However, the question of whether the *ontological truth* from which the patient is suffering is also tolerable for him has not yet been raised. This will be considered in this concluding chapter because unless this question is tackled it remains open whether daseinsanalysis with its psychoanalytically based understanding of therapy may not overtax the patient. Should it prove that the ontological truths to which he is involuntarily exposed by his sensitivity are not at all tolerable for the mentally suffering patient, there would be no justification for the concept of daseinsanalytic therapy proposed here.

To examine this question, it must as a *first step* be explained why daseinsanalysis despite its proximity to psychoanalysis must define the therapeutic goal differently, which is because of the specifically daseinsanalytic linkage of mental suffering with a special sensitivity to ontological truths. It is debatable whether this different therapeutic goal can nevertheless remain an 'analytic' one in Freud's sense or not. As a *second step* an alternative therapeutic goal is therefore contemplated that would change the therapeutic alliance of daseinsanalysis: from psychoanalysis with its hermeneutic method of discovery towards cognitive behavioural therapy or a therapy that involves a positive quest for meaning. Specifically this would either directly involve an ontological desensitisation or an education towards a positive attitude to life based on creating meaning that immunises against the sensitivity.

This alternative therapeutic goal seems at first sight to have the advantage that it is directed against what *causes* the mental suffering, namely the sensitivity. Yet is such a therapeutic goal compatible with how daseinsanalysis views itself? The answer is definitely not because it would mean that an advantage the patient has over the healthy average of the population, namely being especially sensitive to ontological truth, would be evaluated as a pathological one that therefore has either to be eliminated or concealed. The only choice therefore left to daseinsanalysis is either to remain a 'psychoanalysis from daseinsanalytic perspectives' and credit the patient with the truth or to abandon any therapeutic offering of its own. As a *third step*, the existential understanding of anxiety of Kierkegaard and Heidegger is re-examined in terms of this specific question. Only Heidegger's suggestion that anxiety has a paradoxical structure opens the way to a specifically daseinsanalytic formulation of the therapeutic goal that relies on the concept of philosophical experience.

6.1 Is the patient able and willing to tolerate the ontological truth?

The question of whether the truth is tolerable for the patient arises only for daseinsanalysis and not for psychoanalysis. Why? For Freud, mental suffering begins with *repression*: the child represses the wishes that are incompatible with familiar reality and therefore endanger it. The child can only overcome this danger by repressing the wishes. When Freud refers to neurotic suffering 'from reminiscences', he means first and foremost the repressed childhood wishes that have become inaccessible to memory. For daseinsanalysis though, mental suffering begins not with a repression of a person's childhood wishes but with a special sensitivity to the fundamental truths that concern his human being.

This difference must be reflected in the therapeutic goal. For linking mental suffering with the repression of childhood events gives rise to a different therapeutic task from assuming it to result from an absence of the (normal) repression of truths about being and an excess of (ontological) experiences.[116]

The fact that a psychoanalytic therapy involves regaining a truth that has become inaccessible to the patient because of repression is expressed by Freud with three well-known formulations of the therapeutic goal: making the unconscious conscious, recollection of the repressed, remembering instead of acting out (1914, pp. 145–156). The question of whether this truth is appropriate to the patient does not arise here because it is after all a truth of *that time*, with which the patient is credited *today* under entirely different conditions. If the patient nevertheless resists remembering, it is because he deceives himself and believes that this long obsolete threat still exists.

It is different when daseinsanalysis assumes that the patient is sensitive to truths that never become obsolete and therefore also create anxiety throughout life. Here the question of whether these truths are tolerable for the patient must be elucidated. The argument that it can still be left to the individual patient to decide for himself whether and how much truth he wants to take on avoids the problem because this concerns not only an assessment of the treatment suitable for this patient but whether daseinsanalysis can and should fundamentally be orientated towards recognising and accepting ontological truths.

However, there are two serious objections to this. The first relates to the mentally healthy majority of the population that according to the daseinsanalytic view is free of mental suffering precisely because it can successfully repress or trivialise ontological truths in the daily conduct of life. The second relates to the patient who suffers because he cannot tolerate the truths that impose themselves on him because of his sensitivity and therefore struggles despairingly against them.

Both these objections suggest a different therapeutic goal, namely to transmit to the sensitive patient the capacity for forgetting

---

[116] Heidegger does not refer to 'repression', but the 'forgetting' of our own being that he describes also has a volitional quality and can therefore definitely be described as repression. That is shown for instance by the following sentence: 'In order to be able to "really" get to work "lost" in the world of tools and to handle them, the self must forget itself" (*BT*, p. 324).

or art of forgetting that would remove the basis for his suffering. Now there are two therapeutic approaches that offer that, albeit under a different name, and can therefore be conceived as alternatives to a 'psychoanalysis from daseinsanalytic perspectives': behavioural therapeutic desensitisation and logotherapy, which specialises in discovering meaning. With both, the question that arises is whether they are reconcilable with the daseinsanalytic image of the human being and understanding of suffering.

6.2 Desensitisation and discovery of meaning as therapeutic alternatives?

For both these therapeutic alternatives, *sensitivity* would be the object of the treatment, and the goal would be to reduce if not eliminate this or to immunise the patient against it. The means of achieving this objective would be targeted strategic interventions. Both forms of therapy are based on the current notion that a psychotherapy should help the patient towards a life free of mental symptoms and also to greater inner contentment and equilibrium.

The first form of therapy would seek the greatest possible reduction of the sensitivity and would be classified among the cognitive behavioural therapies. For this the procedure of '*desensitisation*' practised there would be available. What it would mean to proceed specifically to achieve a desensitisation of ontological sensitivity in daseinsanalytic terms I can only speculate. It is possible to imagine using mental exercises to limit attentiveness to the concrete-ontical 'here and now' and leave unconsidered all the associations and emotions that go beyond it. This would include corresponding concentration exercises, indeed even the 'mindfulness training' that is so highly praised today, which consistently guide the patient to screen out ontological inclusions.

This ontological desensitisation therapy would be the exact counterpart to the philosophical therapy already discussed and rejected as impractical in Chapter 4.1. While this entailed entering a philosophical conversation with the patient about that to which he is especially sensitive, this would involve using mental techniques to eliminate his reluctant philosophising and protect him from the intrusions of ontological anxiety, guilt and shame.

The same goal of desensitisation could also be achieved in another way, namely by a targeted discovery of meaning. This would be based on the conviction that the supposed sensitivity only arises because a person has lost or never yet found a meaning in life.[117] The patient should therefore become capable of orientating his life towards a *positive meaning*. It is obvious that the concept of meaning used here is not meant in a hermeneutic sense but in terms of practical living: here the patient lacks confidence that life ultimately has a meaning and it is only a matter of being open to this to lead a life that he himself can experience as *meaningful*. Accordingly, a therapy would entail finding the way to a new attitude to life based on a fundamental confidence in meaning.

Unlike a desensitisation therapy, in a therapy based on discovering meaning sensitivity would be combatted only indirectly. The conviction that everything has a meaning would operate here as a *protective shield* against sensitivity or, to put it another way: the belief in meaning would increase the *immunity* towards experiences of meaning*less* facticity and make it more difficult for anxiety to emerge.

Arguments for and against

-   *In favour of a therapy based on ontological desensitisation*
    there is the medical–ethical argument that this is a direct
    and therefore more efficient alleviation of suffering,
    which is reinforced by the economic argument that the
    therapy is shorter in duration and therefore saves costs
    in time and money.[118]

-   *In favour of a therapy based on finding meaning* it can be
    argued that those suffering mentally are lacking an
    existentiell foothold and orientation and that this form
    of therapy would enable them to gain both without

---

[117] This is represented above all by Viktor Frankl's logotherapy, which in the further development by Alfried Längle took on the name existential analysis (*Existenzanalyse*). Despite this name, which suggests a philosophical kinship, existential analysis and daseinsanalysis have little in common because existential analysis is not a hermeneutical-psychoanalytic movement and also does not set out to be, but is classified as a humanistic psychotherapy.

[118] The same arguments can apply to the use of psychotropic drugs, which achieve the same goal of a desensitisation by biochemical methods.

a specific world view being simultaneously imposed
on them. This appears an important advantage that
distinguishes this form of therapy from religious and
pseudo-religious offerings based on finding meaning.
Here the patient is to find his own meaning that appears
suited to him individually, which is well expressed with
the concept of 'authenticity'.

I am not arguing against these two forms of therapy as such but
only against assimilating them into daseinsanalysis and bringing
daseinsanalysis closer therapeutically either to cognitive behavioural
therapy or to logotherapy.

- *Against a daseinsanalytic-ontological desensitisation therapy* is
the argument that sensitivity is explained as a deficiency
to be remedied with mental techniques. This would
remove the patient's advantage over the mentally healthy
average, namely a special openness to his own being.
This greater openness would be sacrificed to help the
patient towards a better social adaptation and to greater
inner contentment.

- *Against a daseinsanalytic therapy based on finding meaning*
it can be argued that ontological experiences of the
meaning-less 'that I am and have to be' to which the
patient is subjected by his sensitivity would be explained
as untrue. While no specific meaning would ideally
be imposed on the patient, the conviction that human
being is fundamentally supported by a meaning and
therefore every opposite experience is pathological in
nature probably would be.

If daseinsanalysis does not want to become cynical, it can adopt neither
of these forms of therapy. For it would be cynical to impoverish the
patient by removing a special sensitivity that belongs to him in full
knowledge that this sensitivity is also a distinguishing characteristic.
Likewise, it would be cynical to suggest to the patient that his
philosophical experiences are mere illusions to which he is enslaved

because he has lacked a meaningful reference—again in full knowledge that these anxiety-inducing experiences convey a truth of being.

Daseinsanalysis would lose credibility by adopting either of these therapeutic offerings because it would knowingly mislead the patient as to the purpose of lessening his suffering and increasing his social adaptation and inner contentment. It would inculcate in him convictions that it does not hold but considers to be therapeutically effective.

Two statements by Freud accord with these considerations. They concern the kind of relationship the psychoanalyst should have with the patient's suffering on the one hand, and with the truth on the other: 'Cruel though it may sound, we must see to it that the patient's suffering, to a degree that is in some way or other effective, does not come to an end prematurely' (1919, p. 162) and 'finally we must not forget that the analytic relationship is based on a love of truth—that is, on a recognition of reality—and that it precludes any kind of sham or deceit' (1937b, p. 247).

6.3 The paradoxical structure of anxiety

The only choice that therefore remains open to daseinsanalysis, if it is to remain true to itself, is either to adopt Freud's conception of therapeutic analysis as 'educating himself to the truth about himself' or to abandon any therapeutic offering of its own. If it does not want to renounce it, then it must be able to justify why it believes that to mentally suffering people not only their individual historical truth but also the ontological truth about the 'nullity' of their own human being is fundamentally tolerable for them.[119] Can it be justified at all? Until now it has seemed difficult to find a plausible reason for this—perhaps because it lies where is least suspected, namely in anxiety itself. Kierkegaard indicated that anxiety is an inherently contradictory force and in connection with this Heidegger was able to show *why* the human being is both repelled and attracted by the truth that anxiety reveals. Daseinsanalysis can therefore rely on the paradoxical effect of anxiety on the human being if it

---

[119] This is distinct from the question of the *individual* appropriateness, which depends both on the respective circumstances and on the patient's capacity and readiness for it.

undertakes a 'psychoanalysis from daseinsanalytic perspectives' with the sensitive patient.

Kierkegaard captures the contradiction in the formulation that anxiety is 'a *sympathetic antipathy and an antipathetic sympathy*' (1980, p. 42)—therefore an emotion we avoid and also want to seek out and experience because we are both attracted and repelled by it. That anxiety constitutes for the human being not only a negative, but also a positive force contains a mysterious paradox that according to Kierkegaard results in the human relationship to anxiety alternating between fleeing from it and being curiously drawn to it. For in anxiety the child is already said to experience freedom in the form of adventure and fairy tale, the world of monsters and mysteries. Yet is Kierkegaard referring here to something more than the particular fear that is termed a 'thrill' in the English language and which can be translated into German as 'Angstlust'?[120] Although Kierkegaard introduced the distinction between fear and anxiety and insisted that anxiety is profoundly different from fear (1980, p. 50), he does not make the difference at all clear. For our question, however, the reference to the 'thrill' or 'Angstlust' in the customary sense does not help any further because the fact that people consciously and voluntarily seek out *specific ontical* dangers to experience 'the thrill' does not actually mean that the human being is also drawn by 'anxiety' and is therefore ready to expose himself willingly to the danger that lies in his own being.

Only Heidegger manages to rediscover the paradox that was more intuited than truly recognised by Kierkegaard in the *structure* of anxiety: '*Angst* is not only *Angst* about..., but is at the same time, as attunement, *Angst* for ...' (*BT*, p. 175). What this means can only be shown by a comparison with fear. For it is obvious that fear is not only *fear about* but always at the same time *fear for*. The person who for example has fears *about* an illness has fears *for* his health, and that applies to all apprehensions because we only have fears *about* a *danger* as long as we at the same time have fears *for* the preservation of what is threatened by the danger, whether that is things or people and in the case of people ourselves or others. Therefore the person who has no *fears for his life* knows no dangers and is therefore free of any

---

[120] Cf. The title of Michael Balint's book: *Thrills and Regressions* (1959), which was translated as *Angstlust und Regression*.

fear. 'Having fears about' therefore has the meaning of 'concerned about': the person who has fears about an illness cares for his health; the person who has fears about family quarrels cares for peace and for harmony in the family—this commonality of fear about and fear for can therefore always be indicated.

Now Heidegger claims that the same applies to anxiety. And yet it is entirely different in the case of anxiety. With fear, that *about which* we fear and that *for which* we fear are always opposite in nature: illness here, health there, quarrels here, harmony there and so on. We always have fear about something negative that can cause damage and fears for something that is endangered and can be damaged. Therefore in every fear lies the hope that the negative thing can be averted, so that the positive thing for which we have fears can safely withstand the danger and remain intact.

Unlike fear, according to Heidegger, that about which we become anxious and that for which we become anxious are the same: 'That *about which Angst* is anxious reveals itself as that *for which* it is anxious: being-in-the-world' (*BT*, p. 176). This is initially hard to imagine and yet precisely here lies the paradoxical relationship to anxiety that was already indicated by Kierkegaard: we want to escape our own being because we have anxiety *about it* and we want to turn to our own being because we have anxiety *for it*. Anxiety therefore not only triggers a movement of flight but at the same time also a movement towards what is making us anxious. In other words, anxiety contains not only the wish to escape the danger that strikes us from our own being but also the wish to listen to what the anxiety discloses about what in truth it means to be a human being and to *concern* ourselves with this truth.

If however it so happens that the anxiety itself gives rise to a genuine *interest* in what it discloses, the daseinsanalytic therapy can assume that the truth is fundamentally *appropriate* to the sensitive patient and conversely the patient is also fundamentally *able to be motivated* for 'educating himself to truth about himself'. To the daseinsanalytic therapist the task then remains of awakening the interest in the truth of being that is dormant in the patient and keeping it alive—whether and how far that can succeed in the individual case also depends on individual and social factors that cannot always be influenced.

6.4 *Having* philosophical experiences in order to become philosophically experienced

If daseinsanalysis can be convinced that the truth about what it means to be a human being is appropriate to the patient who is sensitive to it, its final task is to formulate the therapeutic goal so that it is congruent with the philosophical meaning of mental suffering. For this the concept of experience presents itself in place of the psychoanalytic concept of memory—and more specifically the concept of the *philosophical experience*.[121] This already played an important role in the previous chapter, especially in relation to the analytic relationship (Chapter 4). Based on all the above explanations, the specifically daseinsanalytic therapeutic goal can only lie in having philosophical experiences and thereby becoming philosophically experienced. Yet what does it mean really to *have* an experience?

In his major work *Truth and Method*, Hans-Georg Gadamer gives an impressive phenomenological analysis of experience, from which I am drawing two important considerations (*TM*, p. 360ff.). *First* Gadamer distinguishes between the many experiences that confirm our earlier experiences and are therefore added to our expectations and the few experiences that disprove earlier experiences and teach us that something is not as we previously thought it to be. Only the latter experiences, which thwart our expectations, are according to Gadamer 'authentic' experiences because they are the only ones we really have to 'have'. Gadamer therefore suggests a distinction here between experiences that are not experiences at all in the strict sense because they only confirm earlier experiences, and experiences that disprove our previous opinion and therefore require us really to 'have' them. Only experiences that we *had* to have and also really have had result in our being more experienced afterwards than before. *Second*, Gadamer emphasises the fundamentally *negative* quality of every authentic experience. That is the case because every authentic experience 'always involves an escape from something that had deceived us and held us captive' (*TM*, p. 364f).

---

[121] I hope it is superfluous to point out that I am not referring here to the concept of the 'corrective emotional experience' that the psychoanalysts Alexander and French both emphasised in 1946 as the most important factor at work in a successful psychoanalysis.

With both considerations Gadamer questions current notions about how experience is gained and how someone becomes an experienced human being. For instance, no one can be considered 'experienced' merely because he is old and has seen and experienced a great deal. An old person is only 'experienced' if what he has experienced also *became an experience*, if he was willing to learn from experiences and if necessary to see through his cherished opinions as illusions. With his thesis that all authentic experiences are negative in nature, Gadamer also invalidates the current distinction between 'positive' and 'negative' experiences. For now unexpectedly a 'positive' experience is also negative if it contradicts negative expectations. Only this complication explains why many people refuse to believe in positive experiences as such but reinterpret them as negative ones. It is less threatening for them to hold on to the usual negative expectations than really to 'have' a positive experience and admit that something is not as they thought it to be.

For Gadamer an experienced person knows that he cannot become set on any one past experience but must remain open to the possibility of it being disproved at any time by a new experience. In scientific empirical research, this is the prevailing attitude because here progress consists by definition in knowledge going out of date and being superseded by new knowledge that is already known from the outset to be liable to be superseded in turn the very next day. Yet with personal experiences it is different. Here young people are referred to as still being inexperienced because they have not yet 'gathered' any experiences and accordingly a human being is called 'experienced' when he has a rich store of experiences available. For Gadamer though the truly experienced person is distinguished specifically by his knowing that 'he is master neither of time nor the future' (*TM*, p. 365) and that future experiences await him that may contradict all previous experiences. The person therefore who has truly become experienced will not insist on how experienced he is, will not proudly declare that as the saying goes *nihil humanum mihi alienum est* and that therefore nothing more in life can surprise him but he will constantly remain open to unexpected and surprising experiences in the knowledge that 'nothing returns' (*TM*, p. 365).

Gadamer does not explicitly distinguish between specific ontical experiences and experiences of being. He nevertheless emphasises that a specific experience that is truly 'had' is always simultaneously an experience of human finitude: 'Thus experience is the experience of human finitude' (*TM*, p. 357). But if a person really becomes aware of his finitude, he has had an experience of being. Through Gadamer's experiential analysis, it becomes possible to understand the goal of therapy daseinsanalytically as the goal of enabling the patient to 'have' the experiences of being to which he was previously involuntarily subjected by his sensitivity.

From Sisyphus to the philosophically experienced person

I have already twice made recourse to the mythical figure of *Sisyphus* (in Part III, Chapters 2.4 and 5.2). Now this figure becomes important again because it symbolises the person who repeatedly fails in carrying out his (ontological) intention and yet holds unswervingly to this goal and thus refuses really to 'have' the experience of the failure. The figure of Sisyphus epitomises what Freud discerned as the 'repetition compulsion' in mental suffering. I assume though that the patient is not merely subordinated to this 'compulsion' but adheres stubbornly to the unfulfillable wish to become free of human conditions of being by his 'acting out'.

If the patient really has a philosophical experience, he simultaneously experiences the failure of his previous 'acting out' because his mental suffering had the hidden meaning of changing what cannot be changed. Really to 'have' a philosophical experience involves the admission of its truth and its irreversibility. Therefore 'having' a philosophical experience also has a transformative power. It liberates from the temptation to further acting out.

The kind of philosophical experience the patient has to have mainly depends on that to which he is especially sensitive. But it always involves the experience of not being able to cross a boundary—and not on the basis of an individual incapacity but as a human being. For this limitation that belongs to human nature Heidegger uses the concept of 'nullity' and emphasises that this nullity may in no event be confused with a privation or a lack. Human *dasein*, Heidegger repeatedly emphasises, does not suffer from a lack, for his being although 'thoroughly permeated with nullity' (*BT*, p. 263) is in no way deficient in the usual sense. Although this sounds paradoxical, this distinction between 'lack' and 'nullity' is still very helpful for being clear also as a daseinsanalytic therapist about which illusion the patient has to free himself from: from the illusion that what makes him anxious about his own human being is a mere 'lack' and that he can therefore escape anxiety if he only succeeds in correcting this lack or rendering it harmless.

It cannot therefore be stated in general what philosophical experiences a patient has to have, but it always involves the experience of an irresolvable 'nullity' of our own existing. The experience of not being able to become master of the future as a human being, as Gadamer emphasises, is only one example of the philosophical experiences that it becomes possible to 'have' through a daseinsanalytic therapy. Other examples are found in the preceding chapters.

As the patient in a daseinsanalytic therapy 'has' philosophical experiences, he changes from a 'reluctant philosopher' into a 'philosophically experienced human being', but he does not explicitly become a philosopher. His philosophical experience will be expressed much more in a different—more honest, more independent but also more committed—relationship to the entirely concrete reality. Does his 'philosophically experienced' relationship to concrete reality and to specific fellow human beings also differ from the relationship to reality of those who owe their mental health to the normal repression of the truths of being or their reinterpretation as truths about meaning? It seems likely in any case that the same, namely more honest self-perception, more independent judgement and a more selfless interest in things and other people also distinguish him from the 'healthy average' simply because the collective repression and collective interpretation of meaning on which average mental health is based sets boundaries on the individual relationship with concrete reality and enforces a certain adaptation, even if this is not even noticed by the individual because it is so 'normal'.

On the meaning and function of depressive experiences during the therapeutic process

I cannot conclude this chapter without mentioning the possibility of depressive reactions during an analytic psychotherapy. For this it is important to remember the daseinsanalytic view of depression (cf. Part III, Chapter 5). Unusually, depression has not been set alongside the many other forms of mental suffering but interpreted as the basic form of mental suffering that lies in wait behind all other forms of suffering and is always only more or less successfully averted by them. It can therefore be understood that the danger of a depressive reaction increases when the illusory nature of a patient's previous acting out is unmasked for him in the context of a therapy. Although this disillusionment viewed from outside brings a new freedom, it is initially a loss for the patient. Paradoxical as it sounds, despite the symptoms of suffering life was still previously somehow tolerable because of the cherished illusion—its loss can therefore initially discourage the patient. It is important as the therapist not to be afraid of a possible temporary depressive reaction in the patient, but to understand it as part of the analytic process. Patients need varying amounts of time really to 'have' disillusioning experiences. For one thing, it is not a single action but a process that Freud accurately described as 'working through'. A depressive reaction is usually part of this working through and then has—according to the saying—the meaning of *reculer pour mieux sauter*, a temporary retreat that is necessary to move forward effectively.

Bibliography

Altmeyer M. and Thomä H. (eds.) (2006). *Die vernetzte Seele. Die intersubjektive Wende in der Psychoanalyse* (The interconnected soul. The intersubjective turn in psychoanalysis). Stuttgart: Klett-Cotta.

Aristotle (1936). *Problems and Rhetorica ad Alexandrum.* Trans. W. S. Hett and H. Rackham. 2 vols. London, Heinemann and Cambridge, MA: Harvard University Press.

Aron, L. (1996): *A Meeting of Minds: Mutuality in Psychoanalysis.* New York: Analytic Press, reprinted Routledge 2009.

Balint M. (1949). Early developmental stages of the ego: primary object love. *International Journal of Psychoanalysis,* 1949, Vol. 30: 265–273.

Bernhard, T. (1971). *Gehen* (walking). Frankfurt: Suhrkamp.

Binswanger L. (1922). Über Phänomenologie (on phenomenology). In *Ausgewählte Werke* (Selected works), 1–4, Heidelberg 1992–1994, Vol. 3, pp. 35–69.

—— (1955). *Ausgewählte Vorträge und Aufsätze* (Selected lectures and essays). Bern.

—— (1957). *Schizophrenie* (Schizophrenia). Pfullingen, Germany: Neske.

—— (1986). Dream and existence (trans. J. Needleman). *Review of Existential Psychology and Psychiatry,* 19, pp. 81–105.

—— (1992–1994). *Ausgewählte Werke* (Selected works), Vols. 1–4. Heidelberg: Asanger.

—— (2010). *Eine Einführung in die Probleme der allgemeinen Psychologie.* (Introduction to the problems of general psychology). Republished by Nabu Press (Berlin, Springer Verlag).

Bion, W. (1990). *Brazilian Lectures. 1973 São Paulo, 1974 Rio de Janeiro.* London: Karnac.

Böhme, G. (2003). *Leibsein als Aufgabe. Leibphilosophie in pragmatischer Hinsicht* (The task of being a body. The philosophy of the body in a pragmatic respect). Zug, Switzerland: Die Graue Edition.

Boss, M. (1951). *Sinn und Gehalt der sexuellen Perversionen. Ein daseinsanalytischer Beitrag zur Psychopathologie des Phänomens der Liebe* (The meaning and content of the sexual perversions. A daseinsanalytic contribution to the psychopathology of the love phenomenon). 2nd edition. Bern: Huber (3rd revised and expanded edition, 1966).

—— (1954). *Einführung in die psychosomatische Medizin* (introduction to psychosomatic medicine). Bern: Huber.

—— (1957). *The Analysis of Dreams.* Trans. Arnold Pomerans. London: Rider.

—— (1977). *I Dreamt Last Night…* Trans. Stephen Conway. New York and London: Gardner Press [distributed by Wiley].

—— (1982). *Psychoanalysis and Daseinsanalysis.* Trans. Ludwig Lefebvre. New York: Da Capo Press.

—— (1994). *The Existential Foundations of Medicine and Psychology.* Trans. Stephen Conway and Anne Cleaves. New York and London: Jason Aronson.

Burston, D. and Frie, R. (2006). *Psychotherapy as a Human Science,* Pittsburgh: Duquesne University Press.

Condrau, G. (1972): *Aufbruch in die Freiheit* (Leap into freedom) Vienna: Europa Verlag

Cremerius, J. (1984). Zur kritischen psychoanalytischen Revision der Abstinenzregel. Vom regelhaften zum operational Gebrauch (On the critical psychoanalytic revision of the rule of abstinence. From the rule-based to the operational use). *Psyche* 9/84: 769–800.

Devereux, G. (1967). *From Anxiety to Method in the Behavioral Sciences.* The Hague: Mouton and Company.

Fichtner, G. (ed.) (2003). *The Sigmund Freud–Ludwig Binswanger Correspondence, 1908-1938.* Trans. A. Pomerans. London: Open Gate Press.

Freud, S. and Breuer, J. (1895). *Studies on Hysteria. S.E.* 2.

Freud, S. (1900). *The Interpretation of Dreams. S.E.* 4-5.

—— (1909). Family romances. *S.E.* 9.

—— (1910). Five lectures on psycho-analysis. *S.E.* 11.

—— (1912). Recommendations to physicians practising psycho-analysis. *S.E.* 12.

—— (1913a). Preface to Bourke's scatologic rites of all nations. *S.E.* 12.

—— (1913b). On beginning the treatment. *S.E.* 12.

—— (1914). Remembering, repeating and working-through. *S.E.* 12.

—— (1915a). Thoughts for the times on war and death. *S.E.* 14.

—— (1915b). Observations on transference-love. *S.E.* 12.

—— (1915c). The unconscious. *S.E.* 14.

—— (1916–17). *Introductory Lectures on Psycho-Analysis. S.E.* 15–16.

—— (1917). Mourning and melancholia. *S.E.* 14.

—— (1919). Lines of advance in psycho-analytic therapy, *S.E.* 17.

—— (1920). *Beyond the Pleasure Principle. S.E.* 18.

—— (1921). *Group Psychology and the Analysis of the Ego. S.E.* 18.

—— (1924). Neurosis and psychosis. *S.E.* 19.

—— (1926a). *Inhibitions, Symptoms and Anxiety. S.E.* 20.

—— (1926b). The question of lay analysis. *S.E.* 20.

—— (1930). *Civilization and its Discontents. S.E.* 21.

—— (1933). *New Introductory Lectures on Psycho-Analysis. S.E.* 22.

—— (1937a). Constructions in analysis. *S.E.* 23.

—— (1937b). Analysis terminable and interminable. S.E.

—— (1938). *An Outline of Psychoanalysis. S.E.* 23.

—— (1939). *Moses and Monotheism. Three Essays. S.E.* 23.

Fromm-Reichmann, F. and Moreno, J. L. (1956) (eds.). *Progress in Psychotherapy.* New York: Grune & Stratton.

Fuchs, T. (2002). Melancholie als Desynchronisierung. Ein Beitrag zur Psychopathologie der intersubjektiven Zeit (Melancholia as desynchronization. A contribution to the psychopathology of intersubjective time). In *Zeit-Diagnosen. Philosophisch-psychiatrische Essays* (Time-Diagnoses. Essays on philosophy and psychiatry). Zug, Switzerland: Die Graue Edition.

Gadamer, H.-G. (1996). Hermeneutics and psychiatry. *The Enigma of Health.* Cambridge: Polity Press 1996, pp. 163-173.

—— (1997). Rhetoric, hermeneutics, and ideology-critique. In *Rhetoric and Hermeneutics in Our Time.* Trans. Richard E. Palmer, ed. Walter Jost and Michael J. Hyde. New Haven: Yale University Press, pp. 313-334.

—— (2004). *Truth and Method.* Trans. rev. Joel Weinsheimer and Donald Marshall. London and New York: Continuum.

Girard, R. (1977). *Violence and the Sacred.* Trans. Patrick Gregory. Baltimore, London: Johns Hopkins University Press.

Habermas, J. (1971). *Knowledge and Human Interests.* Boston, MA, Beacon Press.

Heidegger, M. (1966). *Being and Time.* Trans. Joan Stambaugh. New York: SUNY Press.

—— (1971). Language. In *Poetry, Language, Thought.* Trans. Albert Hofstadter. New York: Harper & Row, pp. 189–210

—— (1988). What is metaphysics? In *Pathmarks,* ed. W. McNeill. Cambridge: Cambridge University Press, pp. 82–96.

—— (2001a). *Zollikon Seminars,* ed. Medard Boss, trans. Franz Mayr and Richard Askay. Evanston, IL: Northwestern University Press, 2001.

—— (2001b). *The Fundamental Concepts of Metaphysics. World, Finitude, Solitude.* Trans. William McNeill and Nicholas Walker. Bloomington, IN: Indiana University Press.

Holzhey-Kunz, A. (2001). *Leiden am Dasein: Die Daseinsanalyse und die Aufgabe einer Hermeneutik psychopathologischer Phänomene* (Suffering from being: daseinsanalysis and the task of a hermeneutics of psychopathological phenomena). Vienna: Passagen Verlag.

—— (2002). *Das Subjekt in der Kur. Über die Bedingungen psychoanalytischer Psychotherapie.* (The subject in the treatment. On the conditions of psychoanalytic psychotherapy). Vienna: Passagen Verlag.

—— (2005). Kann und soll die Liebe in den Fokus zweckrational konzipierter Paartherapie rücken? (Can and should love enter the focus of couple therapy conceived with a rational purpose?) In: Jürg Willi / Bernhard Limacher (ed.): *Wenn die Liebe schwindet. Möglichkeiten und Grenzen der Partnertherapie* (When love fades. Possibilities and limitations of couple therapy). Stuttgart: Klett-Cotta Verlag, pp. 99ff.

—— (2006). Ludwig Binswanger: Psychiatry based on the foundation of philosophical anthropology' in E. Wolpert et al. (Eds.) *Images in Psychiatry. German Speaking Countries*, Heidelberg: Universitätsverlag Winter, pp. 271–288.

Homer (1980). *The Odyssey*. Trans. Walter Shewring. Oxford: Oxford University Press.

Husserl, E. (1931). *Ideas: General Introduction to Pure Phenomenology*. Trans. W. R. Boyce Gibson. London and New York: Allen & Unwin and Macmillan.

Jaenicke, U. (1998). Kein Träumen ohne Leiden und Wünschen (No dreaming without suffering and desiring). *Daseinsanalyse*, 14, p. 200ff.

—— (1999). 'Es träumte mir von M. H. …' (I dreamt about M.H.) Various key questions on the interpretation of a 'healthy' dreaming; in *Sonderheft Daseinsanalyse*, 15, p. 189f.

—— (2008). The issue of human existence as represented in dreaming. A new daseinsanalytic interpretation of the meaning of dreams. *International Forum of Psychoanalysis*, 2008, 17: 51–55.

Kernberg, O. (1975). *Borderline Conditions and Pathological Narcissism*. New York: Jason Aronson.

Kierkegaard, S. (1980). *The Concept of Anxiety*, ed. and trans. Reidar Thomte and Albert B. Anderson. Princeton, Guildford: Princeton University Press.

Kolakowski, L. (1967). Ethik ohne Kodex (ethics without code), in *Traktat über die Sterblichkeit der Vernunft. Philosophische Essays* (Treatise on the mortality of reason. Philosophical Essays). Munich: Piper.

Laplanche, J. (1992). *La révolution copernicienne inachevée* (The unfinished Copernican revolution). Paris: Aubier.

Levinas, E. (1978). *Existence and Existents*. The Hague: Martinus Nijhoff.

Lorenzer, A. (1970). *Sprachzerstörung und Rekonstruktion. Vorarbeiten zu einer Metatheorie der Psychoanalyse*. (The destruction and reconstruction of language. Preliminaries to a meta-theory of psychoanalysis). Frankfurt: Suhrkamp.

May R., Angel, E., Ellenberger, H. (1994). *Existence. A New Dimension in Psychiatry and Psychology*. Northvale, NJ and London: Jason Aronson.

Menninghausen, W. (1999). *Ekel. Theorie und Geschichte einer starken Empfindung* (Nausea. Theory and history of a strong sensation), 2nd edition, Frankfurt: Suhrkamp.

Mentzos, S. (1992). *Psychodynamische Modelle in der Psychiatrie*. (Psychodynamic models in psychiatry). 2nd edition. Göttingen: Vandenhoeck & Ruprecht.

Nietzsche, F. (1977). On truth and lies in a nonmoral sense. In *The Portable Nietzsche*, ed. And trans. W. Kaufmann. London: Penguin.

—— (1978). *Thus Spoke Zarathustra*. Trans. W. Kaufmann. London: Penguin.

Orange, D. M. (2010). *Thinking for Clinicians. Philosophical Resources for Contemporary Psychoanalysis and the Humanistic Psychotherapies*, New York London: Routledge.

Racamier, P.-C. (1992). *Le génie des origines. Psychoanalyse et psychoses.* (The spirit of origins. Psychoanalysis and psychoses). Paris: Payot.

Reik, T. (1948). *Listening with the Third Ear. The Inner Experience of a Psychoanalyst.* New York: Grove Press.

Retzer, A. (2002). Das Paar. Eine systematische Beschreibung intimer Komplexe (The couple. A systematic account of intimacy-related complexes). In: *Familiendynamik*, 27, 1 and 2, pp. 5–42; pp. 186–217.

Ricoeur, P. *(1970). Freud and Philosophy: An Essay on Interpretation,* trans. Denis Savage. New Haven: Yale University Press.

—— (1974). Technique and nontechnique in interpretation. Trans. W. Domingo. In *The Conflict of Interpretations,* ed. Don Ihde. Evanston, IL: Northwestern University Press, pp. 173–191.

Sartre, J.-P. (1965). *Nausea.* Trans. Robert Baldick. London: Penguin.

—— (2003). *Being and Nothingness. An Essay on Phenomenological Ontology.* Trans. Hazel Barnes. London: Routledge.

Scheler, M. (1973). *Wesen und Formen der Sympathie* (the nature and forms of sympathy). Bern: Francke.

Schmid, W. (2004). *Mit sich selbst befreundet sein. Von der Lebenskunst im Umgang mit sich selbst.* (Being your own friend. The art of living in terms of dealing with oneself). Frankfurt: Suhrkamp.

Schmitz, H. (1998). *Der Leib, der Raum und die Gefühle* (The body, space and feelings). Vienna: Sirius.

Seidler, G. H. (1995). *Der Blick des Anderen. Eine Analyse der Scham* (The other's gaze. An analysis of shame). Stuttgart: Verlag Int. Psychoanalyse.

Sennett, R. (2006). *The Culture of the New Capitalism.* New Haven, CT: Yale University Press.

Staude, D. (ed.) (2010). *Methoden Philosophischer Praxis. Ein Handbuch* (Methods of philosophical praxis. A handbook), Bielefeld (transcript).

Stolorow, R., Atwood, G., Orange D. (2002). *Worlds of Experience. Interweaving Philosophical and Clinical Dimensions in Psychoanalysis.* New York: Basic Books.

Tellenbach, H. (1980). *Melancholy. History of the Problem, Endogeneity, Typology, Pathogenesis, Clinical Considerations.* Pittsburgh: Duquesne University Press.

Werthmann, H.-V. (1997). Psychoanalytische Deutung (Psychoanalytic interpretation). In *Schlüsselbegriffe der Psychoanalyse* (Key concepts in psychoanalysis), ed. Wolfgang Mertens, 3rd edition, Stuttgart: Klett-Cotta Verlag.

Woggon, B. (2000). *Ich kann nicht wollen. Berichte depressiver Patienten.* (I've lost my will. Reports from depressive patients). Bern: Huber, 2nd edition.

World Health Organization (2000). *The ICD-10 Classification of Mental and Behavioural Disorders.* WHO: Geneva.

Further reading

Holzhey-Kunz, A. (1994). Einleitung zu Ludwig Binswanger (Introduction). *Ausgewählte Werke* (Selected works), Vol. 4. Heidelberg: Asanger, pp. 13–55.

—— (1997). In die Welt hinaus. Kindliche Entwicklungsschritte als Seinserfahrungen (Out into the world. Children's developmental steps as experiences of being). *Daseinsanalyse* 14/1, pp. 5–15.

—— (1997). What defines the daseinsanalytic process? *Existential Analysis* 8.1, pp. 93–104.

—— (1998). Wie von Seelischem zu reden sei. Zwei neue Sprachen für die Psychoanalyse: Medard Boss und Roy Schafer. (How to talk about the mind. Two new languages for psychoanalysis) *Daseinsanalyse* 15/2, pp. 102–118.

—— (2000). Welche therapeutische Relevanz misst die Daseinsanalyse der Erinnerung von Kindheitserfahrungen bei? (What therapeutic relevance does daseinsanalysis accord to the memory of childhood experiences?). *Daseinsanalyse* 16, pp. 33–49.

—— (2001). Le rêve, une forme d'existence (Dream, a form of existence), in: Hervé Mesot (Ed.): *Des interpretations du rêve* (Dream interpretations). Paris: Presses Universitaires de France, pp. 203–226.

—— (2001). Psychopathologie auf philosophischem Grund: Ludwig Binswanger und Jean-Paul Sartre (A philosophical foundation for psychopathology: Ludwig Binswanger and Jean-Paul Sartre). *Schweizer Archiv für Neurologie und Psychiatrie*, 3, pp. 104–113.

—— (2002). Depression und Subjektivität (Depression and subjectivity). In: Thomas Fuchs/Christian Mundt (Eds.): *Affekt und affektive Störungen. Phänomenologische Konzepte und empirische Befunde im Dialog* (Affect and affective disorders. Phenomenological concepts and empirical findings in dialogue). Paderborn et al. Zurich: Schöningh, pp. 187–198

—— (2003). Ellen West: Binswangers daseinsanalytische Deutung in daseinsanalytischer Kritik (Ellen West: A daseinsanalytic critique of Binswanger's daseinsanalytic interpretation). In: A. Hirschmüller (Ed.): *Ellen West. Eine Patientin Ludwig Binswangers zwischen Kreativität und destruktivem Leiden* (Ellen West. Creativity and destructive suffering in a patient of Ludwig Binswanger). Heidelberg: Asanger, pp. 95–109.

—— (2003). Sartres existenzielle Psychoanalyse als radikale Hermeneutik des Subjekts (Sartre's existential psychoanalysis as a radical hermeneutics of the subject). *Daseinsanalyse* 19, pp. 96–115.

—— (2006). Ludwig Binswanger: Psychiatry based on the foundation of philosophical anthropology, in: *Images in Psychiatry. German Speaking Countries*, ed. Eugen Wolpert et al. Heidelberg: Winter, pp. 271–288.

—— (2006). Unter dem Blick des Anderen. Die Scham als Objekt und Subjekt der Philosophie, in: Georg Schönbächler (Ed.) (Under the gaze of the Other. Shame as an object and subject of philosophy). *Die Scham in Philosophie, Kulturanthropologie und Psychoanalyse* (Shame in philosophy, cultural anthropology and psychoanalysis). Zurich: Collegium Helveticum, pp. 15–22.

—— (2008) *Daseinsanalyse* (daseinsanalysis), in: Alfried Längle, Alice Holzhey-Kunz: *Existenzanalyse und Daseinsanalyse*, facultas wuv UTB, pp. 181–348.

—— Daseinsanalysis: three controversial approaches to mental suffering, in: *Legacy and Beyond*, ed. Laura Barnes and Greg Madison, Routledge 2011, pp. 35–51.

—— Lebendigsein. Existenzphilosophische Überlegungen zur Zweideutigkeit eines Grundgefühls (Being alive. Reflections on the ambiguity of a basic emotion based on existential philosophy), in: Joerg Fingerhut, Sabine Marienberg (ed.): *Feelings of Being Alive*, Berlin (de Gruyter) 2012 , pp. 123–145

—— Leiden an der ontologischen Negativität, in: Emil Angehrn, Joachim Küchenhoff (ed): *Die Arbeit des Negativen. Negativität als philosophisch-psychoanalytisches Problem* (The work of the negative. Negativity as a philosophical-psychoanalytic problem). Weilerswist (Velbrück Wissenschaft) 2014, pp. 99–121

Index

Printed and bound by CPI Group (UK) Ltd, Croydon, CR0 4YY

12/02/2026

02052824-0002